W9-BCO-153

ARCHITECTS · OF · AUSTRALIA

THE · BICENTENNIAL · EDITION
1 · 9 · 8 · 8

Architects and their Architecture – An Observation

"As a Photographer of Architecture I find great
satisfaction in turning the building process full circle.
In the beginning is the Architect's idea then the
production of plans, elevations and working drawings,
all in minute scale in relationship to the final building.
It could be a fifty level edifice arising from a drawing
no more than a metre square.

Finally the camera reduces it all again to similar scale but
with details, textures, design, volume, linear qualities
and perspective – all gleaming in bright sunshine; in the
trade it is known as 'Architect's delight'. I have heard
some of them say the most enjoyable part of the whole
procedure is looking at the photographs. Let's leave it
at that!!"

Max Dupain
December 9th, 1987

ARCHITECTS · OF · AUSTRALIA

The form intends to be an integral part of the spatial scheme of the city as a whole.
It should tell about a fellowship and dignity among citizens which is not accessorial,
but must be conceived as fundamental to democratic life.

THE · BICENTENNIAL · EDITION

1 · 9 · 8 · 8

ISBN 0 9589598 3 8 Casebound

© 1988

Images Australia Pty Ltd
Melbourne, Australia 1988

FOREWORD

Few things vary so much from one country to another as cities and towns. They crystallise the essential elements of the country: the nature of its people, its climate, its size, its history and its natural materials.

Places for work and leisure; places to live; the design of these fundamental components is integral to the character of all communities.

Because of this, architects and developers bear a heavy responsibility. From their technical professionalism and their creativity come not only functionalism but also "soul".

As Executive Chairman of Bond Corporation, an enterprise which was born out of property development and continues to rank property as one of its strategic core operations, I am delighted with the way Australian architects are meeting their responsibility. The buildings they design are distinctively Australian, yet the increasing global demand for Australian architects bears witness to a wider international quality – which I am convinced goes beyond mere passing fashion.

The vigour and spirit of enterprise which has lifted Australian architecture to its present high level needs to be nurtured. Publications such as "Architects of Australia" are a springboard for a healthy competitiveness among architects – and competition is the pathway to improvement.

Alan Bond, A.O.

Acknowledgements

This, the second edition of "Architects of Australia", would not be what it is had it not been for the inspired works, close collaboration and sound advice of all the participants in putting this magnificent volume together.

We would particularly like to thank Daryl Jackson Pty Ltd for allowing us the use of their profile in our promotional material and Mitchell/Giurgola & Thorp Architects for permitting the use of their project, "The New Parliament House, Canberra", on the cover and for providing unique concept sketches by Romaldo Giurgola.

As well, a publication of this nature relies on the co-operation of many other individual experts and professional organisations and, in this regard, we especially wish to thank the Archives Division of the Public Works Department, Victoria and the Parliament House Construction Authority in Canberra. Both of these organisations have been more than helpful in providing photographs and illustrations for "Architects of Australia – The Bicentennial Edition, 1988".

Finally, we must thank Mr. Max Dupaine, one of the finest exponents of Architectural photography in the world, for his intriguing and insightful view of Architects and their Architecture, Mr. Geoff Turnbull for an outstanding Critique, and Mr. Alan Bond, Executive Chairman of Bond Corporation, for providing a stimulating Foreword.

CONTENTS

CRITIQUE

This book is a record of current public and commercial architecture in Australia in the bicentennial year. The book has no single author whose task is to interpret contemporary Australian architecture, but it has as many authors and points of view as there are architectural firms contributing. What they have done and can do is here briefly shown and told. This compilation thus has a candour and directness for there is no argument, as to what should and should not have been achieved in public and commercial architecture in recent years. This is a pattern book for the immediate and continuing, and not an iconoclastic manifesto for beginning again, nor a projection of a distant future.

Turning these pages is rewarding and compelling. The competence and quality of architectural services in Australia today is ably demonstrated, yet the editors did not afford inclusion of every practice and practitioner. The public and commercial realm is the concern and focus of this book, and so only some public housing represents the vast areas of our cities given over to private detached houses.

An astonishing number of viable and lively architectural firms emerge. Their recently built contributions to the city appear in handsome photographs, being but tantalising glimpses of those realities. A brief description of the professional services offered only hints at the hectic activities and obsessive care in the realization of these buildings. Commitment to good building practice and dedication to efficient and ample professional service cannot be differentiated between the entries in this book, but there is a diversity in the appearances or aesthetics of the products. The virtuously prosaic and functionalist building may be adjacent to the brilliant culturally significant and inclusive image. The magnificently set, grandly conceived and beautifully crafted new Parliament House, a building which will gain as much international admiration as the Sydney Opera House, appears in this book equally with quick, expedient, industrialised, modular factory designs.

Some commentators say that there is no singular Australian architecture, but as many architectures as there are architects. Aesthetic intentions in the creation of buildings varies in kind and degree from one architect to another. Each would compose a plan, the structure and form of a building differently even when the same brief is at hand. The results of architectural design competitions are evidence of this. The circumstances of each brief, the site and setting, the needs and desires of the occupants and visitors, the systems of construction and service may profoundly affect the architect's solution. One architect in this way may be quite diverse in approach and modes of composition while another might work constantly in a particular technique and expression. The benefit of this modern encyclopedia of Australian architects, like the pattern books of the nineteenth century, allows the reader interesting and informative access to the diversity that occurs in Australian architecture. From knowledge, empathy can be recognised. This book is a useful and educational reference.

This book is full of urban buildings and reflects that Australians are amongst the most urbanised in the world, albeit that most of us abide in the suburbs. Agriculture and mining are the basis of the economy and we are fascinated by bush lore and rural life but our culture is essentially the culture of cities, the garden city. Nationhood is being reckoned in 1988 to have begun with the foundation of a city settlement on Sydney Cove. This city colony was British rather than French, Dutch or Spanish, as well it might have been, nor was it a trading outpost of the Chinese Empire or a Hindu/Buddhist Kingdom of South East Asia. Captain Arthur Phillip and his charges possessed territory and began agriculture and the rudiments of a Georgian city. The mother country sustained the settlement until Sydney itself became the centre for further colonization and the establishment of European farming and towns. The seaboard city was the generating point for the ruralization of the continent, rather than the great city being the consequence of rural surplus and the urbanization of an agricultural state. By a process a number of seaboard cities became the capitals of sovereign colonial states which federated in a commonwealth in 1901. The majority of projects in this book are located in these capitals, including Canberra, the early twentieth century new federal capital.

The odd place in Australia still carries an aboriginal name, most spots on the map however are named in memory of worthy administrators or British places. The culture of cities with its complex heirarchies and networks of specialists is in stark contrast to the nomadic and animist culture which had kept the continent for thousands of years, attributing a pantheon of spirit souls and narratives to its natural features. The urb, exalting the chief, required the subjection and control of nature and its material transformation in agriculture. This fundamental change continues.

In two hundred years the growth of cities in Australia has been substantial and accelerating. This book accurately conveys the feel of rapid and continuing acquisition of city space. In the past, the engulfment of space for the city has needed an architecture that is already formed, prompt and fashionable. Over the years some architects stand out as having been more idealistic and talented in developing uniquely individualistic work that endures. Quality permeates the work of Francis Greenway, the first, as does the works of John Verge, Joseph Reed and William Wardell. Walter and Marion Griffin's organic ideology that insists upon regional formulations, and their Beaux-Arts training, are the context for the design of Canberra, a city bedded down with axes and circles in the receptive hollows of ancient mountains and river in the hinterland. The Griffins created buildings that grow out of and celebrate the old rock beds of Castlecrag or the hilly undulations of outer Melbourne and the grid, block and cube streetscapes of Melbourne's central business district. Haddon, Annear and Dods in urban settings made imaginative amalgamations of elements they well knew, and they were very inventive as well. Leslie Wilkinson can be admired for his insistence upon the plan and an expression appropriate to Sydney's climate, as can Roy Grounds in Melbourne. Robin Boyd felt so confident of the standards and status of Australian architects that he participated at an international level, believing Australian architecture contributes to universal architectural culture.

Popular nostalgia today for old and existing buildings in our cities may be evidence of cultural maturity, that demands respect and admiration for what has been achieved and established. The city in Australia is no longer necessarily an arena for conquest of what is there, obliterating what has happened before. The existing fabric is recognised to have a life and characteristics that need layering upon and nurturing, and only the most thoughtful and sophisticated intervention and enhancement.

Jeff Turnbull

Jeff Turnbull
Co-ordinator for the Master of Architecture by design,
University of Melbourne.

RAIA Headquarters, Canberra, 1969
Ancher Mortlock Murray & Woolley, Architects

Architecture is part of the story of Man . . . the progressive control of a hostile environment, the transformation of a savage world into a productive and life-enhancing one. Architecture is man shaping his world and being shaped by the world he has created.

Today Architecture is home, office, playground, neighbourhood, city, nation, Spaceship Earth. It is security, shelter, community and something to influence every waking moment. Architecture is a way of life and something taken for granted.

Tomorrow Architecture will help shape the world to come; play a vital part in the use of resources; play a key role in solving increasingly complex problems in our increasingly crowded world. It will be in the forefront of solving problems of the cities, problems of earthly frontiers and problems of frontiers in space.

Architecture is people. It is their needs, desires, skills and abilities. Architecture is also architects and their professional assessment of needs, desires and resources.

And then Architecture is one more thing . . . a single thing greater than all its parts together . . .

The Idea.

THE ROYAL AUSTRALIAN INSTITUTE OF ARCHITECTS

President (top)
Robert Hall LFRAIA

Vice President (left)
Dudley Wilde LFRAIA

National Executive Director (centre)
Donald Bailey LFRAIA

**National Secretary
& Membership Director** (right)
Jack Nelson Hon RAIA

National Information Director (left)
Simon Johnstone

National Education Director (centre)
Judy Vulker

National Practice Director (right)
Margaret Lothian

National Headquarters
2a Mugga Way
Red Hill, A.C.T. 2603

Telephone
(062) 73 1548

Cables
Archroyal Manuka

Telex
RAIA 62 428

Facsimile
(062) 73 1953

Viatel
062 731 5481

RAIA Chapters

Australian Capital Territory
2a Mugga Way
Red Hill, A.C.T. 2603

Telephone
(062) 73 2929

New South Wales
Tusculum, 3 Manning Street
Potts Point, N.S.W. 2011

Telephone
(02) 356 2955

Northern Territory
133 Mitchell Street
Larrakeyah, Darwin, N.T. 5794

Telephone
(089) 81 2288

Queensland
Cnr Mary & Albert Streets
Brisbane, Qld 4000

Telephone
(07) 229 6244

South Australia
1 King William Road
Unley, S.A. 5061

Telephone
(08) 272 7044

Tasmania
1st Floor, City Hall Building
Market Place
Hobart, Tas. 7000

Telephone
(002) 34 5464

Victoria
30 Howe Crescent
South Melbourne, Vic. 3205

Telephone
(03) 699 2922

Western Australia
22 Altona Street
West Perth, W.A. 6005

Telephone
(09) 321 7114

The Royal Australian Institute of Architects is a national organisation with headquarters in Canberra and Chapters in each State and Territory representing architects in private and public practice.

In its concern for the advancement of architecture and the improvement of the built environment, it makes contact with the community at various levels including: vigorous representations to governments on issues relating to the environment, building, and the building industry; the recognition and encouragement of excellence in architecture by national and state awards systems; advice to the general public by 'shop front' architectural advisory services; monitoring and inspecting schools of architecture; the encouragement of high standards of architectural service by ethical codes; constant practice advice to its members; the publishing of books and documents and the conduct of courses and seminars for continuing professional development.

The RAIA and its members contribute to their communities by designing buildings and assisting with the procurement of buildings to give physical form to the building aspirations of individuals, communities and governments.

'Architects of Australia' provides a convenient reference for those who, for various reasons, may be seeking information on the experience and skills available from the architectural profession at large.

The firms whose principals are members of the RAIA have taken that additional step agreeing to abide by a strict code of professional conduct, to continue to study through professional development programmes, by interchange of ideas and experience with fellow members, and to inform their client public of these experiences and skills in a professional manner.

Such firms are identified by the RAIA Trade Mark:

ARCHITECTS

It is important for a building to take on a role of elucidation and manifestation, since what we _are_ has a strong effect on what we _may be_. Before being an abstract artistic gesture, a building is a process of explanation. It is in finding a delicate balance between a building's statement and its ability to explain itself that true classicism lies.

1 Town Hall House and Sydney Square, Sydney, N.S.W.

2 Commonwealth Family Law Courts, Parramatta, N.S.W.

3 Surf Pavilion, Queenscliff, N.S.W.

4 Hotel, Campbells Cove, Sydney, N.S.W.

5 & 6 Cadets Mess, Australian Defence Force Academy, Canberra, A.C.T.

7 'The Anchorage' Townhouses, Tweed Heads, N.S.W.

8 State Library and Museum, Melbourne, Vic.

9 Commercial Offices, Parramatta, N.S.W.

10 & 11 Australian Embassy, Bangkok, Thailand

ANCHER MORTLOCK AND WOOLLEY PTY LTD
Architects and Planners

Directors
Ken Woolley B Arch LFRAIA
Stephen Thomas B Arch FRAIA
Dale Swan B Arch MSc. FRAIA
Noel Lehmann B Arch
Bruce Bowden ASTC (Arch) Dip T & CP LFRAIA

Associates
Tony Allen B Arch ARAIA
Philip Baigent B Arch ARAIA
Walter Barda B Arch ARAIA

Established
1946

Address
40 Collins Street
Surry Hills, N.S.W. 2010

Telephone
(02) 332 1255

Facsimile
(02) 332 2506

Number of Employees
60

Project Types
Government
Defence, Courts, Broadcasting

Community and Civic
Libraries, Museum, Administration

Educational
University, schools, colleges

Scientific and Medical
Laboratories, health centres

Commercial
Offices, hotels

Residential
Medium density housing

Ecclesiastic
Churches

Industrial
Workshops, amenities

Other Disciplines
Research and Planning
Brief Development
Urban Design
Interior Design
Landscape Design

Person to Contact
Ken Woolley, Bruce Bowden

Current and Recent Projects

ABC Radio and Orchestra Complex, Sydney	$85M
Commonwealth Law Courts, Parramatta	$21M
Australian Embassy, Bangkok, Thailand	$30M
Australian Pavilion, Expo 88, Brisbane, Queensland	$6M
State Library and Museum, Melbourne, Victoria	$340M
Sydney Space Theatre, Power House Museum, Sydney	$12M
Australian/Hellenic Memorial, Canberra	$0.5M
Cadets Mess, Defence Academy, Canberra	$7M
Students Union, University of Sydney, Stage 2	$3.5M
Exhibition Glasshouse, Botanic Gardens, Sydney	$2M
International Hotel, Macquarie Street, Sydney	$35M
International Hotel, Campbells Cove, Sydney	$35M
Commercial Office Building, Parramatta	$6.5M
Commercial Office Building, Burwood	$7.5M
Commercial Office Building, Liverpool	$13M
Community Health Centre, Tuggeranong, A.C.T.	$5.5M
Rehabilitation Centre, Isabella Plains, A.C.T.	$1.6M
Scientific Research Facilities, Canberra	$2M
Amenities and Refit Facility, Garden Island Dockyard	$2M
Weapon Systems Workshop, Garden Island Dockyard	$2M
Wharf Support Facilities, Garden Island Dockyard	$2.5M
Medium Density Housing, Tweed Heads	$6M
Medium Density Housing, Linley Cove	$12M
Stepped Housing, Rushcutters Bay	$3M

Prizes & Awards

1945
Sulman Medal for Sydney Ancher's own House at Killara

1958
First prize in national competition for Waverley Town Hall

1959 RAIA Sulman Medal for House at Cronulla

1962 RAIA Wilkinson Award for House at Mosman

1964 Joint award winner, Sunday Telegraph Small House design competition

1967 RAIA Project House Design Awards, 1967, 1968, 1969 (2), 1970 (2), 1973, 1974, 1976 (2), 1977
– RAIA Blackett Award for Union Building, University of Newcastle

1968
– RAIA Wilkinson Award: The Penthouses, Rushcutters Bay
– Competition winner for Great Hall, University of Newcastle
– 'The Age' (Melbourne) House Award
– Western Australia Project House Awards
– Limited Competition for National Gallery, Canberra (Placed second)

1969 RAIA Blackett Award for Staff House, University of Newcastle

1972 RAIA Merit Award for Townhouses, Almora Street, Mosman
– RAIA Merit Award, Wentworth Building, University of Sydney

1976 RAIA Merit Award, Category B, for Attached Housing, Macquarie Fields

1978 Bathurst Orange Housing Competition: Second prize in two-stage competition
– RAIA Merit Award for work of Outstanding Environmental Design, (in collaboration with Noel Bell-Ridley Smith), Sydney Square

1979 Winner of limited competition, new building for Department of Criminology, Canberra
– RAIA Merit Award Town Hall House and Sydney Town Hall Complex

1980 RAIA Merit Award Building conversion for the NSW Nurses Association
– RAIA Merit Award. The Kiosk Gardens Restaurant Design Development and Documentation for Government Architect
– Limited competition winner, 220 townhouses and flats, Lane Cove, N.S.W., for Lend Lease Homes Pty Ltd

1981
– Bronze Medal Award of Victorian Chapter, RAIA for Environmental Design of Melbourne University Complex
– RAIA Merit Award, Woolley House, Paddington

1982
– RAIA Merit Award, West Amenities Refit and Control Building, Garden Island Dockyard
– RAIA Wilkinson Award – Woolley House, Paddington
– RAIA Civic Design Award – Sydney Square
– Winner Limited Competition for the National Archives, Canberra
– Winner RAIA Ideas Competition for the Gateway Site, Circular Quay, Sydney
– Highly commended BHP Steel Award for West Amenities Refit and Control Building and GMLS Workshop, Garden Island Dockyard

1984 RAIA Merit Award, for housing, Canberra, A.C.T. for 26 townhouses at Yarralumla
– RAIA Merit Award for Church of Jesus Christ of the Latter Day Saints, Leura

1985 RAIA Merit Award for GMLS Workshop; Garden Island Dockyard

1986 Winner limited competition, Victorian State Library and Museum, Melbourne
– RAIA Canberra Medallion and Sir Zelman Cowan National Award, Cadets Mess, Australian Defence Force Academy, Canberra (in association with the Department of Housing and Construction)

1987 Winner, limited competition for the Australian/Hellenic Memorial, Canberra
– RAIA Wilkinson Award and Robin Boyd National Award, Woolley House, Palm Beach
– RAIA Blackett Award, Townhouses, Tweed Heads

Background
The practice was begun in 1946 when Sydney Ancher opened a small office of his own. It was formed into the partnership of Ancher Mortlock & Murray in 1951 and practised under that name until 1964 when Ken Woolley left the Government Architect's office to become a partner. The firm of Ancher Mortlock Murray and Woolley was incorporated in 1969 allowing smaller involvement shareholdings by younger directors. Over the years, Ancher, Murray and, recently, Mortlock, have retired.

The current organisation is managed by five directors and three associates. The senior director, Ken Woolley, is responsible for both management policy and design approach, being involved in the design phase of all projects. The other directors and associates work in collaboration with Ken Woolley and assume varying responsibilities depending on the nature of particular projects. Essentially this is a design studio approach based on the concept of personal service to the client.

All work remains under the control of the directors, who are all active, experienced design architects, fully involved in all aspects of the office output. The firm would be classed as medium to large, with the capacity and ability to undertake projects of virtually any type and scale. There is a degree of latent additional capacity in the organisation. The directorate, management structure, office space and equipment are all capable of sustaining increases in staffing, and the reputation of the firm within the profession, gives it access to talented staff when recruitment is necessary. The practice has part-ownership of Cadnet Pty Ltd, a large technical computing organisation with extensive CADD facilities.

During the past 41 years of practice, the firm has been responsible for projects of greatly varying size, cost and function. Commissions have been completed on time and budget for a wide variety of government departments, statutory authorities and a variety of commercial clients.

Approach
The firm has always adopted a consistent approach to its work: to create designs that are totally appropriate for their function and their site, and have a character that strongly reflects the individual objectives of the client. The firm has not specialised in, or been heavily committed to, one type of building. The great variety of projects undertaken have indicated that a solution which is appropriate for one architectural problem is unlikely to be appropriate for another. Therefore the buildings do not comply with a pre-conceived design formula or reflect an applied style. Their character evolves from their own nature.

The firm is also committed to achieving professional excellence at all stages. The record of awards and competition successes is evidence of the belief in excellence and is testimony to the calibre of staff and the degree of thought and effort that is invested in every project.

The consistency in design therefore comes through appropriateness rather than sameness and through excellence rather than the pursuit of personal style.

The firm believes that design quality, constructability and cost planning are the most critical aspects of project development and are integral components of a total management responsibility. The design process establishes a relationship between building size, quality and cost; priorities can be determined and one factor cannot change without affecting the others. Constructability creates a link between design, documentation and construction, qualifying the parameters of cost and time. Accurate cost planning determines the reality of a project. The firm is committed to balancing these factors correctly to ensure that the finished project achieves the highest possible architectural quality while representing the best value for money.

Price Waterhouse Centre, Melbourne
Kino Cinemas, Melbourne
Bay Street Housing, Port Melbourne

BATES SMART & McCUTCHEON PTY LTD
Architecture/Engineering/Interior Design/Project Management

Directors
Robert Dunster B Arch Dip TRP FRAIA FRAPI
Robert Bruce ASTC Arch FRAIA
Struan Gilfillan B Arch FRAIA
Tim Hurburgh Dip Arch M Arch FRAIA
Roger Poole B Arch FRAIA MRAPI
Roger Arnall Dip Mech Eng MIE Aust

Address
One Clarendon Street
East Melbourne, Vic. 3002

Telephone
(03) 417 1444

Facsimile
(03) 419 0429

Telex
AA 31154

Number of Employees
125

Disciplines
Architecture
Structural Engineering
Services Engineering
   Mechanical, Electrical,
   Fire Protection, Lifts, Hydraulics
Interior Architecture & Design
Project Management
Urban Design

Persons to Contact
Roger Poole
Tim Hurburgh
Robert Bruce

Representative Clients
Financial and Professional Services
ANZ Banking Group
Arthur Andersen & Co
Arthur Robinson & Hedderwicks
American International Group
AMP Society
Coopers & Lybrand
Chase AMP
Commonwealth Banking Corporation
Ernst & Whinney
ESANDA Limited
Mallesons Stephens Jaques
Price Waterhouse
Sedgwick Limited
Touche Ross
Corporate
Australian Airlines
Clemenger Harvie
Comalco Limited
CRA Limited
ICI Australia Limited
OTC Australia Limited
Western Mining Corporation
Health Care/Laboratories
Royal Children's Hospital
Royal Women's Hospital
St Francis Xavier Cabrini Hospital
Warrnambool Base Hospital
Western General Hospital
Coronial Services Centre
Hospitality/Retail
David Jones
Kino Cinemas
Regent of Melbourne Hotel
Codesign
Coles & Garrard
Le Cone
Bags Only
Budget Rentacar

Historic/Recycling
Raheen – The Pratt Group
Meat Market Craft Centre
Sale Courthouse
Bendigo Cathedral
Tasma Terrace – National Trust
Residential
BP Australia
Pratt Group
Ministry of Housing
Little Company of Mary
Downhill Ski Club, Mt Buller
Private Clients
Government/Semi-Government
Construction Group
Melbourne City Council
Public Works Department – Victoria
Melbourne and Metropolitan Board of Works

Profile
Bates Smart & McCutcheon is a major Australian and
international practice of architects, engineers, interior
designers and project managers. Founded in 1852, the
practice comprises six directors leading 120 members
working in teams tailored to suit the demands of
individual projects.

Our fundamental concerns are quality and innovation
– we believe that each project must grow from quite
specific client needs and site influences, and that real
innovation emerges from creative responses to the unique
nature of each project. We seek thorough documentation
and management, combined with cost-effective, personal
service. Long standing relationships with clients and
repeat business provide the basis for dynamic growth.

1 The Hill Stand, Flemington Racecourse

2 Spaceframe, Node

3 Betting Ring, Moonee Valley Racecourse

4 National Australia Bank, Braeside

5 Hamer House, Sandringham

EDWARD F BILLSON & ASSOCIATES PTY LTD

Paul Cater, John Sawley, Leo Blyth, Edward Billson Jnr., Edward Billson III

EDWARD F BILLSON & ASSOCIATES PTY LTD
ARCHITECTS

Directors
Edward F. Billson Jnr. B.ARCH (MELB)
F.DIP (RMIT) RIBA FRAIA
John Sawley B.ARCH (ADEL.) FRAIA

Associates
Edward F. Billson III B.ARCH (MELB)
AAIA ARAIA
L. V. Blyth
P. G. Cater B.ARCH (RMIT)
K. S. Teagle B.ARCH HONS (ADEL.) ARAIA

Addresses
Edward F. Billson & Associates Pty Ltd
Architects
106 Jolimont Road
Melbourne, Vic 3002

Telephone
(03) 650 2551

Billson & Sawley Architects Pty Ltd
Architects
257 Sturt Street
Adelaide, S.A. 5000

Telephone
(08) 212 3172

Number of Employees
10

Project Types	Percentage
Commercial	20%
Banks/Offices	
Educational	10%
Public/State Schools	
Recreational	60%
Club Houses/Racecourses	
Residential	10%
Houses, Apartments	

Other Disciplines
Structural Engineering
Interior Design and Space Planning

Person to Contact
Melbourne
E. F. Billson III

Adelaide
J. A. Sawley

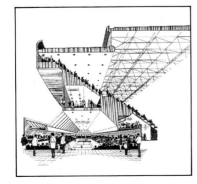

Current and Recent Projects
Commercial

ANL Office Building, South Melbourne	$1.7M
Braeburn Office Building, Jolimont	$1.0M
National Australia Bank, Braeside	
Croydon	$0.6M
Mildura	$1.0M
Rosebud	
ANZ Branch Offices, Mornington	
Ringwood	$1.5M

Educational

Parkwood High School, Ringwood East	$2.5M
Melbourne Grammar, Preliminary Study	
St Michael's Boys Grammar School	$1.0M
St Mary's Boys Regional School	$0.76M

Recreational

Moonee Valley Racecourse, Development	$18.8M
Flemington Racecourse, Development	$22.5M
SAJC Morphettville Grandstand	$9.3M

Racecourse Developments at:

Geelong	$0.95M
Bendigo	$0.8M
Bairnsdale	
Stawell	
Moe	
Wagga	

Consultant Architects:
Hong Kong Turf Club
Macau Trotting Club
Johannesburg Turf Club

Residential
Hamer House, Sandringham
Keir House, Brighton
Billson House, Toorak

Australian National Line, Melbourne

Design Approach
Edward F Billson and Associates understand what the building project means to the Client. Solving the complex relationships of market forces, aesthetic impact and cost, is vital in order to produce a successful building.

Maximising client involvement ensures that client needs are correctly interpreted and their particular problem is solved. To aid this involvement we offer a comprehensive range of services including :

Inspection Services
Feasibility Studies
Quick Conceptual Designs
Architectural, Structural, Interior Design
Documentation, Specification Writing
Expedition of all Permits
Construction Supervision and Contract Administration

Buildings are for people and should enhance the lives of those in and around them. We have consistently built with originality, creating buildings as stimulating and innovative as they are functional and cost effective.

Our engineering and construction expertise allows us to adopt the latest building technology and produce the optimum solution. We are experienced in solving complex functional requirements and building on sites which impose many restrictions. Recognition of our excellent service is rewarded by continued patronage of clients and the satisfaction of new clientele.

Company Profile
The Architectural Practice of Edward F. Billson was established in 1927 and is now entering the third generation of private practice.

Edward F. Billson Snr. was awarded the first ever Degree in Architecture from the University of Melbourne, and gained his early experience in the office of Walter Burley Griffin, the designer of Australia's Capital City, Canberra.

His own practice began when he won the world wide competition for his design of the University of Auckland Arts Building. He also won the first RAIA Medal for excellence in the design of Street Architecture.

Edward F. Billson and Associates have carried out work on a wide range of projects including:

> Recreational Facilities, Banks, Offices, New Houses and Renovations, Warehouses, Churches, Hospitals, Commercial and Domestic Interiors

The firm has a world wide reputation for expertise in the design of Racecourse Grandstands. The Stand at Flemington has the largest cantilevered roof in the Southern Hemisphere, which is praised by the racing industry and public for providing an unobstructed panoramic view of the track, sweeping on over the Maribyrnong River to the towers of Melbourne.

The Adelaide office of Billson and Sawley Architects was founded in 1980, when the Firm was commissioned to replace the Grandstand at Morphettville, South Australia. John Sawley has since carried out an extensive amount of work for the South Australian Jockey Club as well as other commercial and residential projects.

Edward F. Billson III entered the firm in 1978 and after graduating in Architecture from the University of Melbourne went on to spend three years in New York. He worked with the renowned firm of John Burgee Architects with Philip Johnson, gaining experience in the design and construction of skyscrapers. The project he was involved with was an elliptical office tower on 53rd Street and 3rd Avenue. He has returned to Australia, bringing valuable insights to American building development and marketing techniques and new direction in design.

BLIGH JESSUP ROBINSON
Architects

Directors (left to right)
James Grose B Arch (Hons) ARAIA ADIA
Phillip Tait Dip Arch ARAIA
Robert Gardner Dip Arch FRAIA
Jon Voller B Arch ARAIA
Noel Robinson Dip Arch Grad Dip Urb + Reg Plan
  FRAIA RIBA ADIA
Graham Bligh B Arch LFRAIA
Shane Thompson Dip Arch ARAIA

Established
Bligh Jessup Robinson   1987
Bligh Jessup Bretnall   1926
Noel Robinson Architects   1972

Addresses
Brisbane
301 Ann Street
Brisbane, Qld 4000

GPO Box 1007
Brisbane, Qld 4001

Sydney
40 Gloucester Street
The Rocks, N.S.W. 2000

Canberra
Ground Floor
North Wing, Churchill House
218 Northbourne Avenue
Braddon, A.C.T. 2600

Telephone
Brisbane   (07) 229 5266
Sydney   (02) 27 4244
Canberra   (062) 49 8936

Facsimile
Brisbane   (07) 221 0796
Sydney   (02) 27 4554
Canberra   (062) 57 1590

Number of Employees
70

Project Types
Commercial
Office/Retail

Community/Recreational
Pools, Libraries and Malls

Educational
Schools, Colleges and Universities

Health Planning
Hospitals and Research Laboratories

Resort Development
Hotels, Club Houses and Condominiums

Residential
Homes, Public Housing and Apartments

Urban Design
Public Precincts and Urban Planning

Other Disciplines
Bligh Jessup Interiors Pty Ltd
Interior Architects and Space Planners

Interdesign Pty Ltd
Photography, Modelmaking and Graphic
Design

Person to Contact
Brisbane   Jon Voller
Sydney   James Grose
Canberra   Michael Adams

Bligh Jessup Robinson Projects
Commercial
Inns of Court, North Quay, Brisbane
17 Storey Office Building $10M

Kenlynn Centre, Upper Edward Street, Brisbane
5 Storey Office Building $1.5M
RAIA Citation
RAIA Sir Zelman Cowan Award Finalist
CCA Award for Excellence

Redevelopment of 239 Queen Street, Brisbane
14 Storey Office Building $17M

Queensland Law Society House, Ann Street, Brisbane
7 Storey Office Building $5.5M

Brisbane 2000, Queen Street, Brisbane
62 Storey Office Building $100M

Office Building, Eagle Street, Brisbane
24 Storey Office Building $15M

Educational
Applied Science Building and Resource Material Centre
Bald Hills C.O.T.A.F.E.
Science Teaching and Library Blocks

Queensland and Agricultural College, Lawes, Qld
Campus Development

Dalby Agricultural College, Dalby, Qld
Campus Development

Telecom Training School, Chermside, Brisbane $12M

Government Projects
Domestic Terminal Complex at the new
Brisbane International Airport, Eagle Farm, Brisbane
Major Airport Passenger Terminal $70M

Supreme Courts Building, Brisbane
Queensland Law Courts Centre $50M

Queensland Police Headquarters,
Roma Street, Brisbane
8 Storey 40,000 metres square Floor Area $50M

Health Planning
Wynnum Hospital, Wynnum, Brisbane
40 Bed Hospital $1.2M

Arid Zone Research Centre, Longreach, Qld $2.5M

Community/Recreational
Sandgate and District Senior Citizens Centre
Sandgate, Brisbane $0.5M

Queensland Marriage Guidance Council
St Pauls Terrace, Brisbane $0.5M

Bundaberg Airport, Bundaberg, Qld $0.5M

Wacol Juvenile Detention Centre, Wacol Qld
In association with Department of Works $2.5M

Bald Hills Hospital, Bald Hills, Brisbane
Disabled persons and young disabled living unit $2.6M

Keperra Hospital, Keperra, Brisbane
40 Bed Hospital $1.4M

Space Planning and Interior Architecture
Cannan & Peterson, Solicitors,
Riverside Centre, Brisbane
1500 metres square Commercial Office

Lend Lease Corporation, Queensland Headquarters
Riverside Centre, Brisbane
2000 metres square Commercial Office

IBM Australia Limited, Queensland Headquarters
IBM Centre, Brisbane
4500 metres square Commercial Office

Resort Development
Hyatt Coolum, Coolum, Qld
500 Room, 5-Star Hotel $47M

Lizard Island Resort Extensions
Far North Queensland
Major Refurbishment and Extension $3M

Melanesian Hotel, Lae, Papua New Guinea
Refurbishment Existing Hotel $1.5M

Proposed Cairns Casino
In Association with Wimberly Wisenand
Allinson Tong & GH Cairns, Qld $500M

Shute Harbour Marina, Shute Harbour, Qld
Marina Hotel and Shopping Housing

Iwasaki Farnborough Resort, Yeppoon, Qld
Environmental Impact Study, Establishment, Consultation

The Gateway Hotel, Port Moresby, Papua New Guinea
Refurbishment and Extension $3M

Housing
Multi-Unit Housing, Lyneham North, Canberra $2.5M
Aged Persons Housing, Kambah, Canberra $1.2M
Single Persons Housing, Phillip, Canberra $0.8M
Infill Housing, Canberra $1.3M
Northcrest, Maroochydore, Qld
17 Storeys $7M

Profile
Bligh Jessup Robinson brings together two established
practitioners in Queensland and Australian architecture
– Bligh Jessup Bretnall Architects and Noel Robinson
Architects.

Bligh Jessup Bretnall Architects has been a major
architectural presence in Queensland since 1926
with more than 60 years of continuous practice.
Its pre-eminence is apparent throughout the State,
having established a reputation for quality work – a
crucial factor in securing a range of major public and
private commissions, including the Supreme Courts
Building, the New Brisbane Airport and Expo 88.

Over the last 15 years, Noel Robinson Architects
has established a national reputation for innovative
architecture in a range of projects from single houses
to large public and commercial projects – ranging
from the National Anglican Centre on the shore of
Lake Burley Griffin in Canberra, to the pavilion housing
Sir Charles Kingsford Smith's Southern Cross.

The work of the firms has been distinguished with many
awards for architectural excellence, both inside and
outside the profession of architecture. Clients range from
the Australian and State Governments, large and small
private enterprise bodies, developers, local authorities
and other experienced client bodies. These clients have
differing needs in the development of their projects,
resulting in a variety of working methods – from total
management traditional systems, to working with
project management organisations, fast track project
development, construction management and feasibility
and environmental impact studies.

Bligh Jessup Robinson has the depth of 75 years practise,
and the merging of the practices creates the opportunity
to tackle projects with a highly experienced, innovative
yet pragmatic, approach.

Co-ordinated teamwork, logical processes, budget
and design control and construction awareness are
long standing principles reinforced by contemporary
technological resources. With offices in Brisbane,
Sydney and Canberra the practice gains commissions
throughout Australia and internationally.

Bligh Jessup Robinson aims to build appropriate
architecture – buildings and places that rely on
functional determinants, physical and social contexts –
buildings and places that will contribute to the
Australian cultural milieu.

A

BLYTHE YEUNG & MENZIES
Architects Interior Designers

Directors (left to right)
John H. Blythe F.R.A.I.A., F.I.Arb.A.
Patrick Y.F. Yeung F.R.A.I.A., F.I.Arb.A.
David N. Menzies B.A., A.R.A.I.A.
Prudence L. Cotton L.D.A.D. (Lon.),
  S.I.A.D. (Lon.)

Established
1978

Address
17 Morrison Street
Hobart, Tasmania 7000

Telephone
(002) 23 4011

Facsimile
(002) 23 2582

Number of Staff
20

Contact
John Blythe

Measuring Performance
Our performance must be judged by the results we achieve.

In that other measure of excellence – awards – Blythe Yeung and Menzies has recently achieved two firsts.

For our own offices at 17 Morrison Street, Hobart we received the first BOMA (Building Owners and Managers' Association) Award ever presented in Tasmania.

And for the same offices we received the first Interior Design Award presented by the Royal Australian Institute of Architects, Tasmanian Chapter.

Work in Progress
Current projects are valued at more than $30M

Project Types	Percentage
Commercial	40%
Interior Design	15%
Domestic	5%
Institutional	17%
Town Planning	3%
Industrial	20%

Current and Recent Projects

Department of Mines Office & Laboratory Complex, Rosny Park	$5,200,000
Office Building 242 Liverpool Street, Hobart	$1,700,000
Indoor Cricket Centre & Showrooms Moonah	$800,000
Shopping Centre Moonah	$600,000
Office Redevelopment 212 Liverpool Street, Hobart	$500,000
Office Development 15 Murray Street, Hobart	$13,000,000
Primary, Junior & Senior Schools Dominic College	$3,500,000
Elderly Persons Complex Lindisfarne	$400,000
Burnie Technical College Phase 2 Design	$6,000,000
Building Refurbishment & Fitout Telecom, Hobart	$600,000
Refurbishing Gibsons Mill Complex to Offices Morrison Street, Hobart	$700,000
Office Building 175 Collins Street, Hobart	$6,000,000
Bus Building Factory Kingston	$1,200,000
Office Building 54-60 Victoria Street, Hobart	$4,500,000
Classroom Block St. James College, Cygnet	$400,000
Maintenance & Stores Complex Mornington	$550,000
Manual Arts Block and Library St. Virgil's College, Hobart	$500,000
Primary School and Library St. Mary's College, Hobart	$250,000
Administration & Staff Facilities Dominic College Senior School	$400,000
Lindisfarne Sports Centre Lindisfarne	$270,000
T.C.A. Headquarters Bellerive	$950,000
Interior Fitout Executive Building, Hobart	$2,500,000
A.M.P. Offices Salamanca Place, Hobart	$270,000
A.M.P. Offices Argyle Street, Hobart	$260,000
Tasmanian Technopark Glenorchy	$1,000,000
Derwent Entertainment Centre	$12,500,000

The Practice
Blythe Yeung and Menzies has brought together a talented and versatile team of architects, planners and interior designers under directors John Blythe, Patrick Yeung, David Menzies and Prue Cotton.

It has an on-going and diverse history of significant projects undertaken for the private sector, federal, state and local government. These range from major office buildings to schools, shopping complexes, sports centres and industrial buildings.

The Disciplines
Besides a full range of architectural and planning services the practice has established a specific interior design section, headed by Prue Cotton, specialising in this complex and demanding discipline. Interior design is an integral part of the total service we offer.

The practice also is experienced in project management and building arbitration and has completed significant development projects in its own right.

Associations
Blythe Yeung and Menzies has formed associations with leading national project Developers and major Building companies. As a result it can offer a total package covering concept, design, construction and management for appropriate projects.

Our Aims
Buildings, first and foremost, are for people. We strive to design buildings that will be enjoyed by the people who use them and by those in whose environment they are situated. The creative challenge is to produce results which are sensitive, stimulating, sensible, usable and cost-efficient.

To achieve this we like to become involved at the earliest possible stage of a project and to work closely and cooperatively with our clients.

BWD Architects

Office, St Leonards

Office, Artarmon

BWD Space Planning

Studio City

BWD Interior Design

Reception, Clemenger

Board Room, Clemenger

BODDAM WHETHAM + DORTA
Architects & Interior Design

Directors (left to right)
David Boddam-Whetham RAIA B Arch Sydney
Grad Dip Const N.S.W.
  BWD Architects
Jeanette Dorta SIDA B Arch Venezuela
Grad Dip Hosp Planning London
  BWD Interior Design

Established
1976

Address
85 Avenue Road
Mosman, N.S.W. 2088

Telephone
(02) 960 4144

Facsimile
(02) 960 4255

BWD Team
Architects   7
Interior Design   3
Technical Support   4
Support Services   3

Group Services
BWD Architects
Architecture

BWD Interior Design
Interior Design

BWD Space Planning
Space Planning

Inline with Design
Product Design

J&J Mitchell
Landscape

Inline with Design
Corporate Graphics

Bowstring Pty Ltd
Project Development and Management

Current and Recent Projects
Recent projects illustrate the diversity of skills provided:

Commercial Offices
120 Pacific Highway, St. Leonards

407 Pacific Highway, Artarmon

Telecom, Gosford

Studio City, Sydney

Industrial
AG Campbell Distribution Centre, Silverwater

Western Meat Distribution Centre, Blacktown

Retail
Thorby Arcade

Kogarah Refurbishment

Interior Design
Offices – John Clemenger (N.S.W.) Pty Limited, Sydney

Offices – CBS Fox

Offices – APPM

Offices – Connaghan & May, Ayer

Offices – Metal Manufacturers

Offices – IPEC

Offices – BBDO Singapore

Theatres – 'The George', Sydney

Theatres – Manly Cinema

Space Planning
Computer Technology

IPEC

John Clemenger (N.S.W.) Pty Limited

Alto Ford

Project Development and Management
Manly Cinemas

TLE Re-location Study

Product Design
Inline with Design range

Corporate Graphics
Kell & Rigby

Thorby Arcade

Consultancy
Cooks River Environmental Study

Pavillion Hotel, Canberra

BWD Philosophy
BWD was Incorporated in 1976.

The specific Philosophy of BWD is to provide excellence in Architecture and Interior Design.

BWD's projects range from commercial, industrial and residential to theatres, retail centres and hotels. Each requires a specific design skill directed to solving unique problems.

BWD's belief is in direct personal service with accountability and performance being essential between client and designer.

BWD's past and future rests totally on the individual as the creator. Therefore, our internal management is a nexus system where each member benefits from their own productivity and performance. This arrangement is highly motivational, ensures commitment and maintains high skill levels with the Group.

The nexus system is taken externally with BWD being able to provide service throughout Australia and to larger projects.

THE BPA GROUP

BPA Australia Pty Ltd
BPA Interiors + Space Planners Pty Ltd

Directors
Ken W. Bell
Howard R. Puddy
Peter H. Lee
Ian F. Poole

Established
1978

Offices

Australia
BPA Australia Pty Ltd
Sydney
Level 6, 225 Miller Street
North Sydney
N.S.W. 2060
Telephone
61 2 959 4055
Facsimile
61 2 959 3642
Telex
AA75520
Perth
29 Ord Street
West Perth, W.A. 6005
Telephone
61 9 322 5699
Facsimile
61 9 322 2330
Melbourne
337 Moray Street
South Melbourne
Vic 3205
Telephone
61 3 699 8022
Facsimile
61 3 696 1203
Brisbane
Suite 3
17 Henry Street
Spring Hill, Qld 4000
Telephone
61 7 832 3822
Facsimile
61 7 832 3874
New Zealand
Bell Puddy Architects
New Zealand Limited
Suite 303-304
Achilles House
Cnr Customs &
Commerce Streets
Auckland
Telephone
64 9 393 373
Facsimile
64 9 392 848

**Offices in
Association**

San Francisco
Team 7 International
1011 Kearny Street
San Francisco
California 94133
Telephone
1 415 391 5510
Facsimile
1 415 391 5513

Hotel Specialists
Frizzell Hill Moorhouse
Architects
Third Floor
170 Maiden Lane
San Francisco
California 94108
Telephone
1 415 398 7141

Los Angeles
Retail Specialists
McClellan Cruz Gaylord
& Associates
Suite 400
199 South Los Robles
Avenue
Pasadena
California 91101-2457
Telephone
1 818 793 9119
Facsimile
1 818 796 9295

London
Hutchinson & Partners
33 Upper Street
Angel Islington
London N10PN
Telephone
44 1 226 9708
Facsimile
44 1 226 0686

Number of Employees
80

Project Categories
Office
Retail
Industrial
Hotel
Retirement Village
Religious and Community
Health Care
Parking Station
Residential

Person to Contact
Sydney
Ken Bell, Ian Poole

Perth
Howard Puddy, Peter Lee

Melbourne
David Pfaff, Howard Puddy

Brisbane
Andrew Schulz, Mark Leith

New Zealand
Ian Poole, Dorb Connell

San Francisco
Richard Tapp, Bill Moorhouse

Los Angeles
Rick Gaylord

London
Max Hutchinson

Current and Recent Projects
Office
Fourteen major office developments.

Market Street, Melbourne, Victoria
(The Jack Chia Group) $A16.5M

Taxation Office, Dandenong, Victoria
(Consulere Pty Ltd) $A10.0M

436 St. Kilda Road, Melbourne, Victoria
(Pennant Holdings Limited) $A11.6M

Broadlands Centre, Perth, Western Australia
(Pennant Holdings Limited) $A9.3M

St. George's Court, Perth, Western Australia
(Oceanic Pacific Property Trust) $A5M

225 Miller Street, North Sydney, New South Wales
(AFT Property Trust) $A1.6M

Newmarket Fair, Auckland, New Zealand
(Mace Development Corporation Limited) $NZ37.4M

Retail
Forty-three centres totalling 3.7 million square feet.

Bay City Plaza, Geelong, Victoria
(The Perron Group of Companies) $A42M

Booval Fair Shopping Centre, Booval, Ipswich,
Queensland (Woolworths Limited) $A12.0M

Armadale Shopping Centre, Armadale,
Western Australia (Pennant Holdings Limited) $A10.9M

Orange City Centre, Orange, New South Wales
(Pennant Holdings Limited) $A10M

Riverton Forum, Riverton, Western Australia
(Gillon and Osboine) $A8.1M

Fremantle Wool Stores; Fremantle, Western Australia
(Armstrong Jones Property Trust) $A6M

Newmarket Fair, Newmarket, Auckland, New Zealand
(Mace Development Corporation Limited) $NZ37.4M

Henderson Shopping Centre, Henderson, New Zealand
(Realty Development Corporation Limited) $NZ15.0M

Industrial
Wang Computer Pty Ltd, Rydalmere, New South Wales
(Wang Computer Pty Ltd) $A11.0M

Toyota, Kewdale, Western Australia
(Prestige Toyota) $A3.2M

National Panasonic, Kewdale, Western Australia
(The Perron Group of Companies) $A1.7M

Cummins Diesel, Kewdale, Western Australia
(The Perron Group of Companies) $A1.3M

Hotel
'Princes' Hotel, Perth, Western Australia
(The Greetings Group) $A5.2M

Franklin Street Hotel, Melbourne, Victoria
(The Greetings Group) $A19.3M

Derby Motel, Derby, Western Australia
(Northern Lights Pty Ltd) $A3.2M

Retirement Village
Parkland Villas, Woodlands, Western Australia
(Parkland Villas Pty Ltd) Stage I, $A3.4M $A12.5M

'Camelia Court', Bayswater, Western Australia
(Civilian Maimed & Limbless Association) $A10.7M

Churches of Christ Guest Village, Ipswich, Queensland
(Churches of Christ) $A3.3M

Religious and Community
Catholic Church, Gosnells, Western Australia
(Gosnells' Parish Catholic Church) $A0.55M

Langford Community Centre, Gosnells,
Western Australia (City of Gosnells) $A0.5M

Richard Rushton Community Centre, Langford,
Western Australia (City of Gosnells) $A0.45M

Worongary Fire Station, Queensland
(Queensland Fire Board) $A0.8M

Health Care
The Group has completed, in all, seven Health Care
centres to a value of $A6.6 million for private medical
practitioners and community groups.

Parking Station
Flinders Street Carpark, Melbourne, Victoria
(Kings Parking Co. Pty Ltd) $A3.75M

The Group has also developed expertise in retail centre
parking stations.

Residential
Johnson Residence, Point Piper, Sydney, N.S.W.
(Mr and Mrs B. Johnson) $A2.2M

'Princes Tower', Surfers Paradise, Queensland
(Cinco Developments Pty Limited) $A1.8M

'The Pelicans', Mandurah, Western Australia
(Woss Corporation) $A2.2M

Nagappa House, Dalkeith, Western Australia
(Mr and Mrs S. Nagappa) $A0.5M

Profile
The BPA Group
The BPA Group operates throughout Australia and
New Zealand with offices in Sydney, Perth, Melbourne,
Brisbane, and Auckland. BPA has associated offices in
San Francisco, Los Angeles and London.

As a company with an international perspective BPA
promotes, designs, and manages a wide range of projects
for demanding commercial companies operating in diverse
fields and differing economies. The resultant exposure to
a variety of marketplaces and clients, as well as exposure
to international research and trends, places The BPA
Group in a unique position to serve our clients' needs.

BPA chooses to base its reputation on being more
than successful designers of commercial and retail
developments, we offer our clients a range of expertise
embracing –

An understanding of property development and market
trends;

Entrepreneurial skills in identifying development
opportunities;

Design which responds to market demands;

An understanding of design, time, and cost constraints.

Today's commercial environment demands a far greater
balance of commercial understanding and architectural
skills than ever before.

In this respect The BPA Group has made it their
business to explore new ways of translating a
development concept into a design reality.

As a consequence of our entrepreneurial attitude,
we at BPA –

Identify development opportunities;

Prepare basic sketches and financial feasibility models
against which sensitivity studies can be run taking
into account constraints such as the nature of the
development, location, land value, building costs,
development costs, likely tenants, projected income
and project capitalisation, to ensure the viability of the
potential project.

The BPA Group has also been involved in retail and
high-rise commercial refurbishments, in some cases
integrating new structures with historic buildings
and facades.

BPA has kept pace with technology by introducing the
CADAM and MICRO CADAM system to its production
capabilities. The system operates with three terminals
on a double shift basis linked to the AUSTCAD main-
frame giving the documentation process greater
reliability, flexibility and speed.

Through BPA Interiors + Space Planners Pty Ltd, The
BPA Group can offer to its clients a total fitout package
and specialised major retail tenant fitout programmes.

The BPA Group, we believe in balance, not compromise.

the bpa group

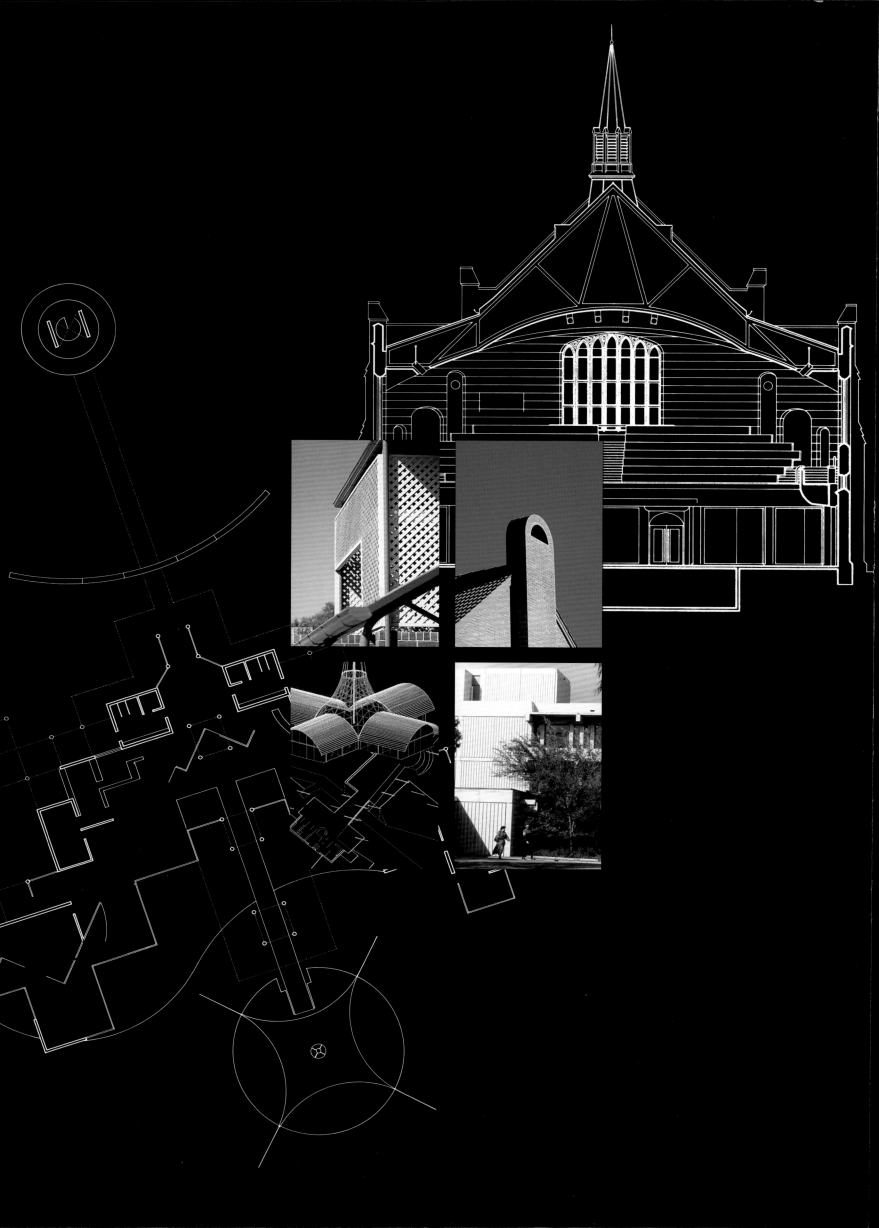

BROWN FALCONER GROUP PTY LTD

Directors
A.C. Reynolds Dip.Arch., F.R.A.I.A.
M.J. Doley B.Arch., F.R.A.I.A.
C.F. Norton Dip. Arch., R.W.A., R.I.B.A.,
   F.R.A.I.A., A.C.I.Arb.
D.G. Risbey R.I.B.A., F.R.A.I.A.
C.R. Wilson Dip.Arch., Dip. T.P., F.R.A.I.A.
A.L.S. Davies B.Arch.(Hons), Grad.Dip.
   A.R.A.I.A.

Established
Gordon Brown commenced sole
practice in 1946.
Brown Falconer Group Pty. Ltd.
formed in 1975.

Address
255 Magill Road
Maylands, S.A. 5069

P.O. Box 330
Norwood, S.A. 5067

Telephone
(08) 332 5655

Facsimile
(08) 333 2142

Regional Office
33 Mackay Street
Port Augusta, S.A. 5700

Telephone
(086) 42 4050

Number of Employees
30-35

Project Types
Health Services
Hospitals, Medical Centres

Aged Care
Nursing Homes, Hostel developments,
Day Centres

Educational Facilities
Schools and Colleges

Community and Recreational Facilities
Civic Centres, Sporting complexes and
Interpretive Centres

Commercial
Office/Retail

Housing

Other Disciplines
Electrical Engineering
Town Planning
Project Management
Interior Design
Graphic Design
Computing Applications

Person to Contact
Andrew Davies

Current and Recent Projects

Health Services
Western Community Hospital
104 Bed Hospital with 30 bed Nursing Home,
20 Semi-dependent units (joint venture with
S.A. Housing Trust), Day Therapy Centre

Mount Barker District Soldiers Memorial Hospital
Redevelopment of existing hospital complex

North-Eastern Community Hospital
Original development and redevelopment

Repatriation General Hospital – Daw Park
Various projects and Master Planning Study

The Brown Falconer Group are Architects for
approximately forty metropolitan and country hospitals

Aged Care
Various projects for the following clients in addition to
projects for a number of Local Government and country
aged care bodies and hospitals

Masonic Memorial Homes Trust Inc.

Southern Cross Homes, Lourdes Valley

Helping Hand Centre Inc.

Resthaven Incorporated

Aged Cottage Homes

Central Methodist Mission

Christian Rest Homes

Salvation Army (S.A.) Property Trust

S.A. Baptist Homes for the Aged Inc.

Educational Facilities
Collegiate School of St. Peter
Preparatory School Development Study
Preparatory School resource centre and classrooms
"Old Prep. Building" restoration and refurbishing
Memorial Hall reconstruction (after fire)
Chapel Refurbishment

Prince Alfred College
Sports Centre, Science Building and Boarding Houses

Scotch College
Sports Centre, Master Planning Study

Walford Anglican School for Girls
Development Study
Science and Junior School classroom buildings
Music and Art facilities, Assembly Hall

Education Department Facilities
Various state schools

Community and Recreational Facilities
The Parks Community Centre
High School, Sports Centre, Performing Arts Centre,
Health Centre

Waikerie Civic Centre

Christchurch Uniting Church
Church on the Parkin-Wesley Theological College
Campus

Payneham Civic Centre

Regional Interpretive Centres
Signal Point – River Murray Interpretive Centre, Goolwa
Wadlata – Outback Interpretive Centre, Port Augusta

Arid Lands Botanic Park

Commercial
Highways Department, Port Augusta
North Regional Office and Depot complex

State Bank of South Australia
A number of branches

Housing
South Australian Housing Trust
Donegal Street Housing,
Various joint venture housing developments

Profile
Brown Falconer Group Pty. Ltd. was formed by the
incorporation of practices of Brown Davies Reynolds
& Doley Pty. Ltd. and Peter Falconer Pty. Ltd.

The Group is now an inter-disciplinary practice
incorporating architects, engineers, planners, project
managers, interior designers and a computing scientist
providing a comprehensive range of professional skills.

Combining a diversity of expertise with a broad base
of experience, the practice is identified with a significant
reputation for proficiency and performance skilfully
applied to a wide variety of successful projects.

Maintaining the ability to respond to the requirements
of private, ecclesiastical, community-based and government clients, the firm has consistently developed a
sound reputation for special expertise in cost-effective
and innovative solutions to Health, Welfare and
Educational projects.

Architectural Methodology
We believe that the most successful solutions are
primarily evolved from a framework of close client
consultation, a cognitive understanding of functional,
technical and emotional requirements and user needs,
combined with a continuity of personnel throughout
the project.

The need for client and user participation in the design
process, to develop and explore concepts and ideas,
and to articulate lateral thinking is of fundamental
importance. This process, constantly reinforced by
an effective programme of post-occupancy evaluation
and review, also promotes an understanding and per-
ception by those who will occupy, manage or use the
environment created.

The practice has developed and adhered to a clear and
simple philosophy of deriving an architectural solution
based on a humanist approach, combining art and technology in logical resolution with the aim of enhancing
the lives of those affected by the built environment.

The continuing success of the Brown Falconer Group
lies in its ability to combine proven expertise with the
enthusiasm and dedication of skilled professionals to
procure architecture that will delight, yet at the same
time satisfy established objectives.

BROWN
FALCONER

Architects
Planners
Engineers +
Project Managers

1 Rialto, Melbourne, Exterior Design
2 North Ryde Industrial Project
3 Pitt and Market Streets Project
4 St Joseph's Church, Croydon
5 Fay Richwhite Building, Auckland, N.Z.

DINO BURATTINI & ASSOCIATES
Architects

Principal
Dino Burattini FRAIA, ARIBA

Associates (left to right)
Anthony W. Price B.ARCH (HONS) ARAIA
Trevor G. Beardsmore B.ARCH. ARAIA
Nicholas Gray DIP.ARCH. COMP ARAIA
Francesco Brundu DIP. G.
Terry O'Rourke B.ARCH UNI NSW

Interior Design
Susan Koedam B.A. Interior Design

Address
720 George Street
Sydney, N.S.W. 2000

Telephone
(02) 212 6844

Facsimile
(02) 281 2256

Number of Employees
In excess of 50

Project Types
Commercial
Industrial
Residential
Refurbishment
Hotel & Tourism
Retail

Other Disciplines
Computer Aided Design & Architectural
Programming
Interior Design

Persons to Contact
Anthony Price
Trevor Beardsmore
Joy Marshall

Current and Recent Projects

City Centre Project –
Pitt and Market Streets, Sydney
26 level office and retail development including
18 office floors and 4 retail floors (35770m² gross area).

Royal Prince Alfred Hospital –
R.P.A.H. Medical Centre, corner Carillon Avenue and
Missendon Road, Camperdown
5 levels of specialist doctors' suites (area 9500m²).
3 levels of car parking for 250 cars (area 8500m²).

155 George Street
Located in The Rocks district, the 13 level commercial
building comprises 9 levels of commercial space (area
10526m²), 2 levels of retail (area 1472m²), and 3 levels of
car parking for 133 cars.

St Martins Tower, 31 Market Street, Sydney
Extensive refurbishment of the building facade to create
a new design philosophy and appearance.

North Ryde office developments at
Waterloo Road, North Ryde
One comprising 17000m² of office space, the other
comprising 18000m² of office/warehouse.

Design for Fay Richwhite Building
151 Queen Street, Auckland, New Zealand
31 storey office and retail development with a car
parking station.

The Royal Exchange Building, 56 Pitt Street, Sydney
Extensive exterior and interior refurbishment.

35-41 Macquarie Street, Sydney
19 storey office development facing Circular Quay and
the Royal Botanic Gardens.

The Church of St Joseph, at Croydon
An imaginative design reflecting the religious
philosophies of the community.

Rockdale Shopping Complex
Princes Highway, Rockdale
Shops and major retail stores (35000m² area). Parking for
2000 cars, with cinema complex including 10 theatres.
4000m² of office space.

Angel Arcade
320 George Street through to 119 Pitt Street, Sydney
Retail and office development comprising 36 level and 24
level towers, includes 6300m² retail area, 69400m²
rentable office space and parking area for 350 cars.

Dixon Street Development
between Goulburn and Liverpool Streets, Sydney
Retail and Hotel complex comprising 15 levels (32700m²
gross area). The complex incorporates Darling Walk
Monorail Station and overlooks Darling Harbour
development.

Mid City Centre, 197-211 Pitt Street and
420-422 George Street, Sydney
Office and retail development. 21 level office tower on
existing Mid City Centre retail complex (50000m²). The
development involves the complete remodelling of retail
area and internal pedestrian malls.

Profile

Dino Burattini has more than 30 years experience in
architecture and has developed in that time a sound
reputation for leadership, innovation and performance.

Having initially studied architectural design in Europe
he developed the ambience and creativity to become
one of Australia's most influential architects.

He is recognised as a leader in the design of major
Hotels and Commercial projects in this country, South
East Asia, the Middle East, and The United States of
America. His work is consistently unique, visually
exciting but practical and has received numerous
awards and citations for excellence.

His firm specialises in high quality design and
documentation for a range of projects including major
Commercial buildings and employs a cohesive team
of professionally qualified and highly experienced staff
to maintain services and production capacity for all
projects undertaken. The core of experienced permanent
staff is supplemented by contract draftspersons in
accordance with the workload.

Several of the firm's senior architects have worked
directly with Dino over a continuous period of more
than 15 years developing a strong working relationship
of teamwork and communication. They are actively
involved in various technical committees and organi-
zations such as B.O.M.A., which assists ongoing research
and development activities to the benefit of all projects
undertaken. Their professionalism and abilities are held
in high regard among major contractors and consultants in the industry.

Computer technology is utilised not only for
administrative, clerical and financial control but also for
design presentation and documentation work. In the
interests of speed, co-ordination and quality of technical
and presentation work, the firm has its own three
dimensional computer-aided drawing system.

To ensure total integration of architecture and interior
design, a comprehensive interior design service is
provided.

As all appointments are equally important in terms of
the firm's objectives, with particular attention given to
the function, operation and commercial viability of each
project, it has established an impressive list of major
corporate and institutional clients as well as prominent
developers and building contractors.

Dino Burattini & Associates will continue to forward its
professional name in Australia and internationally with
ideas and architecture that are imaginative, unique and
professionally implemented and with a high standard of
service to each of its clients.

New Law Courts, Bendigo, circa 1892.

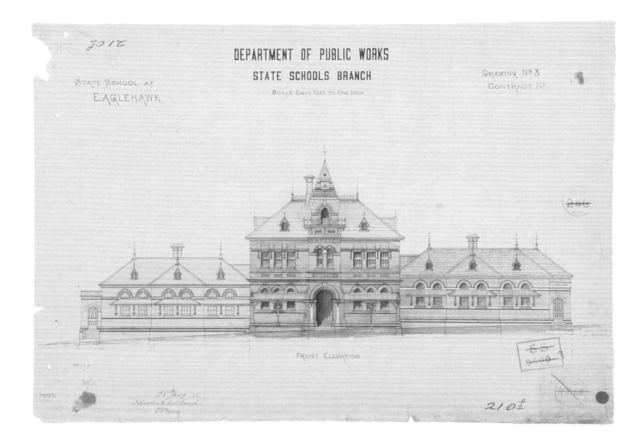

State School at Eaglehawk, circa 1886.

1

2

3

4

1 R & I Bank Tower

2 Carillon Centre

3 W.A. Education Department Headquarters

4 The Alexander Library Building

5 Boans City Centre

6 Wesfarmers House

7 Centennial Plaza, Sydney

8 Argyle House

9 Belconnen Mall, A.C.T.

10 Waterfront Place, Brisbane

11 Australia Place

12 AETNA Life Offices, Chatswood

5

6

7

8

9

10

11

12

CAMERON CHISHOLM & NICOL PTY LTD

Directors (left to right)
Ross Chisholm
Jim Wilkinson
Bill Weedon
Laurie Fuhrmann
Barry Cameron
Tony Swinbourne

Established

Perth	1884
Canberra	1969
Sydney	1982
Brisbane	1987

Perth
Directors
Ross Chisholm APTC(Arch) LFRAIA ARIBA
Jim Wilkinson APTC(Arch) FRAIA ARIBA
Bill Weedon M.Arch(Calif.) APTC(Arch) ARAIA
Laurie Fuhrmann APTC(Arch) FRAIA

Address
Australia Place
15 William Street
Perth, W.A. 6000

Telephone   **Facsimile**
(09) 322 1566   (09) 481 0854

Canberra
Director
Barry Cameron Dip.Arch(APTC) FRAIA ARIBA

Address
16 National Circuit
Barton, A.C.T. 2600

Telephone   **Facsimile**
(062) 73 3922   (062) 73 2603

Sydney
Director
Tony Swinbourne B.Arch(UNSW) FRAIA

Address
5 Norberry Terrace
199 Pacific Highway
North Sydney, N.S.W. 2060

Telephone   **Facsimile**
(02) 922 4677   (02) 922 6415

Brisbane
Associate Director
Henry Peel B.Arch(Hons) Qld ARAIA

Address
1st Floor
Naldham House
Cnr Felix & Mary Streets
Brisbane, Qld 4000

Telephone   **Facsimile**
(07) 221 7422   (07) 221 5473

Associate Directors
Perth
Eddie Goodfellow Dip.Arch(Hammersmith)
   FRAIA ARIBA
Kym MacCormac B.Arch(Adelaide) FRAIA
Rob Strzelecki A.(WAIT) ARAIA
Greg Salter A.(WAIT) ARAIA

Sydney
Manfred Kersch M.Arch.Des(UNSW)
   B.Arch(Hons) UNSW

Manager
Robert Borland B.Comm(UWA) AIMM

Staff
The number of employees in all offices
usually numbers between 65-75

Project Types
Offices
Low, Medium and High Rise
Retail
Regional, Town and Neighbourhood Centres
Civic
Libraries, Municipal Buildings, Transport Facilities
Educational
Schools, Colleges, University Buildings
Resort Developments
Hotels, Casinos, Convention and Exhibition Buildings,
Sports Arenas
Residential
Public Housing, Group Dwellings, Apartments
Industrial
Workshops, Warehouses, Laboratories

Current and Recent Projects
Offices
W.A. Fire Brigades Board
Metropolitan Water Authority
Forests Department
Eastpoint Plaza
Education Department Building
Allendale Square
City Centre
Australia Place
Wesfarmers House
Argyle House
R & I Bank Tower
AETNA Centre, Chatswood, N.S.W.
Centennial Plaza, Sydney
Waterfront Place, Brisbane
Retail
Carousel Shopping Centre
Karrinyup Town Centre
Belconnen Mall, A.C.T.
Whitford City
Noarlunga Colonnades, S.A.
Carillon Centre
Boans City Centre
Morley City
Joondalup Town Centre
Civic
Karrinyup Civic Centre
Melville Civic Centre
Floreat Civic Centre
Alexander Library Building
Transperth Bus Junction
Educational
University of W.A. – Various Faculty
Buildings and Reid Library
Curtin University – Various Faculty
Buildings and School of Nursing
Penrhos MLC College
Prendiville Catholic College
State Public Schools
Resort Development
Burswood Island Resort – Hotel,
Convention Centre, Exhibition Hall
Residential
Belconnen & Fisher Mass Housing, A.C.T.
Freshwater Close Apartments & Town Houses
City Gardens, East Perth
Cromarty Village, N.S.W.
Industrial
Transperth Workshops
Transperth Running Depots
WAGR Road Workshops
SPD Warehouse & Offices, Kewdale
SPD Warehouse & Offices, S.A.
Piccadilly Square

Design Philosophy
The thrust of the firm's design philosophy is "to demonstrate that today's successful buildings can only evolve when human needs, environment, energy and economic concerns are integrated in a simultaneous rather than sequential fashion".

The past 30 years have afforded special opportunities to complete a comprehensive range of projects for a wide variety of clients: governmental, institutional and commercial. From its Perth office the firm has expanded over the years to Canberra, Sydney and Brisbane. Tasks and staffing are handled largely on a project by project basis, drawing upon previous experience where appropriate, always under the direct supervision of a senior director.

The involvement and interest of selected staff members are maintained throughout the total programme of each commission from the initial concept through the various stages of documentation and project management to completion, occupation and use.

Thorough analysis of the client's requirements and needs precede the preparation of the comprehensive design brief. Strong emphasis is placed upon the achievement of the best architectural design solution within constraints of budget and time.

By establishing and maintaining a close personal working relationship with each client or his representative all projects are effectively monitored through the various phases to ensure that programmes, cost control and refinements to briefed information are achieved.

The design process requires effort, organisation and close collaboration between client, architect and the consultant team. Special importance is placed upon working creatively, co-operatively and efficiently with the specialist knowledge and capacities of each team member and with lines of communication open at all times. Shared analysis of the design issues encourages effective interpretation into the built solution.

Progressive answers are sought to architectural challenges via a thorough knowledge of constructional materials, innovative techniques and building services. Fundamental to the firm's existence is the commitment to build well and to seek at all times an understanding and application of the best of technology.

Architectural clarity and a timelessness of form and detail in the built work are design aims which help to make each completed project stimulating and relevant to its users and to generate the widest range of opportunities, immediate and future, in the broader use and care of the built environment.

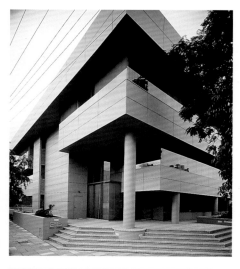

CANN ARCHITECTS PTY LTD

Chairman
Robert J. B. Cann B. Arch (Melb) FRAIA

Directors (left to right)
Neil R. Ross FRAIA HKIA
Tony Schmaehling M.Arch (YALE)
J. Bruce Callow A. Arch (WAIT) FRAIA C.D.
Steven C. Artelaris B. Arch (WAIT) ARAIA
Darryl Parker A. Arch (WAIT)
Rod Marshall B. Arch (UWA) Hons. ARAIA
John Hutchison Dip. Arch (ABDN) ARAIA
  ARIBA
Bevan Johns B. Arch (Adelaide) ARAIA

Finance Director
Colin Logie

Established
1971

Addresses
Perth
23rd Floor
The Forrest Centre
221 St. George's Terrace
Perth, W.A. 6000

Telephone   **Facsimile**
(09) 322 1411   (09) 322 6799

Telex
CANN AA94479

Sydney
17th Floor
Royal Exchange Building
56 Pitt Street
Sydney, N.S.W. 2000

Telephone   **Facsimile**
(02) 251 4078   (02) 251 4312

Queensland
7th Floor
Gateway Building
50 Appel Street
Surfers Paradise, Qld 4217

Telephone   **Facsimile**
(075) 92 0094   (075) 38 2440

Number of Employees
80

Client Services
Architecture
Interior Design
Space Planning
Site Analysis and Project Feasibility
Technical and Consultant Co-ordination
Project Management
Computer Support Services
Contract Documentation
Contract Administration and Inspection
Project Development

Project Types
Architectural   Interior Design
Commercial   Hotel/Resort
Educational   Office
Hotel/Resort   Restaurant
Industrial   Residential
Multi-Residential
Municipal
Recreational
Retaii

Persons to Contact
Robert Cann
Perth
Neil Ross, Bruce Callow
Sydney
Steve Artelaris, Tony Schmaehling
Surfers Paradise
Darryl Parker, Tony Schmaehling

Current and Recent Projects
Architectural/Commercial
'The Forrest Centre,' 221 St George's Terrace, Perth
30 and 8 Storey Office Complex

Bus Junction and 2A Carpark
For Transperth and Perth City Council
In association with Cameron Chisholm & Nicol

'Irwin Chambers', Cnr Hay and Irwin Streets, Perth
6 Storey Office Development

'Markalinga House', 253 St George's Terrace, Perth
8 Storey Office

76 Kings Park Road, Cnr Thomas Street, West Perth
5 Storey Office Development

24 Outram and Ord Streets, West Perth
5 Storey Office Development

28-42 Ventnor Avenue, West Perth
5 Storey Office Development

'Scott House', 46-48 Kings Park Road, West Perth
5 Storey Office Development

26 Colin and Ord Streets, West Perth
3 Storey Office Development

6 Kings Park Road, West Perth
3 Storey Office Development

Spencer Street, Bunbury
2 Storey Office Development

Agricultural Department 'E' Block,
Jarrah Road, South Perth

Educational
Midland Technical College, Stage II

Maida Vale Classrooms and Library
and Resource Centre

Hotel/Recreational
Observation City Resort Hotel, Scarborough

Western Australian Indoor Sports Complex
'Superdrome', Mt. Claremont

Scarborough Surf Lifesaving Club

North Beach Community Recreation Centre

Multi-Residential
'Peninsula Village', Maylands
400 Townhouse Development

Observation City, Scarborough
Beachfront Residential Apartments
Design Development

'Twin Waters', South Perth
23 Luxury Apartments

'Parklane', Crawley
19 Luxury Apartments

'Parkhill', Crawley
17 Luxury Apartments, Refurbishment

'Minderup', South Perth
Luxury Apartments

Interior Design
B.H.P. Offices

W.A. Development Corporation, Offices

British Airways, Perth International Airport
V.I.P. Lounge

Observation City Resort Hotel and Retail
All Public Areas Complete Fit-Out (i.e. Restaurants,
Convention Centre, Ballroom, Bars, Lobby, Reception,
Nightclub and Retail Shopping Arcade)

The Western Mail
4 Floors – Executive Offices

Legal & General
Building Refurbishment

Mitsui & Company, Offices

Oceanic Equity Ltd, Offices

Markalinga Management Ltd, Office Headquarters

Julia Mines N.L., Head Office

Mediterranean Garden Restaurant, Refurbishment

Collison, Hunt & Richardson, Offices

Midland Technical College
Interior Fit-Out Co-ordination

W.A. Sports Complex, 'Superdrome'
Interior Co-ordination

Awards and Competitions
1987 RAIA Design Awards
Commendation 'The Forrest Centre'

Concrete Masonry Association of Australia
Award for Excellence
Commercial Building Category 1984
Office Building: Cnr Colin and Ord Street, West Perth

Residential Building Category 1984
'Parklane Apartments', Crawley

International Besser Masonry Award 1983
3 Storey Office Building
Cnr Colin and Ord Streets, West Perth

NW Housing Award, State Housing Commission

Observation City, Scarborough
Austmark International Ltd
Hotel Resort and Residential complex
limited competition

Markalinga House, 251 St. George's Terrace, Perth
Markalinga Pty Ltd
8 Storey Corporate Office Project limited competition

Western Australian Sports Centre
State Government of Western Australia Sporting
Complex. Limited competition designed in association
with Peter Hunt Architect and using Daryl Jackson
Pty Ltd as consultants

Carr Boyd Minerals
3 Storey Corporate Office Development
Limited competition

Profile
Cann Architects Pty Ltd, formerly Robert Cann and
Associates, has expanded over the last 15 years from
its large Perth base to incorporate offices in Sydney and
Surfers Paradise. Continuing clients include, the State
Government, major corporations, private and public
companies and private individuals. The core staff of the
practice has a collective experience extending across
Australia and overseas.

The nature of projects carried out in recent years has
been varied in both type and value ranging up to $100
million. The success of these projects demonstrates the
versatility of the practice and a progressive approach
in seeking new projects and fulfilling clients' needs.

Cann Architects' philosophy is in building towards
tomorrow; creating not only the built environment but
appreciating users' interaction with their surroundings.
The design approach is directed towards providing
enduring aesthetic standards with sculptural qualities
together with a strong sense of commercial viability.

Direct involvement with, and initiation of, several major
projects demonstrates the understanding and ability of
the practice to relate to their clients' needs aesthetically,
financially and commercially. C.A.D. and financial
modelling computer facilities plus an on-staff financial
adviser provide backup for the complexities of initiating
major projects in today's economic climate.

Cann Interior Design, an autonomous arm of the
organisation, also offers clients a diverse range of
expertise and services. Able to accept commissions
independent of an architectural role, this department
has successfully completed a diverse range of major
projects since its establishment in 1985.

1 Darwin Parliament House – Competition Entry

2 Frank Daniels, Printers

3 Cattell Residence

4 City of Bayswater, Administration Centre

5 Control Tower at Karratha Airport

6 Commercial Offices – Competition Winning Scheme   *7 Fire Station at Karratha Airport*

9 Enterprise Unit Complex at Technology Park – Node 250

8 Rockingham Hotel Tourist Complex   *10 Bayswater Works Depot*

CHRISTOU & VUKO PTY LTD
Architects & Interior Designers

Directors (left to right)
Peter Christou B.Arch (HONS) ARAIA
Brian Vuko APTC (Arch Dist.) FRAIA

Established
January 1981

Address
8 Bowman Street
South Perth, W.A. 6151

Telephone
(09) 367 9714
(09) 367 9661

Facsimile
(09) 474 1652

Project Types
Commercial
Government
Civic
Institutional
Industrial
Resorts
Airports
Educational
Broadcasting
Residential – single and multiple
Community/Recreational
Retail

Services
Full Architectural Services –
including design, documentation,
administration and consultants
appointment and technical
co-ordination.

Feasibility Studies – research, site,
costing and design.

Urban and interior design.

Planning – Town and space.

Project management.

Professional advice.

Other Disciplines
Interior Design
Urban Design
Research and Planning
Project Management

Persons to Contact
Peter Christou
Brian Vuko

Current and Recent Projects
City of Bayswater Administration Centre in Embleton,
Western Australia 1984
Awards:
R.A.I.A. Design Award 1984 – W A Chapter
R.A.I.A. National Sir Zelman Cowen Award Finalist
(1 in 4) 1984
R.A.I.A. Civic Design Award – W A Chapter
– Runner up in 1987
BOMA Awards – Public Building Category and overall
BOMA winner 1986

Cattell Residence
in Carine, Perth, Western Australia 1985 –
R.A.I.A. Design Award 1986 – W A Chapter

Enterprise Unit Complex at Technology Park, Bentley,
Western Australia (1984-87) – comprising 5 buildings
of various tenancies, uses, sizes and layouts

20 Residential Unit Development
in South Perth, Western Australia 1986-87

South Perth Esplanade Commercial Development 1987
– in conjunction with Lawrence Heah Architect

Control Tower at Karratha Airport 1986

Design Proposals for Perth International Mint 1986-87

Fire Station at Karratha Airport 1987

York Tourist Farm on 40ha of land below
Mount Bakewell in the Town of York – 1986

100 single mens accommodation for Mount Newman
1987 – invited competition

Darwin Parliament House 1985 – National Competition
–Scheme selected for exhibition purposes

Master Builders Association (MBA) office
refurbishment, Perth, Western Australia 1987

City of Canning Community/Recreational Centre –
Whaleback, Lynwood, Western Australia 1987

Rockingham Hotel Tourist Complex 1987 –
in association with Krantz, Sheldon, Arndt,
Silbert & West Architects

City of Bayswater Works Depot, Perth,
Western Australia 1987

Technology & Industry Development Authority,
Science and Discovery Centre, Perth 1987

Parry Corporation Development Proposal for extensive
tourist facilities at Mandurah on 37ha of land at Peel
Inlet, Western Australia 1985

City of Kwinana Works Depot, Perth,
Western Australia 1987

Australian Broadcasting Commission
Ongoing projects in Perth and country areas, 1981-1987

Mandurah Hospital for Building Management
Authority, Perth, Western Australia 1987 – second
place in invited Design and Construct competition
with Concrete Constructions

Steedman's Scientific Complex, Perth 1987

Offices for shipping company in Fremantle,
Western Australia 1987

City of Stirling Community Centre – invited limited
competition 1987

Frank Daniels Printers – office and workshops, Perth,
Western Australia 1985

Childrens Services Centre in Fremantle,
Western Australia 1985

Hornibrook Office/Workshop complex, Perth,
Western Australia 1983

Westel Office/Warehouse complex, Perth, Western
Australia 1984

Perth Airport Refurbishment 1983

Leightons Office Refurbishment, Perth,
Western Australia 1984

Several individual residences

Numerous development proposals for commercial,
institutional, resort and multi-residential projects

History
Christou & Vuko Pty Ltd was established in January
1981 following its directors' winning submission in
an open competition for a large and prestigious office
complex overlooking the Swan River and Perth skyline.

The firm based its foundation on this success and
30 years experience on a wide and diverse range of
projects, together with the recognised individual and
complementary design and construction skills of its
two directors, Peter Christou and Brian Vuko.

Due to this unique and complementary partnership,
they provide, each in their own right, a specific and
personalised service to their clients and a direct input
on all projects from inception through to completion.

Profile
Christou & Vuko Pty Ltd is recognised as one of the most
progressive and innovative architectural *design* firms in
Western Australia.

This reputation is based on the firm's rapid emergence in
the profession and its continuing and diversified success
in a number of competitions and awards for residential,
commercial and civic projects.

The successful marriage of these two conflicting and
opposing notions of design excellence versus cost
effectiveness was exemplified in the firm's success in
the Building Owners and Managers Association Award
where C & V was awarded the Public Building Category
prize (6 categories in total) and the overall winner of
the BOMA Award for 1986.

The significance of this award is measured in terms of
its commercial viability.

To quote the Association's judging criteria:

'The BOMA Award is granted only to buildings
which are economically profitable to the owner
and offer good value to the occupants.'

Philosophy
Christou & Vuko have developed an architectural
philosophy whose language and identity will stand the
test of time, particularly in today's highly competitive,
constantly changing and fashionable market place.

An architecture that is:
simple yet elegant
modern yet timeless
exciting yet functional
innovative yet cost effective

The firm's policy of design, attention to detail and
construction is reflected in the simple clean lines of its
buildings which rely on scale, massing and proportion
for meaning and relevance rather than 'applied'
gimmickry and short-lived fashion trends – thus
ensuring not only an enduring quality in their buildings
but a reliable long term capital investment to their
clients as well.

Christou & Vuko are committed to architecture and
to this end have established a corporate policy of
undertaking projects of a varied nature and size rather
than concentrating on, or being identified with, a
specific building type or field.

C & V will continue to maintain this flexibility and the
pursuit of excellence.

The Salvation Army National Secretariat

Australia's Wonderland, Blacktown

Waterman Centre, C.C.E.G.G.S.

A.C.T. Health Commission Building

Hornsby T.A.F.E.

Ray Rosbrook Hall, Moore Park

COLLARD CLARKE & JACKSON PTY LTD
Architects and Planners

Directors (left to right)
Guy Clarke, B.Arch. (Hons), F.R.A.I.A.,
 F.I.ARB.A.
Peter Cook, B.Arch., F.R.A.I.A., R.I.B.A.
Robert Beverley, B.Arch., F.R.A.I.A.
Tim McNamara, B.Arch. (Hons), A.R.A.I.A.
Ross Maxwell, B.Arch., A.R.A.I.A.
Stephen Doney, B.Arch., (Assoc. Director)

Established
1947

Sydney Office
40 Miller Street
North Sydney, N.S.W. 2060

P.O. Box 77
North Sydney, N.S.W. 2059

Telephone
(02) 92 0637

Facsimile
(02) 92 1191

Canberra Office
55 Woolley Street
Dickson, A.C.T. 2602

Telephone
(062) 47 2077

Facsimile
(062) 47 3507

Number of Employees
24

Project Types
Education and Research
Schools and Special Schools
College & University Buildings
Research Laboratories

Industrial and Commercial
Offices & Tenancies
Warehouses & Special Repositories
Bakeries

Residential and Health Care
Group Housing
Aged Care Housing
Nursing Homes
Health Services

Recreation & Leisure
Gymnasiums & Sports Halls
Theme Park Development

Other Disciplines
Master Planning
Consulting on Building Controls
Landscape Architecture in association with
Robb Gourgaud & Associates

Director to contact
Sydney
Peter Cook

Canberra
Robert Beverley

Current and Recent Projects
Education and Research
Master Planning, Trinity, Summer Hill

Master Planning, C.C.E.G.G.S., A.C.T.

Research School of Earth Sciences,
Australian National University, Stage 4

Hornsby College, T.A.F.E., Stages 3 & 4
for N.S.W. Government Architect

Werrington College, T.A.F.E., Stage 1
for N.S.W. Government Architect

Industrial Arts, Art Buildings & Art Gallery,
Trinity, Summer Hill

Tamworth College, T.A.F.E. Stage 6 for
N.S.W. Government Architect

Cranleigh Special School, Stage 3, A.C.T.

Research Buildings, A.N.S.T.O., Lucas Heights

Art/Design Centre, C.C.E.G.G.S., A.C.T.

Industrial and Commercial
Orion Park Industrial Estate, Stages 1, 2 & 3,
Lane Cove

Salvation Army National Headquarters, Barton, A.C.T.

Industrial Estate Redevelopment, Stages 1, 2 & 3,
Brookvale

Bakery for George Weston Foods, Canning Vale, W.A.

Bakery for George Weston Foods, Dry Creek, S.A.

Commercial Offices for Tekmat Investments, A.C.T.

Food Manufacturing Plant, Fairfield

Department of Local Government and Administrative
Services, Civic, A.C.T.

Australian War Memorial Repository, Mitchell, A.C.T.

George Weston Foods Head Offices, St. Leonards

Recreation and Leisure
Gymnasium, C.C.E.G.G.S., A.C.T.

Moore Park Multi-Purpose Hall for Sydney City Council

Gymnasium, Trinity, Summer Hill

Indoor Entertainment Centre, Belconnen, A.C.T.

Australia's Wonderland, Theme Park, Blacktown

Indoor Sports Centre, Holroyd

Residential, Health and Municipal
Ainslie Village Redevelopment, Stages 1 & 2, A.C.T.

National Medical Cyclotron Project, R.P.A.H.,
Camperdown

Fire Station, Chisholm, A.C.T.

Family Centre, Charnwood, A.C.T.

Nursing Home upgrading for Ashfield Homes Trust

Albert Residence, Woollahra

St. Johns Ambulance Headquarters, Deakin, A.C.T.

Group Housing, Scullin, A.C.T.

Profile
The Practice of Collard Clarke & Jackson Pty. Ltd. has evolved from the office established by Max Collard in Sydney in 1947. Guy Clarke joined the firm in 1955 and Phillip Jackson in 1962. Peter Cook and Robert Beverley became Directors of Collard Clarke & Jackson Pty. Ltd. in 1980 and Tim McNamara and Ross Maxwell in 1984.

Since its formation the company has provided services to numerous government departments and statutory authorities, public and private companies, developers and charities in a wide range of building types.

Ability
Collard Clarke & Jackson is unique in running fully integrated offices in Sydney and Canberra achieving significant output of quality work with small teams of dedicated professionals and with the Directors intimately involved throughout each project. Work load is restricted to maintain this mode of operation which is central to our philosophy of design and documentation and communication of ideas with our clients.

We have experience in projects with varying contractual arrangements including project management and negotiated contracts and in techniques such as fast tracking for both new work and upgrading of existing buildings.

Collard Clarke & Jackson has worked in association with a number of other architectural practices and with the architectural offices of major building procurers such as the National Capital Development Commission and the New South Wales Public Works Department and has completed projects throughout Australia and overseas.

Approach
The wide range of our experience with a team approach to building allows us to tackle difficult projects with confidence.

We see the development of rational solutions to design problems flowing from cost effective construction and a rational framework of regulations. To this end we are committed to the industry in which we work and serve on numerous committees and working groups, particularly in relation to building and planning controls, regulations and industry standards.

We place importance on cost planning and appropriate technology to achieve budgets and building programs. We see good architecture as responding naturally to the environmental and spatial context of each site and above all expressing the classic values inherent in thoughtful design in resolving the complex and conflicting demands of the contemporary urban fabric.

CONRAD & GARGETT PTY LIMITED

Directors
W.A.H. Conrad B.Arch FRAIA RIBA
P.R. Gargett B.Arch FRAIA RIBA
J.D. McPhee B.Arch FRAIA
F.R. Holmes Dip Arch FRAIA
G.J. Cumming Dip Arch FRAIA
K.R. Whiteoak Dip Arch FRAIA
J.L. Blanshard B.Arch Dip HFP FRAIA
R.B. Henderson B.Arch M.A. HFP FRAIA
M.D. Williamson FRAIA
E.D.F. Wyeth ASTC (Arch) FRAIA
D.E. Winsen Dip Arch FRAIA

Associates
P.J. Keatinge Dip Arch FRAIA
Sipen B.Arch FRAIA ADIA
P.W. Wilkes B.Arch ARAIA
G.D. Meiklejohn Dip Arch ARAIA
M.C. Stephensen B.Arch ARAIA
R.I. Hadgraft Dip Arch M.A. HFP ARAIA
J.I. Bennett B.Arch ARAIA

Consultants
L.H. Hailey B.Arch DQIT (Land Arch) FRAIA
J.M. Orange Dip Arch FRAIA RIBA

Established
1890

Addresses
Suncorp Centre
Albert & Turbot Streets
Brisbane, Qld 4000

Box 170 GPO
Brisbane, Qld 4001

Telephone
(07) 229 3555

Telex
CG ARCH 42769

Facsimile
(07) 221 7878

C. & G. Buildings Brisbane (Photo left)

1 *Princess Alexandra Hospital*
2 *Mapping & Surveying Building*
3 *ANZ Special Services Building*
4 *Queensland Government Printer*
5 *Parliament House Renovations*
6 *Q.I.T. Physics & Paramedical*
7 *State Executive Building*
8 *The Gardens Apartments*
9 *National Mutual Centre*
10 *Santos House & Rowes Arcade*
11 *ANZ Bank Building*
12 *National Bank House*
13 *Sheraton Brisbane Hotel*
14 *Central Station Development*
15 *Commonwealth Bank Capital Building (under construction)*
16 *IBM Building*
17 *Commonwealth Bank, King George Square*
18 *Suncorp Building & Theatre*
19 *Craigston*
20 *Watkins Medical Centre*
21 *Brisbane Administration Centre*
22 *Comalco Building*
23 *The Ansett Centre*
24 *Centaur House*

Gold Coast Office
Suite 3, 23 Orchid Avenue
Surfers Paradise, Qld 4217

Telephone
(075) 50 3300

Number of Employees
80

Value of Commissions 1986-1987
$185M

Project Types	Percentage
Commercial	50%
Industrial	4%
Health Care	28%
Hotels/Recreational	5%
Governmental/Educational	4%
Restoration	5%
Interior/Fitout	3%
Landscape	1%

Other Disciplines
Interior Design & Space Planning
Landscape Architecture

Person to Contact
Peter Gargett or John Blanshard

A Selection of Current and Recent Projects
Commercial
Brisbane GPO Redevelopment (Stage 1 Study)
Commonwealth Bank Capital Office
85 George Street
IBM Centre
Santos House
National Mutual Centre
National Bank House

Industrial
Queensland Newspapers Pty Ltd
Graphic Arts Complex
Norman Kepple Printing

Health Care
The Prince Charles Hospital, Cardiac Intensive Care Block
Royal Brisbane Hospital, Bone Marrow Transplant Unit
Princess Alexandra Hospital, Magnetic Resonance Imaging Unit
Spinal Injuries Unit
St. Martin's Nursing Home
Abri Home Southport

Hotels/Recreational
Sheraton Brisbane Hotel
in association with Wimberley, Whisenand, Allison, Tong & Goo
Lennons Hotel Refurbishment

Government/Educational
Mapping & Surveying Building
Embassy for the Arab Republic of Egypt, Canberra
in association with Cameron McNamara
Warwick TAFE College
Anglican Church Grammar School

Restoration/Renovation
All in association with State Works Department
Parliament House, Brisbane
The Mansions
Harris Terrace
Printing Building

Interior/Tenancies
BHP
CRA
CSR
Suncorp Centre
Commonwealth Director of Public Prosecutions
Rowes Arcade
Queensland Newspapers Pty Ltd
Japan Airlines

Landscape
Roma Street Fountain
Suncorp Centre Plaza
City Plaza

History
Conrad & Gargett is one of Australia's oldest and most prestigious firms of architects.

In 1890, H.W. Atkinson founded the firm which has been known successively as:
H.W. Atkinson (1890-1907);
H.W. Atkinson & Chas McLay (1907-1917);
H.W. Atkinson & A.H. Conrad (1917-39);
A.H. Conrad & T.B.F. Gargett (1939-1965);
Conrad, Gargett & Partners (1965-1972);
Conrad, Gargett & Partners Pty Limited (1972-1982);
Conrad & Gargett Pty Limited (1982).

The professional association between Arnold Conrad and Bren Gargett developed into a unique partnership that spanned two generations and almost half a century.

Today, a new generation of Directors is guiding the firm. They adhere to a tradition of training the right people and contributing to the development of one of the largest architectural practices in Queensland.

In Brisbane, C&G designs continue to shape the central city. Throughout Queensland, a significant number of buildings and public areas for commerce, industry, education and medicine have been created first, in the office of Conrad & Gargett. All are a response to client needs and a reflection of the changing face of Queensland.

C&G offers an integrated and professional service over the full range of building types. The firm's abilities are further enhanced by enviable expertise in the following specialist design fields.

High Rise Commercial Design
Specialists in high rise development, C&G designs create distinctive corporate images for clients.

Interior Design
The expertise of C&G's Interior Design Section ensures effective space planning within a distinctive environment.

Health Facilities
The firm has specialist staff well versed in all aspects of design and planning for hospitals, laboratories, nursing homes and aged persons homes.

Restoration and Renovation
C&G combines science and art in the restoration of historic buildings as well as the tasteful renovation of older properties to make them commercially viable.

School Design
C&G has had 50 years experience in the design and development of some of Brisbane's finest schools.

Urban Design
C&G is an award-winner in the design of public places which enhance the urban environment.

Landscape Design
C&G undertakes separate landscape projects such as parks and playgrounds as well as designs which complement new and existing buildings.

1 Port Maree Boat harbour, Cairns

2 Darling Harbour, Masterplan, 1983

3 Chipping Norton Lakes

4 Wollongong Mall

5 Rainbow Pacific CAD Masterplan

6 Opal Cove, Coffs Harbour

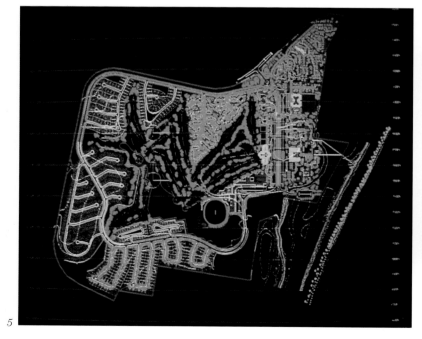

TONY CORKILL PTY LTD

Director (top left)
Tony Corkill FRAIA MRAPI

Associate Directors (left to right)
Warwick Newall B L Arch NZCTP
Michael Spackman AILA MRAIPR
Tim Throsby B Sc Arch ARAIA

Address
223 Liverpool Street
East Sydney, N.S.W. 2010

Telephone
(02) 332 1996

Facsimile
(02) 360 1253

Branch Office
McDonald Brickman Corkill Pty Ltd

Address
32 Villiers Street
Grafton, N.S.W. 2460

Project Types
Community/Recreational
Civic plazas and malls; amusement
parks; sports camps; golf courses

Educational Planning
Technical colleges; secondary schools

Resort Development
Convention centres; hotels; resorts

Residential
Sub-division planning; private houses
and apartments

Marinas
Boat harbours; dry boat storage;
Waterfront developments

Other Disciplines
Feasibility studies; environmental impact
assessments; interiors

Person to Contact
Tony Corkill

Design Approach

Tony Corkill's design team provides specialist services ranging from Master Planning of comprehensive projects through design documentation of civic and corporate facilities, to feasibility studies, environmental and conservation planning.

The firm seeks to create innovative solutions based on astute analysis, and the synthesis of opportunities with objectives to produce clear statements of urban design. It is important that long term objectives are realised for the client while maintaining public interest and relevance to social structure.

This approach has been translated into design for public and corporate projects on the east coast of Australia. Response to the recent surge in Australian tourism is illustrated in the portfolio of major hotels and leisure resorts at Coffs Harbour, Cairns and Philip Island while the current trend in revitalisation of urban centres is reflected in the Wollongong City Mall and Maitland Heritage Mall. These projects reflect the broad range of expertise of Tony Corkill's design team and their ability to produce a dynamic architectural statement within a total environmental plan.

Principal Staff

Tony Corkill

An established architect and urban designer, his experience encompasses projects throughout Australia, the Americas and Europe.

The nature of these projects is varied. They range from environmental impact studies, through cost/revenue analysis to design for international tourist resorts and community development schemes.

His experience in the United States included working on major government projects. He was Planning Director for the Hudson River Valley Commission, preparing urban design and land suitability studies and planning representative in Venezuela for the United Nations.

Warwick Newall

Contemporary entertainment facilities on which this experienced Landscape Architect has worked include the Darling Harbour Redevelopment and Australia's Wonderland.

He has designed golf courses at Port Macquarie and Philip Island and undertaken visual impact analysis on tourist projects and marina planning at Cairns.

As a town planner, he has worked on major government and entrepreneurial developments in Australia and New Zealand.

Michael Spackman

An experienced Landscape Architect and Urban Designer, he has worked on projects throughout Australia and Japan. His portfolio spans major urban redevelopment schemes in Tokyo and sports and recreation centres for the Australian Government.

Australian sporting and leisure projects include masterplanning a boat harbour and resort near Cairns. He was also involved through the design development of the Tasmanian international Velodrome.

Tim Throsby

A career in architectural design, building conservation and project administration has been established in Australia and the United Kingdom.

Sydney's Martin Place pedestrian plaza and Dunk Island resort (Qld) are two of the Australian projects for which he has provided design and documentation.

The rehabilitation of the Argyle Arts Centre in Sydney's historic The Rocks area amplifies his conservation experience.

Current and Recent Projects

Port Maree

A recreation tourist resort and residential community in Cairns. Focus of the development is a Boat harbour for small craft linked to Trinity Bay. Major elements around the harbour provide entertainment, accommodation and services for visitors and residents. There is a tavern and shopping centre on the promenade, family restaurant, hotel and apartments with water access.

Darling Harbour

In 1982 Cox and Corkill were commissioned by the Premiers Department to undertake pre-planning and urban design of the redevelopment scheme for Darling Harbour. The resultant Master Plan proposed a number of inter-related elements centred around education and entertainment with a large open space network of plazas and terraces extending from the water through to Haymarket. Within the Open Space Structure Plan a range of development sites were identified to secure economic return for developers and the Government.

Chipping Norton Lakes

In 1977 the Public Works Department engaged Cox and Corkill to design a regional recreation facility on gravel extraction pits on the Georges River. Controls on further extraction were recommended to ensure the most desirable lake configuration for flood conveyance, ecological habitat and recreation. The water body was broken up to minimise wave action and create islands as wildlife preservation areas. Recommendations for artificial fish reefs, a fish nursery, silt traps and management of wildlife habitats were also part of the Master Plan to be implemented over the 15 year extraction period .

Wollongong City Mall

Cox and Corkill were winners of a limited competition to produce a design for the CBD shopping area. The result is a strong urban solution providing a dynamic setting for the city's future growth while re-establishing its link with the past. The Mall features 14m high steel arch frames behind a portal gateway creating a comfortable microclimate for shoppers in the main street. Other components include an amphitheatre stage with 15 metre high sound shell, kiosk restaurants, interactive fountains, children's playground and commercial stalls. Cost of the conversion was $7.4 million taking 20 months to complete.

Rainbow Pacific

Located 17 kilometres south of Port Macquarie the concept is to create a development where facilities and components reinforce each other. The development comprises an International Resort, Championship Golf Course, Village Shopping Centre, Sports Village and a range of housing including courtyard houses, town-houses and apartments. Housing areas are grouped into neighbourhoods defined by landscaped open space linking to recreation facilities and the Shopping Centre.

Sports and leisure facilities comprising golf, tennis, swimming, athletics, football, cricket and bowls are available to visitors and residents.

Capital cost is $300 million and the project is currently under construction.

Opal Cove Resort

The site occupies rolling coastal hills fronting Hills Beach, six kilometres north of Coffs Harbour. Two hotels, serviced apartments, villas and bures are supported by recreation and leisure facilities overlooking Korora Lagoon and Hills Beach. Significant natural features are retained in reserves while built forms are low rise and staggered to reduce visual impact. Site planning ensures seclusion to those wanting a retreat while offering entertainment to those seeking social activity.

Total capital cost amounts to A$93 million with construction of the major Resort Hotel being undertaken in 1988.

Maitland Heritage Mall

A design concept by Cox and Corkill resulted in a Government grant for construction. Tony Corkill Pty Ltd then won a limited competition for design of the mall.

The proposal creates a focus for the Shopping Centre that is unassuming yet elegant allowing significant historic buildings to be an integral feature of the proposal while screening non-contributory buildings.

Tony Corkill Pty Ltd are currently undertaking design documentation for the Mall which will be opened in September 1988 at a cost of $1.2 million.

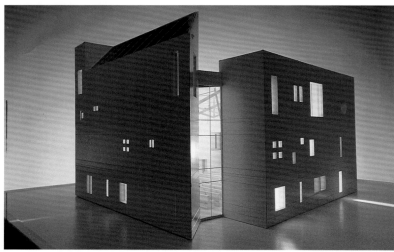

1

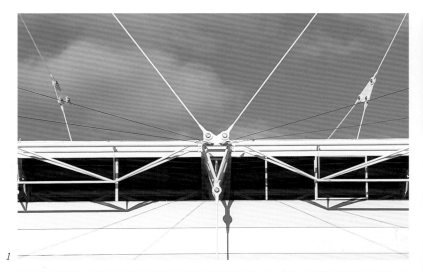

5

2

3

4

6

PHILIP COX, RICHARDSON, TAYLOR & PARTNERS PTY LTD – SYDNEY, CANBERRA
PHILIP COX, ETHERINGTON, COULTER & JONES PTY LTD – PERTH
PHILIP COX, SANDERSON & PARTNERS PTY LTD – MELBOURNE

Directors: Sydney/Canberra Offices
(left to right)
Philip Cox B.Arch FRAIA Dip T&CP Hon. FAIA
John Richardson B.Arch ARAIA
Philip Taylor B.Arch FRAIA

Hank Den Ouden B.Arch FRAIA
Eric Martin B.Arch ARAIA M.B.Env
Ian McGilvray B.Arch ARAIA
Michael Rayner B.Arch ARAIA
Trevor Armitage B.Arch ARAIA
Jon Johannsen B.Arch ARAIA
Peter Reed B.Arch ARAIA
Harry Street B.Arch ARAIA

Directors: Perth Office
Murray Etherington B.Arch ARAIA
Ross Coulter B.Arch ARAIA
Paul Jones B.Arch ARAIA AA.DIP

Directors: Melbourne Office
John Sanderson ARAIA

Established
1964

Addresses
Civic House 477-481 Kent Street
Sydney, N.S.W. 2000

49 Jardine Street
Kingston, A.C.T. 2604

1006 Hay Street
Perth, W.A. 6000

92 River Street
South Yarra, Vic. 3144

Telephone
Sydney (02) 267 9599
Canberra (062) 95 1903
Perth (09) 481 1221
Melbourne (03) 240 1010

Facsimile
Sydney (02) 264 5844
Canberra (062) 95 0964
Perth (09) 324 1816

Number of Employees
75

Project Types	Percentage
1 Sport and Recreational	25%
2 Tourism	20%
3 Commercial	20%
4 Educational	10%
5 Health	10%
6 Residential	10%
7 Restoration	5%

Other Disciplines
Urban and Town Planning
Interior Design
Graphic Design

Persons to Contact
Sydney Philip Cox, Michael Rayner
Canberra Eric Martin
Perth Paul Jones
Melbourne John Sanderson

1-2 *Darling Harbour Exhibition Centre, Sydney*

3 *Haileybury College Chapel, Melbourne*

4 *N.S.W.I.T., Haymarket Campus, Sydney*

5 *Sydney Football Stadium*

6 *Yulara Tourist Resort, Northern Territory*

Current and Recent Projects
Sport and Recreational
Darling Harbour Exhibition Centre, Sydney for the Darling Harbour Authority and Leighton Contractors.

Australian National Maritime Museum, Darling Harbour for the Darling Harbour Authority and Leighton Contractors.

National Tennis Centre, Melbourne for Victorian Government and Civil and Civic Pty Ltd.

Sydney Sports Ground Redevelopment, Moore Park for Sydney Cricket and Sports Ground Trust and Civil and Civic Pty Ltd.

World Cup Athletics Stadium, Canberra for the National Capital Development Commission.

Sydney Aquarium, Darling Harbour, Sydney for Jonray Limited.

International Athletics Stadium, Lidcombe Oval, Sydney for Department of Sport and Recreation.

National Athletics Stadium and Indoors Sports Centre, Bruce, A.C.T. for National Capital Development Commission.

Tourism
Yulara Tourist Resort, Ayers Rock, N.T. for White Industries Limited and N.T. Government.

Canberra National Convention Centre, Hotel and Convention Centre for White Industries Limited.

Manly Pavilion Hotel, The Corso, Manly for Leighton Properties Pty Ltd.

Milton Park Country Hotel and Village, Bowral, N.S.W. for Milton Park Hotels Pty Ltd.

Commercial & Offices
Canberra National Convention Centre for White Industries Limited.

Galleria Development, AML&F Woolstore, Darling Harbour for Austland Ltd/Hazama Gumi Ltd.

No. 1 Pacific Highway, North Sydney for Schroder, Darling and Co. Ltd.

Victoria Cross Development, North Sydney for White Industries Limited.

Farrix Offices, Mounts Bay Road, Perth for Multiplex Pty Ltd.

Manly Pavilion, The Corso, Manly for Leighton Properties Pty Ltd.

National Heart Foundation Headquarters, A.C.T. for National Heart Foundation.

Educational
Markets 3 Campus, Haymarket, Sydney for N.S.W. Institute of Technology.

Macarthur Institute of Higher Technology, Campbelltown, N.S.W.

Macquarie University Graduate School of Management for Civil and Civic Pty Ltd.

Haileybury College Chapel, Melbourne for Haileybury College.

Calwell High School, A.C.T., for National Capital Development Commission.

Health
Teluk Intan Hospital, North Malaysia for the Malaysian Government.

Belconnen Health Centre, A.C.T. for the National Capital Development Commission.

Kambah Health Centre, A.C.T. for the National Capital Development Commission.

Residential
Residence, Dalkeith, Perth for Mr and Mrs L. Connell.

Housing, Brougham Street and Forbes Street, Woolloomoolloo for Housing Commission of N.S.W.

Housing, Forbes Street, Newtown for Housing Commission of N.S.W.

Housing, Illawarra Road, Marrickville for Housing Commission of N.S.W.

Housing, Egan Street, Richmond, Vic. for Ministry of Housing.

Housing, Philip, A.C.T. for National Capital Development Commission.

Restoration
Norfolk Island Restoration, Norfolk Island for Norfolk Island Administration.

Restoration of AML&F Woolstore, Darling Harbour, Sydney for Austland Ltd and Hazama-Gumi Ltd.

Restoration, Buildings 37, 89 & 90, Garden Island for Department of Housing and Construction.

Old Supreme Courts, Phillip Street, Sydney in association with N.S.W. Government Architect for Dept. of Public Works.

Major Awards
Sir Zelman Cowen Award, Royal Australian Institute of Architects, for Yulara Tourist Resort.

Sir Robert Matthew Award, Commonwealth Association of Architects, for Innovative Contribution to Architecture.

Gold Medal, Royal Australian Institute of Architects to Philip Cox.

BHP Australian Steel Award for Yulara Tourist Resort.

Canberra Medallion, Royal Australian Institute of Architects for Kambah Health Centre.

Sulman Medal, Royal Australian Institute of Architects for St Andrews Presbyterian College, Leppington, N.S.W.

Conservation Award, Royal Australian Institute of Architects for Norfolk Island Restoration.

Wilkinson Award, Royal Australian Institute of Architects for House, Cheltenham.

Blacket Award, Royal Australian Institute of Architects for C.B. Alexander Presbyterian College, Hunter Valley, N.S.W.

Philip Cox
Philip Cox, was awarded the RAIA Gold Medal in 1984 and became the first recipient of both RAIA Gold and Silver Medals.

He is a member and former Vice Chairman of Visual Arts Board of the Australia Council and is committed to the development of Australian Design. He is currently chairman of the National Education Committee, Royal Australian Institute of Architects.

His books include Australian Colonial Architecture (Landsdowne), Rude Timber Buildings in Australia (Angus and Robertson), Building Norfolk Island (Nelson), Historic Towns of Australia (Landsdowne) and he is currently preparing The Functional Tradition (5 Mile Press). In 1987, he was appointed Honorary Fellow, American Institute of Architects.

Philip Cox, Richardson, Taylor & Partners
The architecture of Philip Cox, Richardson, Taylor & Partners and its associated offices is the collective aspiration and philosophy of a group of people dedicated in their ambition to create an architecture relevant to Australia. With European settlement now 200 years old, we believe that Australia has an emerging national identity and our design work is relentless in the pursuit of an appropriate architectural identity.

Through a wide range of important projects, we have had many opportunities to develop and demonstrate our philosophy. These projects are exemplary of our ability to simultaneously satisfy our client's needs, solve urban and contextual issues and produce high quality architecture within cost and time constraints.

In order to achieve these objectives we maintain a multi-disciplinary approach with expertise in urban planning, interior design, graphic design, restoration as well as in architecture.

DAVENPORT CAMPBELL

Established
1977

Addresses
Sydney
287 Elizabeth Street
Sydney, N.S.W. 2000
Telephone
(02) 261 2077
Facsimile
(02) 267 8621
Person to Contact
Graham Smith

Brisbane
229 Elizabeth Street
Brisbane, Qld 4000
Telephone
(07) 221 6077
Facsimile
(07) 221 1645
Person to Contact
Ian Dove

Perth
44 St George's Terrace
Perth, W.A. 6000
Telephone
(09) 325 1344
Facsimile
(09) 325 1852
Person to Contact
Lindsay Colwill

Singapore
135 Cecil Street
Singapore 0106
Telephone
(65) 221 4144
Facsimile
(65) 224 8956
Person to Contact
Charlie Weress

Hong Kong
22 Queen's Road Central
Hong Kong
Telephone
852 (5) 24 2126
Facsimile
852 (5) 20 0919
Person to Contact
Ross Kelly

Number of Employees
200

Disciplines
Architecture
Interior Design
Facility Management
Facility Planning
Furniture Ergonomics
Graphics
Project Management
Computer Aided Design

History

Davenport Campbell, one of the largest and most widely recognised architectural, planning and interior design firms in Australia and Asia was established in 1977.

Since its inception, Davenport Campbell has enjoyed a substantial rate of growth as a result of its emphasis on commercial pragmatism and its insistence on maintaining the higher quality standards of design and project management service to its clients.

The firm's greatest measure of its own performance is the fact that in excess of 50% of its work each year is generated by way of repeat clients.

Davenport Campbell has designed and completed a number of new hotels for a range of international operators and has also undertaken more than 30 projects involving the refurbishment and restoration of hotels throughout Australia, South East Asia and the Pacific Islands.

In addition to hotel projects, Davenport Campbell have a sound reputation for the design and planning of commercial offices throughout Australia and South East Asia.

Davenport Campbell was one of the first Australian design companies to make a total commitment to computer aided design and drafting systems, but more particular, develop the potential of the electronic systems to become the market leader in strategic facility planning.

Although structured as a professional practice owned by its working partners, Davenport Campbell apply the commercial standards and management controls of a dynamic corporation.

As designers and project administrators the firm's culture is to operate as a team, whether inhouse or in association with other architects, but most importantly to work as a team with their clients.

Current & Recent Projects
Commercial
Pitt & Liverpool Streets, Sydney
KMS Project, Sydney
70 Pitt Street, Sydney
Uniting Church Offices, Canberra
Melbourne Street, South Brisbane
Robell House, Elizabeth Street, Sydney
State Bank Computer Centre, N.S.W.
Pirie Street, Adelaide
Retail
Campsie Centre, N.S.W.
Macquarie Shopping Centre, N.S.W.
Tuggeranong, A.C.T.
McDonnell & East Qld
Duty Free Shoppers
Australia & Asia
Karrinyup Shopping Centre, W.A.
Hospitality & Tourism
Hilton International
Sheraton Asia Pacific Division
Southern Pacific Hotel Corporation
Menzies at Rialto, Melbourne
Southpoint, Sydney
China Merchants Hotel, Hong Kong
Qantas Airways facilities worldwide

MICHAEL DAVIES ASSOCIATES PTY LIMITED
Architects/Planners

Directors (left to right)
Michael Davies B Arch (NSW) FRAIA
Mark Shoolman B Sc (Arch) B Arch (Hons) NSW
   ARAIA
Grant Chellew B Sc (Arch) B Arch (NSW)
   ARAIA

Established
1975

Address
280 Pitt Street
Sydney, N.S.W. 2000

Telephone
(02) 264 5599

Facsimile
(02) 264 1159

Number of Employees
Currently 24
Varies as required

Project Types
Commercial
Industrial
Local Government and Community
Retail
Leisure and Tourism
Sport and Recreation
Recycling
Educational
Interiors
Residential
Rural

Associated Activity
Sport and Recreation Planning Unit

Other Disciplines
Urban Planning
Interior Design
Landscape Design
Specialist skills in sport
and recreation facilities

Person to Contact
Michael Davies

Current and Recent Projects
Commercial and Retail
Big Bear Redevelopment, Neutral Bay, N.S.W.

500 Pacific Highway, St Leonards, N.S.W.

Australian Federal Police Headquarters,
110 Goulburn Street, Sydney, N.S.W.

24 Young Street, Neutral Bay, N.S.W.

Industrial
Urban Transit Authority Bus Depot,
Neutral Bay, N.S.W.

NEC Warehouse and Office Building,
Alexandria, N.S.W.

Eickhoff Factory, Warehouse and Office Building,
Seven Hills, N.S.W.

Datamail Distribution Centre, Alexandria, N.S.W.

Local Government and Community
Administration Building, Cultural Centre and Library,
Bega, N.S.W.

Community Centre, Brewarrina, N.S.W.

Senior Citizens Centre, Camden, N.S.W.

Narellan Community Hall, Narellan, N.S.W.

Bowral Central Library, Bowral, N.S.W.

Retail
Big Bear Redevelopment, Neutral Bay, N.S.W

Woolloomooloo Neighbourhood Shopping Centre,
Woolloomooloo, N.S.W.

Merimbula Centrepoint, Merimbula, N.S.W.

Sutton Place, Drummoyne, N.S.W.

Leisure, Tourism, Sport and Recreation
Southern Cross International Hotel, Sydney, N.S.W.
(180 rooms)

Gorokan Leisure Centre, Gorokan, N.S.W.

Tourist Development, 32 Bathurst Street, Sydney, N.S.W.

Leisure Centre and Indoor Pool, The Entrance, N.S.W.

Recycling
2 Barrack Street, Sydney, N.S.W. (Pinnacle House)

2 Bond Street, Sydney, N.S.W. (MBF House)

2 Bridge Street, Sydney, N.S.W. (Anchor House)

Kinselas Theatre Restaurant, East Sydney, N.S.W.

Apartments, 44 Bridge Street, Sydney, N.S.W.

Southern Cross International Hotel, Sydney, N.S.W.

N.S.W. Department of Housing, 13 Houses,
Waterloo, N.S.W.

Educational
Sydney Japanese School, Terry Hills, N.S.W.

St Clair No 4 Primary School, St Clair, N.S.W.

Bossley Park Primary School, Bossley Park, N.S.W.

Multipurpose Halls for Secondary Schools (6)

Yasmar Youth Facility, Haberfield, N.S.W.

Riverina Youth Facility, Wagga Wagga, N.S.W.

Interiors
3 Apartments "Oceania", Elizabeth Bay, N.S.W.

Williams Business College, Sydney, N.S.W.

Southern Cross International Hotel, Sydney, N.S.W.

Kinselas, East Sydney, N.S.W.

Residential
Student Housing, University of N.S.W.

10 Townhouses, Hardie Street, Neutral Bay, N.S.W.

5 Townhouses, Doohat Avenue, North Sydney, N.S.W.

House, 25 Tunstall Avenue, Kingsford, N.S.W.

House, 3 Wybalena Road, Hunters Hill, N.S.W.

Rural
Arrowfield Stud Farm, Hunter Valley, N.S.W.

Allandale Winery Development, Cessnock, N.S.W.

Clients
The Company is proud of the opportunity it has had
to work with major government and private clients
and can arrange for references to be provided.
Some of the clients are:

Department of Housing and Construction

Department of Public Works, N.S.W.

Department of Sport and Recreation, N.S.W.

Macarthur Development Board
   (Department of Decentralisation and Development)

Department of Housing, N.S.W.

Brewarrina Shire Council

Bega Valley Shire Council

Willoughby Municipal Council

Wyong Shire Council

Camden Municipal Council

Byron Shire Council

Wingecarribee Shire Council

University of New South Wales

Arrowfield Group Limited

Civil and Civic Pty Limited

Comrealty Limited

Equitable Group Limited

Euronational Properties Limited

Jennings Industries Limited

Leighton Contractors Pty Limited

Leighton Properties Pty Limited

Lend Lease Developments Pty Limited

NEC Information Systems

Shimizu Australia Pty Limited

Southern Cross Hotel (Sydney)

About the Practice
Michael Davies Associates Pty Limited is a multi-
disciplinary Company providing a range of professional
consulting services in the fields of architecture, planning,
interior design, landscape design, research and
construction management.

The Practice commenced early in 1975 after Michael
Davies left Harry Seidler and Associates where he had
been a Senior Project Architect since 1967.

The company evolved from the sole practice established
in 1975, was incorporated in March 1981 and has
experienced steady and sustained growth by adapting
to the changing requirements of clients and the
environment in which they operate.

The Directors believe that the effective solution of a
Client's building and development needs relies on a
close personal liaison between Client, Architect and
Consultants. Full and comprehensive understanding
of the Client's needs, aspirations and objectives
including funding, and investment criteria is therefore
of fundamental importance.

The Company is able to bring together a highly qualified
team of engineering and other consultants and directs
and integrates their work towards an effective solution
of the client's requirements within a predetermined
programme and within budget.

The Company can assist in all stages of the building
programme, from analysis of development potential
and determination of brief right through to building
handover. Alternatively, we can contribute independently
to any part of the design and procurement process.

The Royal Australian
Institute of Architects

Commercial Development, Liverpool, N.S.W.

Factory Development, Campbelltown, N.S.W.

Town Houses, Lane Cove, N.S.W.

Proposal for new grandstand, Randwick Racecourse, N.S.W.

Library and Community Centre, Liverpool, N.S.W.

DE ANGELIS TAYLOR & ASSOCIATES PTY LTD
Architects and Designers

Directors (left to right)
Glorio De Angelis B.Sc (Arch)., B.Arch (Hons),
 Chartered Architect
Stephen R. Taylor Designer

Associates (left to right)
David L. Rumps B.Arch. (U.S.A.), A.R.A.I.A.,
 Chartered Architect
Alan W. Hall B.Sc (Arch)., B.Arch (Hons),
 A.R.A.I.A., Chartered Architect
Els Dirickx A.S.T.C. Dip Int., Interior Designer

Established
1979

Address
Macquarie Terrace
88 Bathurst Street
Liverpool, N.S.W. 2170

P.O. Box 68
Liverpool, N.S.W. 2170

Telephone
(02) 601 1011

Number of Employees
10

Value of Commissions 1986-87
$60M

Project Types	Percentage
Commercial (Retail/Office Buildings)	25%
Residential (Medium Density)	20%
Industrial	15%
Institutional (Churches/Education/ Health)	15%
Recreational/Clubs/Hospitality	10%
Municipal	5%
Interior Design	5%
Residential	5%

Current and Recent Projects
Commercial
Renovations to the Queen Elizabeth Stand,
Randwick Racecourse
for the Australian Jockey Club

Commercial Retail Development, Carlingford

Renovations to the 'Town Centre' Development,
Blacktown

Five New Office Buildings, Liverpool

Camden Valley Inn Tourist Centre

Shop Development, Cabramatta

Ingleburn Fair Shopping Centre

Horse Stud Complex, Mudgee

Residential
Medium Density
'Meadow Courts' 119 unit Residential Complex,
Liverpool

'Brundah Gardens' 100 unit Development, Strathfield

Villa Development, Carlingford

Townhouse Development, Lane Cove

Industrial
El Toro Industrial Estate, Liverpool

New Vehicle Dealership for McGrath Holden, Liverpool

Industrial/Commercial Development, Campbelltown

Industrial/Commercial Development, Liverpool

Institutional
New Retirement Complex,
Griffith for Scalabrini Village

New Multi Purpose Hall for John Therry High School,
Campbelltown

New Accommodation Block for St. Gregory's College,
Campbelltown

Additions to Scalabrini Village, Austral

St. Joseph's Catholic Church, Moorebank

Aged Persons Units, Moorebank

Aged Persons Units, Mt. Pritchard

Retirement Village Complex at Chipping Norton

Recreational/Clubs
Alterations to Belmont 16' Sailing Club

Alterations to Maroubra R.S.L.

Alterations to Castellorizian Club

Extension of facilities at Murrumbidgee Turf Club

Extension to Grandstand at Bathurst Turf Club

New Motel at Bathurst

New Motel at Crossroads

New Motel and Function Complex at Campbelltown

Additions to Existing Motel at Casula

Municipal
Library and Community Centre, Moorebank

New Community Halls for Liverpool City Council

Cabramatta Police Station

History
The firm began in Liverpool in 1979 as a small suburban practice to serve the needs of the builders and developers of the area with buildings that were not only well designed but also cost efficient. Since that time, the practice has grown considerably, drawing on the experiences gained from the many and varied projects that have been undertaken.

This growth has not been confined to the Western Sydney area, but has also required us to extend to many country areas of New South Wales and the ACT, designing horse studs at Mudgee and the Hunter Valley, a nursing home in Griffith, medium density developments in Muswellbrook, Port Macquarie, Kiama and Byron Bay, a motel development in Bathurst and renovations to numerous clubs throughout the state.

At De Angelis Taylor and Associates, we believe that it is important to maintain contact between our clients and one of the Directors of the firm as well as with senior members of the staff assigned to the project. This contact ensures that each project receives the same care and attention to detail that has demonstrated itself for all of our clients over the years. With the addition of an interior designer into the practice, greater emphasis has been placed on integrating "interior and exterior" architecture, resulting in our firm winning, in conjunction with various builders, a number of M.B.A. Housing Awards for project homes and large individual homes.

Having worked with clients on a wide range of projects, we have developed a flexible attitude towards the practice of architecture. This has come through exposure to diverse types of projects of varing scale and complexity. Numerous projects have required us to use innovative design solutions for the "recycling" of older buildings while other projects require a more straightforward solution in their design.

Recently, De Angelis Taylor and Associates has expanded its services to advise developers and estate agents on project viability and feasibility studies. In the case of estate agents, this has often assisted in the sale of the property and we have often continued our relationship with the new owner in assisting them to further develop their new property.

In a like manner, we have also been associated with several builders in the area of Design/Construct, Project Management and Construction Management projects. Several of the clubs, commercial and industrial projects we have been associated with have been developed in this manner.

We are continually striving to improve the quality of architecture in our environment, at the same time ensuring that our projects are cost effective and lasting. To this end, we have developed many progressive office operations, such as extensive use of computers to assist in design and analysis of a project. Just as the tools of our profession are constantly changing, we believe that we must maintain a flexible attitude towards the changing role of the architect within the entire construction industry in order to provide a complete service of the highest standard to our clients.

dt

DEMAINE PARTNERSHIP PTY LTD

Directors
Dominic Kelly
Ian Hunt
Roger Burden
Simon Hanger

Associate Director
Christopher Millen

Established
1938

Address
1 Darling Street
South Yarra, Vic. 3141

Telephone
(03) 266 3721

Facsimile
(03) 266 4351

Number of Employees
20

Project Types
Commerce
Recreation and resort
Education
Health
Industry
Residences

Other Disciplines
Master Plan
Interior Design

Person to Contact
Dominic Kelly

Current and Recent Projects

Commerce
468 St. Kilda Road, Melbourne
Office Building for Leighton Properties Pty. Ltd.
$14M

165 Bouverie Street, Carlton
Office Building for Medical Defence Association of Victoria
$1.33M

31-33 Albert Road, Melbourne
Computer centre for BP Australia Limited
$2.4M

3a Queens Road, Melbourne
Office building for Leighton Properties Pty. Ltd.
$30M

Recreation and Resort
Country Club at Healesville for the Royal Automobile
Club of Victoria

Officers' Mess, Support Command, South Melbourne

Education
Royal Melbourne Institute of Technology
Technical College
Master planning and design of three stages of a
multi-stage development:
Frederick Campbell Building, Victoria Street
Ronald McKay Building, Queensberry Street
Edward Jackson Building, Lygon Street

Holmesglen College of TAFE, Block D Stage 2
Administration and Student
and Staff Services Building

Footscray College of TAFE
Documentation, in association with the Public Works
Department of Victoria, of DISP facility,
Hoppers Crossing

Victoria Police Training Academy, Glen Waverley
Contract administration, in association with the
Public Works Department of Victoria, of Education
and Accommodation Building

Health
The Queen Elizabeth Geriatric Centre, Ballarat
Various projects including:
Acute Assessment Unit
New Kitchen
Bulk Store and Engineering Workshops
Linen handling facility
Rehabilitation Unit
Aged Persons Hostel (Sebastopol)

East Gippsland Hospital, Bairnsdale
Boiler House and Engineering Services Building
20-bed Children's Ward
Kitchen renovation
Casualty Department
Medical Ancillary Complex

Lyndoch Home & Hospital for the Aged, Warrnambool
Stage 2 and Stage 3 of 100-bed radial ward units

Wimmera Base Hospital, Horsham
Intensive Care Ward,
30-bed Nursing Home

West Gippsland Hospital, Warragul
New Laundry facility
30-bed Nursing Home
Kitchen refurbishment

Central Gippsland Hospital, Traralgon
New Pathology Department

Stawell District Hospital
Nursing Home

Orbost & District Hostel Society
Aged Persons Hostel

Carnsworth Garoopna Nursing Home, Kew
Alterations and additions

Gisborne & District Bush Nursing Hospital
30-bed Nursing Home

East Bentleigh Community Health Centre

Master Plan Studies
have been completed for the following Hospitals
Omeo
Orbost
Morwell
The Queen Elizabeth Geriatric Centre
Stawell
Wimmera Base
Dimboola
Nhill
Camperdown
Penshurst
Maroondah
Moorabbin
Warrnambool

Industry
Metal Processing Plant for Commonwealth Aircraft
Corporation

Administration building and factory for the
Victorian Egg Marketing Board
in association with Jennings Industries Ltd.

Residences
Kepper residence at Wonga Park

History
Demaine Partnership Pty. Ltd. was founded by
Robert Snowdon Demaine in 1938. It established
itself firmly in the planning and design of buildings
in the health field, and then extended its field of
activity into industrial and commercial architecture
in the late 1950's, particularly with its involvement
with BP Australia Limited in the design and
construction of their new headquarters building at
Albert Road, Melbourne. The practice is now a multi-
faceted practice, with expertise in the planning, design
and documentation of a wide range of building types.

The practice engages the services of external Consultants
in the related disciplines of structural, civil, mechanical
and electrical engineering, as it believes that by so doing
its clients' interests are best served.

The company has installed extensive facilities for
computer aided drafting, and all substantial projects
are now documented using this system, thereby
providing considerably increased scope and flexibility
for the inclusion of clients' changing requirements.
The system has now been tested in both the commercial
and educational areas of the practice and does offer
substantial benefits to the 'fast tracking' of these
projects.

1 Tiered balconies at Amory Gardens

2 DEM Atrium

3 IBM Australia Limited, Headquarters

4 The Chatswood Connection

5 Lord Ben Stables

6 Devine Erby Mazlin Directors and Associates:
(back row) Graham Murray, Mark Bennett, Peter Joscelyne,
Peter Doddrell, Peter Dunn, Trevor de Waal

(front row) John Ladd-Hudson, Richard Turner,
Warren Marsh, Silvija Smits, David Hollander,
Alan Hession

DEVINE ERBY MAZLIN AUSTRALIA PTY LIMITED

Directors (left to right).
Jonathan G.W. Erby A.M. B.Arch., F.R.A.I.A.
Bruce F. Pryor M.Arch., F.R.A.I.A.
Brian W. Mazlin A.S.T.C.(Arch), F.R.A.I.A. Dip. L.D.

Established
1962

Address
115 Sailors Bay Road
Northbridge, N.S.W. 2063

Telephone
(02) 958 2388

Facsimile
(02) 958 5677

Telex
AA 72998

Number of Employees
160

About the Firm

Founded in 1962 as a partnership between Jonathan Erby and Grant Devine, Devine Erby Mazlin Australia (DEM) is now one of the country's leading firms of architects and enjoys a unique reputation within the architectural profession and the property development industry.

The three long-time principals, Jon Erby, Brian Mazlin and Bruce Pryor have guided the company through a period of continuous growth and expansion, without affecting DEM's ability to fulfil its professional commitments.

By pursuing a philosophy to provide the most comprehensive range of services to DEM clients, the company principals have extended the traditional boundaries of the architectural profession with the incorporation of the Devine Erby Mazlin Group of building design and development-related companies.

Devine Erby Mazlin Australia is the major subsidiary of the DEM Group with a staff of more than 160, providing clients with professional services, from the assessment of the original brief, through all stages to the completion of the project.

DEM offers design and documentation expertise for institutional, commercial and private clients, and the success of the practice is demonstrated by its design of high quality projects and major awards.

The awards include the Royal Australian Institute of Architects (NSW Chapter) Merit Award for Outstanding Architecture for IBM Australia Limited's national headquarters; the Building Owners Managers Association Award for the Devine Erby Mazlin building; and The RAIA/ACROD Award for the MS Society's Western Region Centre.

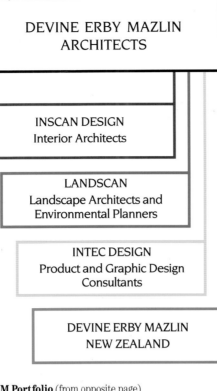

DEVINE ERBY MAZLIN ARCHITECTS

INSCAN DESIGN
Interior Architects

LANDSCAN
Landscape Architects and
Environmental Planners

INTEC DESIGN
Product and Graphic Design
Consultants

DEVINE ERBY MAZLIN
NEW ZEALAND

DEM Portfolio (from opposite page)

1 **Amory Gardens** – a staged office park development in Ashfield, in Sydney's inner west, comprising two five-storey buildings with tiered balconies and terraced garden walls complementing the tree lined grounds.

2 **DEM Office Building** – a 1986 BOMA award winner and located on Sydney's lower north shore, this three-storey office building is planned around an atrium naturally lit by large, pyramid shaped skylights.

3 **IBM Australia Headquarters** – a multi-award winning high tech complex set on 25 hectares and accommodating 2,000 employees. The complex incorporates many innovative energy-efficient systems, and its design is in total harmony with its Cumberland Forest setting in Sydney's West Pennant Hills.

4 **The Chatswood Connection** – one of the largest Australian urban projects, comprising two high-rise office towers, a low-rise office building, an international hotel, a multi-cinema centre, specialty shops and an ice skating rink, connected by a landscaped pedestrian boulevard. The entire complex sits astride Chatswood Railway on Sydney's north shore.

5 **Lord Ben Stables** – a new stable complex to replace existing stables to house 40 horses, service and staff areas, client lounge and staff accommodation, at Sydney's Rosehill.

$m	350	500	650	875	1100
	'83	'84	'85	'86	'87

+43% +30% +35% +26%

Value of Commissions

Current and Recent Projects

Office Buildings
IBM Australia Headquarters
Amory Gardens
The Chatswood Connection
Pymble Corporate Centre
Leighton Headquarters
146 Arthur Street, North Sydney
210 George Street, Sydney
12 Help Street, Chatswood
60 Dixon Street, Sydney
321 Kent Street, Sydney
McDonalds, Thornleigh
Campbelltown Court
Macarthur Park Offices
Australia Post, Sydney
Thomas Holt Drive, North Ryde
307 Pitt Street, Sydney

Health and Education
Multiple Sclerosis Society, Lidcombe
Mater Hospital Redevelopment
Port Macquarie Technical College
Pymble Ladies College
Knox Grammar School
The Kings School
Loreto Convent
Wenona School
St. Ignatius' College
Monte Sant' Angelo
Cranbrook School
St. Patrick's Primary School
Masada College

Hotels and Tourism
Sheraton Hobart Hotel
Potts Point Hotel (formerly Chevron)
Noosa Beachcomber Resort
Noosa Quays Resort
Darling Harbour Hotel Proposal
Sheraton Wentworth, Sydney – Refurbishment

Sport and Recreation
White City Grandstand
Hoyts Cinemas
P.L.C. Gymnasium and Pool
Lord Ben Stables
Nebo Lodge, Rosehill
Woodlands Stud
Warwick Farm Stables

Retail
Warringah Mall – Additional Stages
Victoria Plaza, Chatswood
Penrith Centre Court
Taronga Zoo Park, Restaurant

Renovation and Refurbishment
Commonwealth Bank – 48 Martin Place
Digital House, Sydney
Northpoint, North Sydney
M.L.C. Building, North Sydney
A.G.L. Building, North Sydney
Elf Aquitaine Building, North Sydney

Computer Centres
IBM, West Pennant Hills
AWA, Homebush
M.W.S. and D.B., Sydney
R.D.C., Auckland, N.Z.
Telecom, North Sydney

1   313 Adelaide Street, Brisbane

2   Cathedral Square – Ann, Turbot and Wharf Streets, Brisbane

3   'Chinatown' – Duncan Street, Brisbane

4   BHP Headquarters – Cnr. Wharf and Turbot Streets, Brisbane

5   671 Gympie Road, Chermside

6   'Cats Tango' Restaurant – Hawken Drive, St. Lucia

7   'Windsor Tower' – Cnr. Ann and Wharf Streets, Brisbane

DOUGLAS DALY BOTTGER ARCHITECTS PTY LTD

Directors (left to right)
Bill Douglas Dip. Arch. (UQ) FRAIA
Peter Daly Dip. Arch. (QIT) ARAIA
Ray Bottger Dip. Arch. (QIT) ARAIA

Established
1955

Address
37 Merivale Street
South Brisbane, Qld 4101

Telephone
(07) 844 7402

Facsimile
(07) 846 1002

Project Types
Commercial
Catering
Recreational
Industrial
Retail
Multi-Residential
Carparking Centres
Public Works
Interior Fitout

Person to Contact
Any Director

Current and Recent Projects
Cathedral Square
Commercial Offices, Public Carpark, Public Landscaped Plaza

Chinatown
Public Theme Shopping and Pedestrian Mall

'Leckhampton' (Stage 2)
Commercial Building in 19th Century Style

Admiralty Wharf
Retail, Restaurants, Commercial Offices, Hotel, Theatres, Marina

Other Commercial Developments
313 Adelaide Street

Windsor Tower

67 Astor Terrace

502 Queen Street

BHP House

History and Design Philosophy
Douglas Daly Bottger Architects Pty. Ltd. have a background of more than 30 years architectural history in Queensland with Bill Douglas commencing practice in 1955 and the present directors forming together in 1977. From that extensive experience base has developed a strong, innovative partnership with the expertise and skills to design and administer the construction of a wide range of building projects.

The partners are supported by an experienced group of architects, technical and administrative assistants who all work closely together as a team following the philosophy that 'architecture is a consulting profession which requires us to listen to and interpret our client's needs to produce a pleasing and functional design within an established budget, which we as architects and our clients as owners are proud to acknowledge'.

The team approach is important in our design of a project and all staff members are actively involved in most facets of the practice, wherein we have the ability to advise on each phase of the architectural process from concept to completion, offering the following services:
– site selection
– feasibility studies
– project budgeting
– design and planning
– materials evaluation
– artists drawings and perspectives
– consultant co-ordination
– contract administration
– interior design and fitout
– building remodelling
– development controls
– model making
– construction techniques
– contract negotiation

Individual development research is carried out within the office and has taken members of our design team overseas in order to thoroughly understand the underlying design philosophy and planning associated with particular projects.

Research and study of the unusual is exemplified by our concept of a totally new and authentic Chinatown in Brisbane, with the design based on the TANG DYNASTY of 600 to 900 AD resulting in a successful pedestrian and shopping mall and world class tourist attraction.

DDB is involved in the full spectrum of the built environment with proven abilities in recreation and theme areas, high and low rise commercial, institutional, governmental, retail, hospitality, and interior fitout.

EDWARDS MADIGAN TORZILLO BRIGGS INTERNATIONAL PTY LTD
Architects & Planners

Directors (left to right)
Colin F. Madigan A.O. L.F.R.A.I.A.
David Briggs F.R.A.P.I. F.R.A.I.A. A.A.I.L.A.
Greg Scott-Young B. Arch. (Hons). A.R.A.I.A.

Associates (left to right)
Penleigh Boyd B. Arch. A.R.A.I.A.
Clark Ingram B. Arch. A.R.A.I.A.
Colin Wilkinson B. Arch. (Hons) A.R.A.I.A.

Established
1951

Addresses
Sydney Office
211 Pacific Highway
St. Leonards, N.S.W. 2065

Telephone
(02) 436 2888

Facsimile
(02) 436 2270

Telex
AA74060 EMTB

Canberra Office
66 Elimatta Street
Braddon, A.C.T. 2601

Telephone
(062) 48 5563

Facsimile
(062) 47 2064

Associated Offices

Architectural Information Services
22nd Floor, St. George's Building
Hong Kong

Number of Employees
65

Computer Aided Drafting & Design System
Intergraph

Project Types
Commercial
Office/Retail/Industrial

Public & Civic
Libraries/Civic Centres/Galleries

Educational
Schools/Colleges/Universities

Health & Science
Research Facilities/Hospitals

Recreational
Entertainment Facilities/Hotels

Transportation
Railway Stations/Workshops

Residential
Private & Public Housing

Other Disciplines
Town Planning
Urban Design
Interior Design

Person to Contact
Sydney
Colin Madigan, David Briggs,
Greg Scott-Young

Canberra
Penleigh Boyd

Current and Recent Projects
Commercial: Office/Retail

1 Margaret Street, Sydney Costain Australia (1983 value)	$25M
Johnson & Johnson Headquarters, St. Leonards Civil & Civic (1975 value)	$10M
Retail & Residential Group, Mosman Mosman Municipal Council	$2.0M
Retail Group, Chatswood Willoughby Municipal Council	$1.0M
Architects Head Office, Gore Hill Edwards Madigan Torzillo Briggs	$0.45M
Shopping Centre, Mount Druitt Civil & Civic	$10.0M
Export House, Refurbishment Export Finance Corporation	$1.5M

Public Authorities: Office/Civic

Australian Government Offices, Parramatta Leighton Major Projects	$80M
Australian National Gallery NCDC	$50M
High Court of Australia NCDC	$45M
Administration Building, Randwick Bus Depot, Randwick Urban Transit Authority of N.S.W.	$3.0M
Offices & Council Chambers, Chatswood Willoughby Municipal Council	$3.0M
Offices & Council Chambers, Hunters Hill Hunters Hill Municipal Council	$3.0M

Industrial

Tangara Maintenance Centre, St. Marys State Rail Authority of N.S.W.	$100M
Stage 1 Elcar Redevelopment, Chullora State Rail Authority of N.S.W.	$4.5M
W D & H O Wills National Manufacturing Plant, Pagewood Leighton Major Projects	$50M
Redevelopment of Waggon Maintenance Centre, Clyde State Rail Authority of N.S.W.	$50M
Steel Fabrication Shop, Randwick Urban Transit Authority of N.S.W.	$5.0M
Project Administration Centre & Dock Refit Berth Facility, Garden Island Dept Housing & Construction	$10M
Misdy Computer Installation, Garden Island Dept Housing & Construction	$1.0M
XPT Service Centre, Sydenham State Rail Authority of N.S.W.	$10M
FFG Maintenance Workshop, Garden Island Dept Housing & Construction	$6.0M
Bottle Washing Plant, Wetherill Park Overmyer Management Pty. Ltd.	$5.0M

Educational: Schools/Colleges/Universities

Tuggeranong College, Canberra, NCDC	$17M
Arts/Maths College, Australian Defence Force Academy, Canberra, NCDC	$50M
Graduate School of Management, University of N.S.W. Civil & Civic	$9.0M

Health: Medicine, Research Facility

Sports Science Medicine, Canberra NCDC	$4.5M
John MacArthur Agricultural Institute, Camden Park Dept Public Works	$20M

Community: Recreation/Transportation Buildings

Sydney Entertainment Centre, Hay Market Sydney Entertainment Co., John Holland Constructions Pty. Ltd.	$50M
Railway Stations at East Hills, Holsworthy, Moorebank & Glenfield State Rail Authority of N.S.W.	$8.0M

Municipal
Libraries
at Muswellbrook, Warringah, Warren,
Mona Vale, Mosman, Lane Cove & Chatswood

Tourist Information Centre, Glenbrook Blue Mountains City Council	$0.25M

Interior Design

Australian Government Offices, Parramatta Department of Local Government & Administrative Services	$6.5M
Australian National Gallery & High Court of Australia NCDC	$8.0M
Coopers & Lybrand Regional Office, Parramatta Coopers & Lybrand	$0.35M

Bank Branch Offices (Various) Sydney
Commonwealth Banking Corporation

Landscape Design
Parliamentary Triangle, Canberra NCDC

Station, Modal Interchange & Carpark
for East Hills & Holsworthy Railway Stations,
State Rail Authority of N.S.W.

Bus Depot (Staged Implementation) Randwick
Urban Transit Authority of N.S.W.

Architects Head Office, Gore Hill
Edwards Madigan Torzillo Briggs

Town Planning Studies
Bankstown Station & Environs Master Plan, Bankstown
State Rail Authority of N.S.W. & Bankstown City
Council

Local Environmental Plan & Development Control
Plan for Pulpit Point, Hunters Hill,
Hunters Hill Municipal Council

Awards
Royal Australian Institute of Architects
NSW Chapter

Sulman Medal (1967) for Dee Why Library
Sulman Medal (1971) for Warringah Shire Council
Chambers
Blacket Award (1970) for Warren Library

ACT Chapter
Canberra Medallion (1980) for High Court of Australia
Canberra Medallion (1984) for Australian National
Gallery

Federal
Architects Gold Medal (1981) to Colin Madigan

Profile
When Edwards Madigan and Torzillo formed a
partnership in 1951, the received model of work practice
owed its origin to the classical codes of professional
behaviour operating early this Century. The Architect
identified with the Master Builder. Since then, 35 years
of experience in Architecture and Planning has seen the
design profession evolve to incorporate computers, Value
Managers, Project and Construction Managers, 'Fast
Track' Entrepreneurial Development, the Professional
Client et. al.

EMTB evolved accordingly as a flexible design atelier
responding to the accelerating social and technological
changes, always maintaining a commitment to the
cultural origins of Architecture.

People ask do we specialise in, say, Hospitals – we say
our profession and subject is Architecture. We specialise
in our subject, and, we are idealistic enough to recognise
that Architecture, even more than the other arts is
concerned with ethics, social justice, technology, politics
and finance, and the lofty desire to improve the human
condition. A commitment to such principles has
generated the success and growth of Edwards Madigan
Torzillo Briggs International Pty. Ltd.

Whilst EMTB is indeed International, our home base is
Sydney and Canberra, and we care for the environment
and the impact our specific Design Briefs have on their
immediate surroundings, be they National works, like
the Australian National Gallery, High Court of Australia
and the Parliamentry Triangle design or setting the
scene for the 21st Century in the CBD of Sydney where
commercial design will complement the well established
icons of Sydney Town, the Harbour, the Opera House
and the Harbour Bridge. Sydney has International
status. Our Designs for entertainment, recreation,
education, industry, transport infrastructure and
commerce will maintain this standard.

The images opposite reflect EMTB's design philosophy
and the ability to complete both large and complex
projects within budget and on time.

FIGGIS & JEFFERSON PTY LIMITED
Architects and Interior Designers

Directors (in descending order)
Stephen L. Figgis B. Arch ARAIA
Loyal Figgis Dip. Arch FRAIA (absent)

Associates (in descending order)
Leo Tam B AAS (Hons) B.Arch (Dist)
  ARAIA RIBA HKIA
Audrey Thomas B. Sc (Arch) B. Arch (Hons)
  ARAIA
Eugene Martinov B. Arch

Established
1950

Address
220 Willoughby Road
Crows Nest, N.S.W. 2065

Telephone
(02) 438 5555

Facsimile
(02) 439 5163

Number of Employees
15

Project Types
Commercial Offices
Commercial Retail
Industrial
Community Facilities
Sporting Venues
Private Medical Facilities
High Quality Residential

Other Disciplines
Interior Design
Project Management
Project Appraisal

People to Contact
Stephen Figgis
Audrey Thomas
Leo Tam
Eugene Martinov

Significant Clientele
Figgis & Jefferson gratefully acknowledges the loyalty shown by its clients, some of whom have enjoyed more than two decades of association.

Clientele
Clayton Robard Limited
Dalgety Developments
Australian Fixed Trusts
National Mutual Life Association
Associated National Life
Advance Asset Management
Dainford Limited
Westpac

JRA Limited
CSR Limited
BMW Australia

New England Credit Union
Permewan Wright
Farmers & Graziers
Custom Credit
Woolworths

City Automobiles
Rowley Motors
Scotts Motors
Colby Engineering
Roland Corporation
Crystal Pools

Christian City Church
Wakehurst Christian School
Congregational Church

State Mines Authority
Coalcliff Collieries
Munmorah State Mine

Warringah Shire Council
Manly Municipal Council
Fairfield City Council
Lithgow City Council
Wellington Shire Council
Goulburn City Council
Hornsby Shire Council
Holroyd Municipal Council
Darling Shire Council
Canterbury Municipal Council
Dubbo City Council
Parramatta City Council
Bathurst City Council
Cootamundra Shire Council
Holbrook Shire Council
Temora Municipal Council

Government of Bangladesh
Commonwealth of Australia
Department of Housing and Construction
Department of Public Works

Dubbo RSL
Ettalong Beach War Memorial Club
Goulburn Workmans Club
Central Mangrove Country Club

Firm Background
Figgis & Jefferson was founded in 1950 and has maintained a strong reputation in the design of local government and community facilities for several decades. In later years, the practice has developed a further capacity and technique to handle a wide variety of work, sometimes of an unusual nature and including residential, industrial, sporting venues and multi-storey commercial office towers.

The present management has been responsible for the design output since 1973, during which time the practice has expanded and further developed its reputation for quality and reliability.

Work in Hand
Current projects in 1987 exceed $60 million in value and illustrate the diversity of skills; significant examples are:

Auditorium, Community Hall and Library combined with a 22 storey office tower at Bondi Junction

Church and Global Headquarters for the Christian City Church

Establishment of Showroom Standards for JRA Cars

Multiple Day Surgeries for Dalgety Developments

Design of Headquarters and Regional Offices for Associated National Life Insurance

Bulky Goods Retailing Centre covering 20,630 m² of showroom and exhibition space

Figgis&Jefferson

96 Pacific Highway, St Leonards

Harrison Communications, Neutral Bay

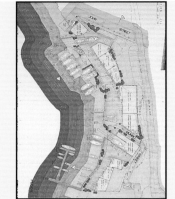
Berrys Bay Marina, North Sydney

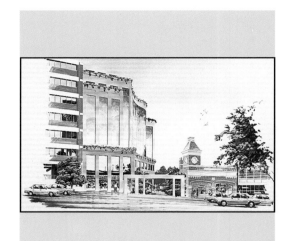
767 Pacific Highway, Chatswood

Central Coast Fair, St.2. Erina

Sharp Australia, Blacktown

CCH, New Zealand

Wellcome Australia, Cabarita

96 Pacific Highway, St Leonards

FIRTH, LEE + PARTNERS PTY LTD

Directors

Associate Director

Directors left to right)
Bill Firth B.ARCH., (UNSW'69) A.R.A.I.A.
Geoffrey Lee B.ARCH., (UNSW'79) A.R.A.I.A.
Ian G. Scott B.ARCH., M BLDG (Sc) F.R.A.I.A.
Robert Douglass B.E. M.I.E. AUST A.A.I.M.
Nick Nikolic S.T.S.B. A.R.A.I.A.

Associate Director
John T. Stefanatos B.Sc ARCH., B.BLDG.
   GRAD. A.I.B.

Established
1969

Address
96 Pacific Highway
St. Leonards, N.S.W. 2065

P.O. Box 1645
North Sydney, N.S.W. 2060

Telephone
(02) 439 8300

Facsimile
(02) 438 3947

Number of Employees
20

Project Types	Percentage
Commercial	30%
Industrial	30%
Residential	5%
Retail	10%
Recreational/Resort	10%
Educational	5%
Government & Civic	10%

Other Disciplines
Urban Planning
Interior Design
Materials Handling and
   Needs Analysis
Project Feasibility
Construction Management

Value of Commissions 1986 – 1987
$35M

Persons to Contact
Bill Firth
Geoffrey Lee

Current and Recent Projects
Commercial
96 Pacific Highway, St. Leonards
(Firth Group Offices)
40 Pacific Highway, Chatswood
477 Pacific Highway, Crows Nest
767 Pacific Highway, Chatswood
60 Archer Street, Chatswood
Sloane Street, Summer Hill
Avoca Street, Randwick
Ebley Street, Bondi Junction
CCH New Zealand
Cnr. Pacific Highway and Whiting Road, Artarmon
Imagineering commercial development, Waterloo
National Bank, Cessnock and Newcastle
Industrial
Schroeder Darling, Rydalmere
Sharp Australia, Blacktown
CCH N.Z., Auckland
Wellcome Australia, Cabarita
Berry's Bay Redevelopment, North Sydney
Lego Australia, Lane Cove
Canterbury Road, Punchbowl
Residential
Villa Homes, Myrtle Street, Blacktown
Townhouses, Westmead
St.Ives Gardens Retirement Village
House, Lindfield
Project Home Design, Long Homes
Retail
Central Coast Fair, Stage 2 – Erina
Mosman Centre, Brady and Heydon Sts, Mosman
Recreational/Resort
Hotel Resort, Ballina
Hotel Resort, Blackheath
Hotel Resort, Rarotonga and Aitutaki
Interior Design
CCH Reception, North Ryde
Henry Davis York, MLC Building
Sharp Australia, Blacktown
Citicentre Investments, St. Leonards
Japanese Consul, Sydney
General
PWD School, Peterborough
RANTEWSS HMAS Albatross, Nowra
AJAAC HMAS Albatross, Nowra
CCH Reception, North Ryde, Interior Design

Design Philosophy and History
Firth, Lee and Partners Pty Ltd (formerly Bill Firth & Partners Pty Ltd) was established as a partnership in June 1969. The change of name in November of 1987 coincided with Mr Geoffrey Lee taking over responsibility as Managing Director.

The objective of the firm is to be innovative in project initiation, design, management, cost control and construction techniques.

During the years, these objectives have been successfully demonstrated and the resulting skills refined to enable us to provide a service not only as the traditional Architect/Planner but also as the client's confidant and working partner.

The variety and complexity of projects successfully completed by the practice includes Housing, Commercial, Industrial, Civic, High Density Residential, Retail, Club, Hotel, Motel, Educational Projects and planning projects ranging in size from $30,000 to $300,000,000.

Since its inception, the group has expanded its activities and professional associations to cover the widest possible range of services associated with any sphere of building and property development. These include feasibility studies, planning advice, cost plans, critical path analysis, site evaluations, local authority liaison, ordinance interpretation and town planning.

In addition to our Sydney office, architectural services are available in Melbourne, Brisbane, Fiji, Auckland and San Francisco. This facility allows us to assist any company wishing to expand interstate or overseas.

Materials handling and needs analysis is now offered through an associated company, Gardner, Cooper & Associates Pty Ltd. This service covers new and existing buildings, assisting companies in economising and rationalising their plant and warehousing requirements.

In 1986, the construction and completion of our premises at 96 Pacific Highway was very satisfying, and marked the start of a new exciting era.

Finally, our architecture is generally known for its efficient, market oriented quality designs. This aspect of our work will continue, and we are extending the virtues of our traditional work, concentrating on a more refined design aesthetic.

1

2

3

4

5

FORBES AND FITZHARDINGE

Directors (left to right)
Mike Fitzhardinge FRAIA MRAPI
Graeme Paynter FRAIA

Established
1946

Address
1064 Hay Street
West Perth, W.A. 6005

P.O. Box 7013
Cloisters Square
Perth, W.A. 6000

Telephone
(09) 322 3644

Telex
Forfit AA95941

Facsimile
(09) 322 1664

Forbes and Fitzhardinge

Forbes and Fitzhardinge is a multi-disciplinary firm which offers a full range of Architectural services together with the support disciplines of Urban Planning and Interior Design.

Located in Perth, Western Australia, it is one of the most respected practices in the State. The present firm was established in 1946 but has historic associations going back to the 1880's. The firm is comprised of two principals and a full-time staff of Architects, technical draughtsmen, administrative and programming personnel.

The firm has won numerous awards and achieved national recognition for its innovation, consciousness, and contribution to the built environment. Co-ordination, cost control, efficiency and imagination are elements in the problem solving process considered in a balanced approach to each project, moulding innovation and enthusiasm with practical experience. The importance of achieving all critical dates in the design, documentation and contractural process is fully appreciated and the firm has achieved an enviable record in respect of "on time, on budget" projects.

No matter what size of project, whether a feasibility study or a multi-million dollar development, creativity is encouraged and allowed to flourish without being flaunted.

Although acting primarily as consultants directly responsible to the client, the firm has been involved as secondary consultants on major engineering projects, both within Australia and overseas.

Architecture

Much of Architecture as practised today is essentially an exercise in maximising space and solving technical problems of lighting, air-conditioning, etc. all without recognising the individual's need for identity. Considerations of adaptability, flexibility, and maximising nett area all too often take precedence over the design and disregard any human reference.

Forbes and Fitzhardinge believe in designing for the optimum environmental character. Structure, services, spaces, etc. are all evolved within a budgetry constraint and a design concept then formed which creates spaces with a sense of identity and human reference, and which are not arbitrary but depend on one another. This holistic approach is used to vitalise the Architecture and create buildings which are a delight to the user and hence increase productivity, maximise returns and are on budget. Architectural services provided include: Investigation, identification and documentation of project requirements and design criteria.

Schematic design drawings and other documents to illustrate the Architectural and Planning concepts permitting evaluation prior to major commitments of documentation.

Design development of the detailed Architectural and Planning concepts.

Documentation and specifications to define the work of and provide the basis for construction contracts.

Administration of all contractural aspects of principal and sub-contracts including financial and quality control.

The management of the entire design/construction process enables the firm to monitor progress of all consultants and regularly report to the client in terms of quality, cost and time. Advice on contractural arrangements is supported by considerable experience in preparing and administrating various formats including those applicable to "fast tracking" and negotiated bids.

Urban Planning

Urban Planning in reality is "Macro" Architecture and is complementary to the design of individual projects. An intimate working knowledge of the problems and particularly the potentials of the wider Urban Planning aspects has proved of considerable environmental and economic benefit to the firm's architectural clients. Specific skills and experience relate to central city development co-ordination and water related developments including marinas. The firm also undertakes specific Urban Planning tasks of a more general nature and in particular matters requiring innovative approaches to problem solving.

Interior Design

To further support the concept of total Architecture the firm has established an Interior Design group. One of the most important areas during the conceptual design work and so often ignored is the analysis to the internal needs of the building user, not in general terms but in the finite microcosm of desk and telephone locations, work station requirements, etc. The creation of an internal environment which allows the user to fully utilise the building's space and energy as well as providing higher staff productivity levels, show significant cost benefits over a period of time due to the correct and efficient use of all the building's services.

Computer Applications

Computer aided draughting enables two and three dimensional images of alternative building concepts to be investigated. The designer can make informed judgements on structural, aesthetic and budgetry constraints minimising time consumption and hence spend more time on innovative thinking. As the design proceeds to production drawings, all established information is utilised eliminating any repetition. Building contract administrative software has been pioneered and developed on a commercial basis. And internal administration and accounting is computerised along with word processing.

Current and Recent Projects

1 Central Park Developments
This 65,000m² commercial development and 1000 vehicle carpark is the final stage in an urban planning scheme maximising commercial benefits for the developers and civic amenity for the City. Buildings already completed in this scheme are the A.M.P. Tower and Commonwealth Bank.

2 Forbes and Fitzhardinge Office

3 S.G.I.O. Office, Geraldton

4 Woodside Petroleum Office

5 Technology Centre, W.A. Technology Park

Other recent commissions include:
N.M.L. Redevelopment
C.R.A. Research and Development Facility
Augusta Hotel Development
Perth International Gold Refinery
Mater Redevelopment, North Sydney
Metropolitan Security Prison
S.G.I.O. Office, Perth
I.B.M. Office, Perth
Gurney Gardens Development, Penang
R. & I. Bank Centre
S.E.C. Control Centre
Wesfarmers, Bassendean
Perth Airport Control Tower
Barwon & Ararat Prisons, Victoria
Greenough Prison
St. John of God Hospital
Wesley Centre
Challenge Bank, Headquarters
Westpac, State Office
Secret Harbour Coastal Development
St. Louis Aged Persons Housing
Wesley College Sports Centre

FORBES
AND
FITZHARDINGE
Architects & Planners

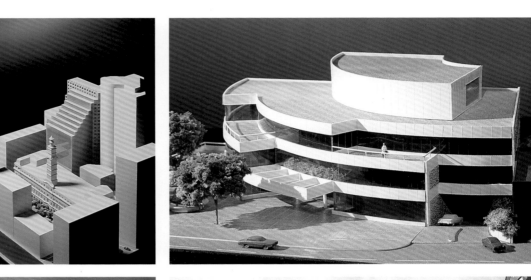

Frank Kolos and Partners Pty Ltd
Architects

FRANK KOLOS + PARTNERS PTY LTD

Directors (left to right)
Frank Kolos B.Arch., F.R.A.I.A., A.R.I.B.A.
Brian Nicholson A.S.T.C. (Arch), F.R.A.I.A.
Alexander Blank
John Bakker M.T.S. Holland
Mark Haywood B.Arch., A.R.A.I.A.

Associate Director
John Robertson B.Arch. (Hons)

Established
1976

Address
110 Pacific Highway
North Sydney, N.S.W. 2060

Telephone
(02) 929 0511

Facsimile
(02) 929 4403

Number of Employees
25

Project Types
Commercial
Office/Retail

Restoration & Refurbishment
Commercial, Institutional and Hotel

Industrial
Factory, Warehouse and Administration

Leisure and Recreation
Cinema/Restaurant and Marina
Complexes

Tourism
Hotel, Motel and Convention

Community
Municipal Facilities,
Schools, Colleges, Telecommunications

Residential
Homes and Medium-Density Housing

Health Planning
Private Hospitals

Other Disciplines
Development Economics
Construction Management
Interior Design
Building Survey Services
Urban Planning
Graphic Design

Person to Contact
Any Director

Current and Recent Projects
Commercial: Office/Retail
10-14 Barrack Street, Sydney

159-171 Pitt Street, Sydney
Development Study

130 Pitt Street, Sydney

374-376 George Street, Sydney
Development Study

35-43 Clarence Street, Sydney
Development Study

875-893 Pacific Highway, Pymble

174 Pacific Highway, Artarmon

810-814 Pacific Highway, Gordon

41-45 Rickard Road, Bankstown

Restoration and Refurbishment
G.P.O. Martin Place
Development Study

343 George Street, Sydney

333 Kent Street, Sydney

154-158 Sussex Street, Sydney

Industrial
38 Boorea Street, Lidcombe

1 Rosebery Avenue, Rosebery

46-62 Dickson Avenue, Artarmon

142 Wicks Road, North Ryde

Leisure and Recreation
Twin Cinema Complex, Mosman

Quad Cinema Complex, Cronulla

Casino Proposal, Darling Harbour

Tourism
Resort Hotel Proposal, Darling Harbour

Hotel, Kings Cross

Hotel, Potts Point

Health Planning
North Gosford Private Hospital

Medical Centre, Ryde
Development Study

Fairfield Private Hospital
Development Study

Quakers Hill Private Hospital
Development Study

Company Profile

Frank Kolos + Partners Pty Limited developed from a practice founded in 1957 that was re-structured in 1976 with the on-going objectives of innovation in project initiation, design management and cost control.

Since its inception, these objectives have been gratifyingly realised through a number of successful projects that embrace a variety and complexity of building types.

The expertise developed by the firm in planning advice and feasibility studies has resulted in a close liaison with institutions, developers and financiers and has instigated numerous major projects in recent years.

Our commitment to a mutually rewarding client/architect relationship ensures the pursuit of achieving a high level of design quality for each project, while closely co-ordinating with each of the engineering disciplines to produce a building that recognizes the construction and economic constraints of today. We are committed to a philosophy of producing design solutions that acknowledge functional, spatial, contextual and marketing requirements, while maintaining an aesthetic integrity that will stand the test of time. This approach ensures individual assessment of each project to produce the correct ingredients for a successful venture.

Our ability to translate clients' briefs into realistic design concepts, combined with a reputation for providing superior documentation and administration services have been the major contributors to the firm's success. We also recognise the need to respond to the changing requirements of clients and their markets, and aim to accommodate their needs by providing the most appropriate design solutions, supported by a commitment to producing quality buildings within functional and economic parameters.

The examples illustrated opposite demonstrate the credibility of our philosophy and reflect the pride we place in the realisation of projects from concept through to successful development.

Other work by the practice has involved a successful membership of The Urban Collaborative which marketed architectural, engineering and planning services in the Middle East, and earned an Export Development Award in 1977 for the planning, design and construction management of a major new industrial city in Iran.

In addition, First Prize, from 94 submissions, was awarded to the firm for our entry in the R.A.I.A. organised national competition for the Majestic Hotel site in Perth, W.A.

The Directors and staff pride themselves on their ability to solve problems and generate alternative ideas. This approach has always endeavoured to produce the best solution for a client, in order to achieve and maintain a successful and mutually gratifying relationship. To this objective we continually strive.

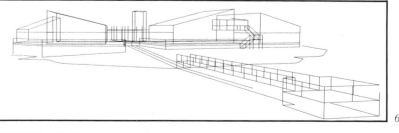

1   The Mining Museum, The Rocks, Sydney

2   'Batemans Bay International' Hotel, N.S.W.

3   'Batemans Bay International' Hotel, N.S.W.

4   Corporate Offices, North Ryde, N.S.W.

5   T'Cap Housing Programme, Bourke, N.S.W.

6   Computer Sketch, Tennant Creek Yacht Club

7   Tennant Creek Yacht Club, Tennant Creek, N.T.

GIBBON HAMOR & ASSOCIATES
Architects, Planners, Interior Designers and Project Managers

Directors (left to right)
Barry Gibbon BSc (Arch), BArch (Hons), ARAIA.
Harry Hamor BSc (Arch), BArch, MTCP,
 ARAIA, ARAPI, AIArbA.

Established
1982

Address
1 Lee Street
Sydney, N.S.W. 2000

Telephone
(02) 211 3122

Facsimile
(02) 281 2434

Number of Employees
7 professional, plus support staff

Project Types	Percentage
Commercial	35%
Industrial	15%
Interior Design	10%
Government	20%
Residential	5%
Tourism & Recreational	15%

Other Disciplines
Town and Regional Planning
Interior Design and Architecture
Development Feasibility Studies
Urban Planning
Arbitration and Contract Dispute
 Resolution
Refurbishment and Restoration
Landscape
Project Management
Building Pathology and Research
Graphic Design
Photography

Persons to Contact
Harry Hamor or Barry Gibbon

Current Value of Work in Progress
$15M

Associated Practice
MJW Associates
Structural and Analytical Engineers

Current and Recent Projects
Batemans Bay International Hotel Complex

Mining Museum, The Rocks, Sydney

Bourke Town Campers Project, Bourke, N.S.W.

Baulkham Hills, Subdivision and Site Development
Plan for 230 Homesites

Festival of Sydney, Public Area Programme

Three Building Commercial Complex,
North Ryde, N.S.W.

Tennant Creek Yacht Club and Hotel/Motel, N.T.

History
Founded in Sydney in 1982, Gibbon Hamor & Associates
has developed a multi-disciplinary approach to architecture, interior design, planning and project management.
This approach is continually being refined, and has been
a guiding principle for the firm's direction of growth.

The partners established the practice after post graduate
studies as well as extensive professional experience, both
with private practitioners and with government and
academia. Additional experience was also gained during
a period of overseas study and employment, principally
in London.

The firm, located in the city, has a wide range of clients,
including commercial, industrial, government (at all
three tiers), and a broad range of smaller private clients.
Projects have been undertaken in all the eastern states,
particularly N.S.W., as well as the Northern Territory.

Philosophy
The firm is young and has a fresh, innovative and
professional attitude to all its commissions.
Gibbon Hamor & Associates strives to provide clients
with excellence in both design and execution of all its
projects, in all disciplines.

The firm recognises, and prides itself, on working closely
and continually with its clients to achieve an integrated,
consistent, cost effective and responsible result to the
particular brief in train.

It is this underlying approach that is the basis for the
studio's approach, and now, after establishing a working
group with a unified and co-ordinated direction, the
practice is building up a deserved recognition for
originality, integrity and efficiency in the projects
undertaken.

Approach
The firm has undertaken to combine the full extent
of professionalism, expertise and responsibility,
occasionally found in the larger, longer established
offices with the responsiveness, originality and freshness
that can only be found in a smaller, moderate firm.

Coupled to the principle of working closely with, and
thoroughly understanding each client's needs, with a
Director's continued input, the firm is able to bring to
bear a consistent and professional approach. This both
reflects our clients' demands, and takes heed of the
limitations of the brief, advantage of the complexities of
Local and State conditions, so providing a Planning or
Building product that maximises the opportunities
available, and is responsive of scheduling and budgetary
constraints.

The firm realises the need to be effectively informed
of current practice and management and is, accordingly,
active with a number of professional organisations.
These include the Royal Australian Institute of Architects,
the Royal Australian Planning Institute, the Association
of Consulting Planners, the Institute of Arbitrators, the
Building Science Forum and the National Trust.

Further, the firm maintains continued professional
relations with a variety of sub-consultants and affiliate
practices, on whose expertise it may call, should the
need arise.

The firm believes that more than merely successful
design and planning is needed to provide a client with a
quality of service that is essential in today's competitive
climate, and so combines environmental awareness with
social, political and economic responsibility, resulting in
designs and buildings that are appropriate to their
function, need and environment.

GIBBON HAMOR
& ASSOCIATES

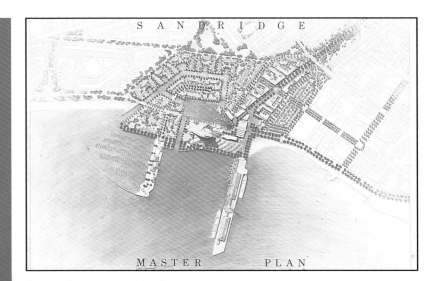

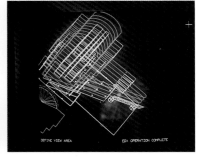

GODFREY AND SPOWERS AUSTRALIA PTY LTD

Architects, Planners, Interior Designers

Directors (left to right)
John Davidson AM B ARCH LFRAIA RIBA
  Hon FAIA
Bryan Fitchett Dip Arch FRAIA
Eric Taylor Dip CE FRAIA MAAS AMASA
Peter Macdonald FRAIA RIBA
Barry Axtens B Arch FRAIA
David Blanche B Arch FRAIA

Established
1896

Addresses
577 Little Collins Street
Melbourne, Vic. 3000

Telephone
(03) 614 6144   (03) 614 4655

Facsimile
(03) 62 6791

Telex
33226

Canberra Office
Godfrey and Spowers Australia Pty Ltd
13 London Court
London Circuit
Canberra City, A.C.T. 2601

Telephone
(062) 47 6533

Facsimile
(062) 47 3465

Canberra Director
Eric Taylor

Sydney Office
Godfrey Spowers and Hallen Pty Ltd
133 Alexander Street
Crows Nest, N.S.W. 2065

Telephone
(02) 439 5488

Facsimile
(02) 439 2738

Sydney Director
Hans H. Hallen ARAIA RIBA

Number of Employees
127

Project Types
Commercial
Educational
Health
Industrial
Interior Design
Recreational
Residential
Retail
Town Planning
Urban Design

Current and Recent Projects

Como Project, South Yarra (formerly South Yarra Project) Mixed use development (Stage 1 with South Yarra Collaborative)	$1,000M
Bourke Place, Bourke Street, Melbourne Investment Offices	$150M
Riverside Quay Project Offices/Residential South Bank – Redevelopment	$300M
Sandridge City, Mixed use/Marina Bayside development, Port Melbourne In association with Robert Peck & Co.	$600M
Victoria Gardens, Office Park Victoria Street, Richmond In association with Robert Peck & Co.	$200M
55 King Street Office Building	$18M
State Mail Centre, Port Melbourne	$8M
303 Collins Street, Melbourne Office Refurbishment	$8M
Melbourne Remand Centre In association with Daryl Jackson Pty Ltd	$45M
Maribyrnong Medical Centre, Sunshine In association with Mitchell Walker Wright Pty Ltd	$73M
The Walter and Eliza Hall Institute of Medical Research, Parkville In association with Daryl Jackson Pty Ltd	$25M
Office Fit-Out, Rialto Project Education Department	$10M
Philip Institute of Technology Library and Computer Building, Bundoora In association with Daryl Jackson Pty Ltd	$6M
441 St. Kilda Road Office Building	$16M
509 St. Kilda Road Office Building	$25M
615 St. Kilda Road Office Building	$15M
601 St. Kilda Road Office Building	$14M
Investment Building 565 Lonsdale Street, Melbourne	$12M
600 Collins Street Office and retail accommodation	$9M
Office Park Burwood Road, Hawthorn	$12M
Jolimont Centre, Office building and Post Office Canberra	$22M
Insurance Offices Burwood Road, Hawthorn	$8M
National Bank House 500 Bourke Street, Melbourne	$39M
Collins Wales House 360 Collins Street, Melbourne	$40M

Recent Awards
BOMA Merit Award 1986
601 St. Kilda Road

RAIA Merit Award 1987
601 St. Kilda Road

The Firm
Reputation
Godfrey and Spowers has been in business since 1896 and for most of that time has been one of the largest practices in Australia. An architectural firm does not survive for almost 100 years unless it has established a reputation for success and continues to work hard to maintain that reputation.

A large firm of enthusiastic and committed people, Godfrey and Spowers brings to each project a wide range of complementary skills at all levels of the organisation. The firm's long and successful history reflects both its stability and dynamism in the rapidly changing building industry.

Reputation and experience offer much to a client but also carry an obligation for the architect. Godfrey and Spowers recognises the obligation and strives to maintain its position at the forefront of the profession.

Knowledge
The skill and 'know-how' demonstrated by this architectural practice is based on its accumulated and collective knowledge. This knowledge is continually being added to, as a result of constant investigation into the techniques and procedures adopted with each new project.

One particular area where this knowledge is crucial is in dealing with authorities. To the uninitiated, the plethora of regulatory controls on a project can be daunting. Knowledge of the authorities' requirements and constant dealings with the people involved have placed Godfrey and Spowers in an enviable position to save its clients time and money.

Technology
The expertise of the firm was enhanced in 1985 with the introduction of the "Intergraph" system of computer aided design and documentation (CADD).

Godfrey and Spowers has an integrated approach to CADD, with this system offering far more than a simple computer draughting programme. The CADD workstations at Godfrey and Spowers are used increasingly to interface with computer design systems in the offices of consultants and clients; providing data based information on all elements of the project.

The Client
Godfrey and Spowers is committed to the success of its clients' projects. A successful project is founded on a close business and personal relationship between owner and architect. Such a relationship engenders frank communication and an understanding of the roles each undertakes in creating a successful project.

Good architecture is a response to the client's needs and aspirations, and results from a rewarding collaboration between client and architect.

The Project
Design
Godfrey and Spowers believes careful and attentive design is another of its professional responsibilities, to the client and community alike.

Good design begins with a considered response to client needs and a synthesis of many pragmatic factors. The result is a development creative and inventive in its solutions to problems and in its appearance.

The Project
The firm's reputation for sound management has its basis in three areas: the close relationship fostered with clients; the efficient management of professional activities; and the adroit control of budget and program during the course of the project.

Godfrey and Spowers consults with the client from the outset to establish priorities and limits for the size, quality and cost of works.

The project is carefully monitored to ensure there is no departure from these agreed standards without the total involvement of the client.

The result is satisfaction and success.

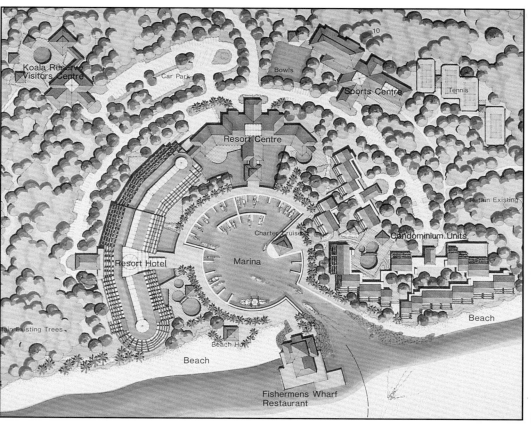

1 Netanya Noosa

2 Resort Master Plan

3 Seahaven Resort, Noosa Heads

4 Lighting and Restoration,
   St. Philips, Sydney

5 Pacific Bay Beach and Golf Resort,
   Coffs Harbour

6 Hillside Residential Units,
   Noosa Heads

GOODWIN AND SOUTHWELL ARCHITECTS

Partners (left to right)
Graham R. Southwell B. Arch(Hons) FRAIA
Clive B. Goodwin B. Arch, FRAIA

Established
1968

Address
20 Loftus Street
Sydney, N.S.W. 2000

Telephone
(02) 251 2566

Facsimile
(02) 251 4170

Number of Personnel
10

Project Types
Resorts
Hotels, Motels, Condominiums
& Apartments

Sport & Recreation
Golf Courses, Tennis Courts,
Fitness Centres, Watersport Facilities,
Marinas, Club Houses

Retail & Commercial
Restaurants, Specialty Shops, Offices

Residential
Townhouses, Low & High Rise Units,
Penthouses, Retirement Housing

Health & Welfare
Private Hospitals, Public Hospitals,
Accommodation for the Disabled,
Day Care Facilities, Assessment &
Rehabilitation Centres

Community & Educational
Schools, Libraries, Community Centres,
Churches

Interior Design
Hotel, Resort, Restaurant, Commercial,
Multiple Residential, Health & Welfare

Person to Contact
Graham Southwell
Clive Goodwin

Current and Recent Projects
Resort Developments
Seahaven, Noosa Heads, Qld
Beachfront resort incorporating 46 self contained units,
"Gingers" restaurant, shops and recreational facilities
Netanya, Noosa
Boutique hotel comprising 29 luxury suites,
"Michelles" restaurant and shops
Pacific Bay Beach & Golf Resort, Coffs Harbour, N.S.W.
Multi-stage resort development on 60 ha of beachfront
land, comprising hotel and condominium accommodation,
beach club, golf course, and comprehensive sporting and
recreation facilities, Stage 1 $40M
Black Bear Inn, Thredbo, N.S.W.
Extension and comprehensive renovation of 36 bed
lodge, restaurant and bar
Report, "Design Criteria for Hotel Developments of
International Standards" prepared for Queensland
Tourist and Travel Corporation
Tennis Centre, Hastings Street, Noosa Heads

Residential
Terraced Hillside Apartments, Noosa Heads, Qld
Townhouses, Hunters Hill, N.S.W.
Luxury Residential Units at St. Ives and Lindfield,
N.S.W.

Health & Welfare
Wolper Private Hospital, Woollahra, N.S.W.
51 beds and operating theatre
Sir Moses Montefiore Jewish Home,
Hunters Hill, N.S.W.
Self care accommodation, hostel, nursing home and
intensive care hostel totalling 350 beds. Physiotherapy
and Day Care Centre
Shellharbour Hospital for N.S.W. Department
of Health, in conjunction with Armstrong
Joyce & Associates
Beverley Park Residential Accommodation,
Campbelltown, N.S.W.
Independent living accommodation for the N.S.W.
Society for Crippled Children

Conservation and Rehabilitation
St. Philips Church, York Street, Sydney
External and internal restoration, and lighting of
Gothic Revival Church
Juanita Neilsen Community Centre, Woolloomooloo,
for the Council of the City of Sydney
Industrial building recycled to community use
74 Clarence Street, Sydney
Refurbishment for restaurant,retail and commercial use

Educational
Projects in conjunction with the
N.S.W Government Architect:
Extensions to Barrenjoey High School
Standard Library Building for use in state high schools

Projects Completed prior to 1982 include
Rohini Village, Turramurra, N.S.W.
100 self contained retirement units
Wentworth Gardens, Parramatta, N.S.W.
17 storey building comprising 204 apartments
Mathew Bligh, Manly, N.S.W.
8 storey strata title unit building
Flinders Village, Castle Hill, N.S.W.
180 hostel and 40 self contained retirement units
Church and Hall at Moorebank, N.S.W.
Assessment and Rehabilitation Unit,
Bega Hospital, N.S.W.
Factory and warehouse, Dee Why, N.S.W.
Noosa Court, Hastings Street, Noosa Heads, Qld
Addition of penthouse and shop
Townhouses, Winnie Street, Cremorne, N.S.W.
and Sunshine Beach, Qld
Terrace Gardens, Hastings Street, Noosa Heads, Qld
Self contained resort accommodation and restaurant
St. Philips Parish Centre, York Street, Sydney
Projects carried out in conjunction with the N.S.W.
Government Architect:
Alterations and extensions to various High Schools and
Public schools throughout N.S.W.
Staff accommodation and services buildings at Jenolan
Caves, N.S.W.
Demountable Schools Programme for the N.S.W.
Department of Education

Company Profile
Goodwin and Southwell Architects was established
by the present principals in 1968 to provide the highest
standard of professional service in the practice of
architecture. The firm is based in Sydney, is active in
New South Wales and Queensland, is also registered
in Victoria, and maintains overseas associations.

The practice has developed special expertise in the
design of resort projects, health care buildings, medium
and high density housing developments, and retirement
communities, and has experience in the restoration and
rehabilitation of buildings.

Clients include property investors and developers,
charitable and religious organisations, government and
semi-government agencies, health care professionals,
and resort operators.

Organisation and Services
A partner directly controls each project, and is the
point of contact with the proprietor, enabling the firm
to provide clients with personal attention and prompt
and efficient service. Quality of design and documentation is of the utmost importance. Effective cost control
and a high standard of integrated management during
the total period of architectural service is essential for
a successful project.

The practice offers its clients a comprehensive range
of services for building procurement. Services available
include involvement in identification of suitable sites,
pre-purchase feasibility studies, preparation of the brief,
conceptual planning, rezoning applications, development and building applications, cash flow projections,
cost monitoring and control, co-ordination of consultants, tendering procedures, negotiation of contracts,
administration of the building contract, furnishing and
equipping to 'ready to occupy' stage, commissioning,
and project accounting including depreciation schedules.

1

2

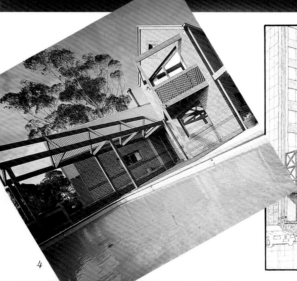

3

4

5

1 Engineers Offices, Auburn Road

2 City Baths, Melbourne

3 Bourke Chambers

4 Vleugel House

5 Celsius House

6 Capita Centre

7 Bryant & May

6

7

GREENHATCH & PARTNERS PTY LTD

Directors (left to right)
Kevin Greenhatch
Geoff Hooke
Leo de Jong

Established
1979

Address
405 Little Bourke Street
Melbourne, Vic. 3000

Telephone
(03) 670 6688

Facsimile
(03) 670 6516

Number of Employees
15

Staff and Office
Professional and Personal
A principal of the firm works directly
on every project.

In addition to the directors a talented
architectural core staff is employed and
complemented with contract professionals that are familiar with the firm's
standards and operations.

Our secretarial facilities also service
a professional group which consists
of Landscape and Urban Designers,
Project Managers and Interior Designers.

Professional Services

Problem definition and analysis

Retail and office development analysis

Residential development studies

Project and Economic studies for leisure
and recreation facilities

Site selection and evaluation

Building appraisals and reports

Formulation of detailed briefs

Concept analysis

Architectural design

Interior design

Tenancy requirements and design

Restaurant and Cafe design

Historic building reports and
restoration proposals

Commercial and residential renovations
and restorations

Contract documentation

Contract administration

Current and Recent Projects

Commercial
Capita Centre, 459 Collins Street, Melbourne
Capita Financial Group
New 16 storey Office Building and Renovation
of 30 storey Tower, in association with
Perrott Lyon Mathieson $52M

Celsius House, 150 Lonsdale Street, Melbourne
Celsius Investments Pty. Ltd.
Renovation of 28 storey Building $8M

266 Auburn Road, Hawthorn
New Office Building $0.7M

Bryant & May Estate, 560 Church Street, Richmond
New Office Building and Renovation
of Historic Building to Offices $12M

Porsche Cars Australia, 550 Church Street, Richmond
New Office Building, Renovation
of Historic Buildings and Existing Factory Service
and Distribution Centre $4M

'Parlez' Restaurant,
401 Little Bourke Street, Melbourne $0.5M

'Pelaco' Building, Goodwood Street, Richmond
Renovation of 5 storey Building to Office Use $6M

Bourke Chambers, 405 Little Bourke Street, Melbourne
Renovation and Tenancies for 5 storey Building $1.8M

Niagara House, 370 Little Bourke Street, Melbourne
Renovation to Offices and Retail $1.2M

390 Toorak Road, Toorak
Renovation of Historic Church Building and
New 4 storey Office Building $7M

Restoration
City Baths, Swanston Street, Melbourne
Restoration and Redevelopment to
Sports Leisure Complex,
Merit Award R.A.I.A (Vic. Chapter) 1984,
Lachlan Macquarie Award R.A.I.A. (National) 1984 $4M

Seabrook House, Lonsdale Street, Melbourne
Conversion of Historic Bluestone Warehouse to
Barristers Chambers $0.7M

Queen Bess Row, East Melbourne
Restoration of Terrace Houses $0.6M

Morning Star Estate, Mornington
Restoration of Historic Mansion
and Thoroughbred Horse Stud $0.75M

Health
Live-in Centre for the Australian Cancer Patients
Foundation, Yarra Junction $3M

Residential
Westbourne Road, Kensington
16 houses for the Ministry of Housing

Ayllene Avenue, Armadale
7 Town House development

Aberdeen Road, Prahran
3 Town House development

New Houses
Yared House, Shoreham

Vleugel House, Mount Martha

Launder House, Cape Schank

Donald House, Mount Eliza

Traynor House, Mount Eliza

Approach

Practical and Co-Operative
Greenhatch & Partners adopts an approach to projects
that is not limited by a consistency of style, but is open
and appropriate to the particular task.

Both Directors play an important role on each project,
offering an integrated consultancy and architectural
design service. Kevin Greenhatch has a primary concern
in the establishment of the project brief, the conceptual
and economic analysis and management of the process.
Leo de Jong has the task of interpreting the requirements
and producing the physical expression in a built form.
Associate Director, Geoff Hooke is mainly responsible
for technical and programming aspects together with
documentation on major projects.

It is recognized that most successful projects reflect a
high level of co-operation between Architect, Client and
other professional consultants. We also believe that it
is increasingly impossible for architectural work to be
produced in a vacuum and that the profession is called
on to be at least part of the financial risk, the emotional
strain, competitiveness and unpredictability that is an
integral part of conducting business in our pluralistic
society.

Project Management
In response to clients' requirements for pre-architectural
analysis and overall management of the process we have
established a Project Management division which is
headed by Michael Cockcroft, an experienced architect
who has had ten years experience in property management with a large Australian public company.

Project Management appointments include:
Porsche Australia
Richmond Office Estate
Pelaco Development
Church Offices Toorak
Niagara House Offices
Elsternwick Retail Arcade

The Practice

Perceptive Analysis and Excellent Design
The emergence and establishment of the firm in
1979 followed an extensive experience gained by
the directions in Architecture, Property Development
and Housing.

We believe that this span of experience and our
involvement in consulting, property investment
and architecture allows us to provide an incisive
and commercial approach to projects.

Although we recognise and appreciate technical,
economic and social influences we are clear that our
cardinal task is producing an architecture that always
has a substantive idea and that respects not only the
visual aesthetic but also the contextural and functional
aspects of the building.

Our work therefore expresses a set of values through
both the consideration and formulation of the brief and
the physical execution of the work.

The intent of the practice is to work on significant
projects and we find our firm competent with both
traditional commissioned work that demands a
committee or working group process and also with
commercial projects that demand solutions tailored
to accommodate a diverse range of conflicting
requirements.

We perceive that urban problems are becoming more
complex and often require a broad range of skills
working in a team approach. There is a need to analyse
and interpret the requirements of the Corporate
Managers, Municipal Councils and Entrepreneurs and
to then link these with Planning, Financial Analysis
and Architecture of the highest professional standard.

Another important characteristic of the practice is the
calibre of working relationships that have been formed
with firms that offer a wide range of professional
expertise. It is our policy to engage the top specialist
consultants that are appropriate for the specific project.

COURT OF AUSTRA

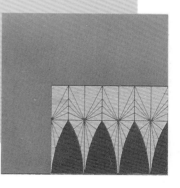

HARKNESS GROUP

Directors (left to right)
Dr Edward L. Harkness B.Arch., M.Bdg.Sc., M.Arch., PhD., FRAIA, MAAS, MASA
Picture top right on facing page
Andrew J. Tweedie B.Sc.(Arch.), B.Arch.
John S. Bailey B.Sc.(Arch.)
Norhisham Bin Mohamed Noori Dip.Arch., B.Arch.
Richard M. Jacombs B.Sc.(Computing Science & Mathematics), B.E.(Aeronautical)
Shirley Byron Secretary

Established
1982

Address
4th Floor
ANZ Bank Chambers
16A Bolton Street
Newcastle, N.S.W. 2300

Telephone
(049) 29 5333
(049) 26 4290

Number of Employees
6

Project Types
Commercial
Educational
Medical
Legal
Recreational
Tourist
Residential

Other Disciplines
Acoustics
Energy Studies
Sunscreen Design
Patent Development and Marketing
Writing of Technical Literature for Manufacturers
Contract Research/Product Development
Electronics Design to brief
Computer Programming to brief

Persons to contact
Dr Edward L. Harkness
Andrew J. Tweedie

Current and Recent Projects

Commercial: Office
Computer energy analysis of heating and cooling loads carried out on behalf of mechanical engineers D.S. Thomas Weatherall and Associates for the $90M Commonwealth Centre, Parramatta (Edwards Madigan Torzillo Briggs International, Architects) and for the MacNamara Building, Parramatta (John Andrews, Architect).

Medical
Building envelope design advice on the $120M New Teaching Hospital, Newcastle.

Legal
Acoustics for the Dubbo Family Law Courts and the Newcastle Family Law Courts.

Recreational/Tourist
$6M Black Marlin Marina, Nelson Bay, with Architect Lan Yap.

Residential
Solar houses designed for clients in the Hunter Valley and Port Stephens.

Other Disciplines
Acoustics
Noise control surveys, reports and expert witness appearances in court proceedings.

Energy
Computer simulation of the energy cost effectiveness of building design options.

Sunscreens
Scientifically designed sunscreens that are free form and sculptured in appearance and exclude sunlight as specified by the architect, client and mechanical engineer.

Patent Development and Marketing
Patent applications prepared in association with patent attorneys, guidance on leasing agreements and marketing.

Writing of Technical Literature
Technical literature is written for manufacturers, e.g., "Precast Concrete – energy cost effective facades", a 24 page booklet researched and written for the Precast Concrete Manufacturers Association of N.S.W. (1987).

Contract Research and Product Development
This service includes architectural products which a client might require to be invented from a written brief or developed beyond a stage already reached.

Profile
Dr Edward L. Harkness for 17 years lectured, researched and wrote on the topics related to the sciences in architecture.

Latter years in teaching revealed to him the possibility of applying science to define form in architecture.

Thus developed his interest in designing buildings and in particular the fenestration texture of buildings (sunscreens) in accordance with the relative movement of the sun to a building and the definition of form in auditoria to the needs of performers.

His book "Solar Radiation Control in Buildings," co-authored by Madan Mehta, now Professor of Architectural Engineering in Saudi Arabia, was published in English in 1978 and in Russian in 1984.

The international interest in Dr Harkness's application of the sciences to define form in architecture in facade design and in acoustic design of auditoria caused him to travel in every continent and to be invited to lecture in overseas countries including Malaysia, Singapore and the United States of America.

Evidence of the marketability of this approach to architecture is illustrated by the major projects on which the Group has worked in recent years; projects in Australia and overseas.

Dr Harkness gave papers to the 1986 Annual Conference of the Australian and New Zealand Architectural Science Association held in Auckland, New Zealand, entitled:
(a) "Experiments in adjustment of stage acoustics by musicians" and
(b) "Energy consequences of building design options".

The activities of the Group are broad, keeping staff fresh and up-to-date with the latest technological innovations and in sharing knowledge with others through publications.

The research background of Dr Harkness has been continued into the Group with the members involved in a continual process of learning new skills and techniques both in Architecture and other fields.

The aim of the Group is to bring together all the architectural sciences. In this way they hope to achieve functional, energy efficient, comfortable and aesthetically pleasing and exciting architecture. This may be achieved by the Group by either controlling the entire design of an environment or by acting as consultants to other architects and mechanical engineers.

It is expected that employees of the office, while achieving expertise in particular areas of interest of the Group, will also be knowledgeable in all other aspects of the Group's activities.

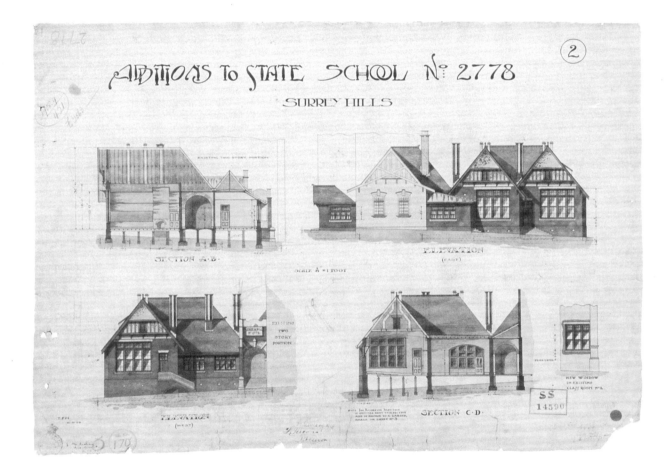

Additions to State School, No. 2778, Surrey Hills, circa 1908.

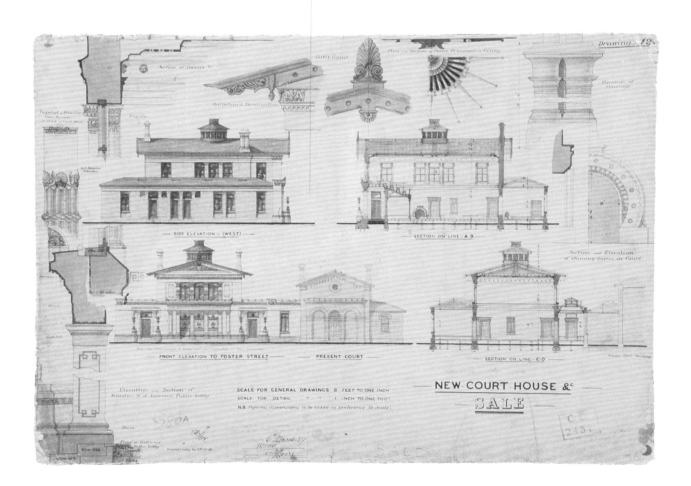

New Court House, Sale, circa 1889.

1 Graham Residence

2 Rumpoles Restaurant

3 Mid-City Walk

4 Mariner Shores Beach Resort

5 Hall Chadwick Centre

6 Bookworld

7 Glaskin Residence

8 Lindeman Island Resort

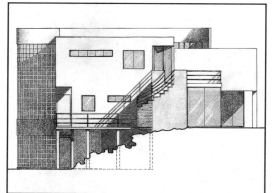

HAYSOM GROUP ARCHITECTS

Directors (left to right)
Edward Haysom
Susan Nutting
Christopher Everding

Established
1987

Address
14th Level
Hall Chadwick Centre
46 Edward Street
Brisbane, Qld 4000

Telephone
(07) 229 8088

Facsimile
(07) 229 6616

Number of Employees
13

Project Types
Commercial
Industrial
Recreational
Residential
Restoration
Retail

Other Disciplines
Graphics
Interior Design

Current and Recent Projects
Commercial
Behnfeld Group

Beneficial Finance

Hall Chadwick Centre, 46 Edward Street

Leighton Contractors, Queensland Office

New Zealand Consulate-General

Sunny Queen Egg Farms

Resort
Mariner Shores Beach Resort, Gold Coast

Lindeman Island Resort, Whitsunday Passage

Restaurants
Jo-Jo's, Brisbane

O'Neills, Brisbane

Rumpoles, Brisbane

Retail
Bookworld Stores

Residential
Glaskin Residence, Gold Coast

Graham Residence, Gold Coast

Spencer Residence, Ascot

Profile
Haysom Group Architects was formed in November 1987. The new Brisbane-based firm evolved from the former company, Haysom + Middleton Architects. Most of the professional personnel from the former company joined Haysom Group Architects, including two of the three directors of Haysom + Middleton.

The directors have an extensive portfolio of experience in Australia, the Pacific and the United States.

The company specialises in the design of resorts, restaurants, commercial office buildings, office interiors, commercial residential complexes and exhibits.

The philosophy of Haysom Group Architects and By Design Pty Ltd, its subsidiary company, is based on the need to integrate the design of both the outside and the inside of buildings. This results in the provision of professional services which cover the complete design process, from initial concept and building construction through to fitout.

This is achieved with a strictly personal approach in which the directors are involved in all stages of a project.

Good design and space planning evolves from comprehensive analysis of a client's expectations, needs and budget.

While offering practical services, emphasis is placed on high quality design solutions which are aided and backed by the latest in computer technology, including the CAD system.

Computers are used during all stages of a project, starting with a comprehensively analysed client brief, through design and scheduling, to cost analysis. Computers also provide a broad data base for information such as the analysis of town planning requirements as well as pricing.

The philosophy of Haysom Group Architects is to create building styles that do not specifically relate to current architectural preoccupations, but rather endure on their own merits.

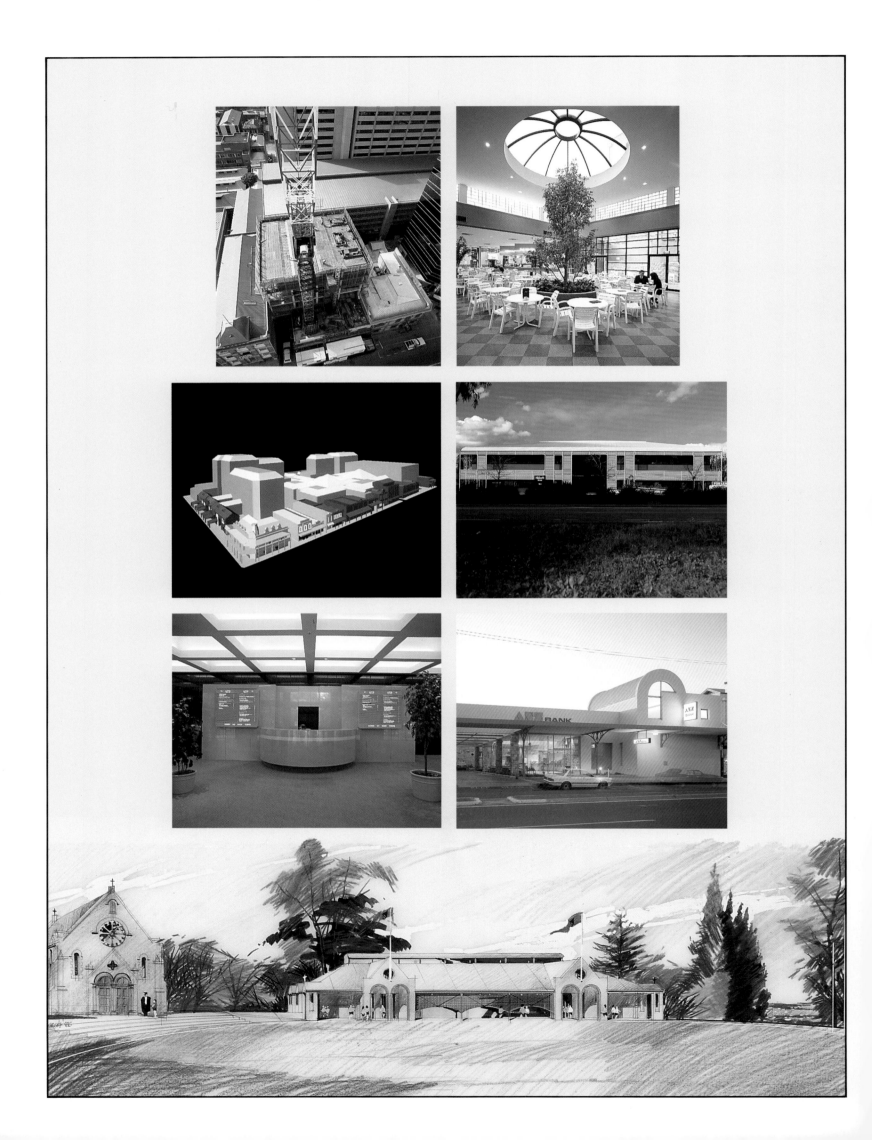

HODGKISON MATTHEWS & PARTNERS PTY LTD
Architects

Partners (top to bottom)
Robin Hodgkison
Barry Matthews
Peter Gray
Rod Matthews
Robert Battersby

Associate Partners
Philip Nayda
Geoff Jarvis

Associates
David Whittaker
Barry O'Connor

Addresses
Adelaide
262 Melbourne Street
North Adelaide, S.A. 5006

Telephone
(08) 267 4766

Facsimile
(08) 267 3105

Melbourne
83 Rathdowne Street
Carlton, Vic. 3053

Telephone
(03) 663 3255

Facsimile
(03) 662 1283

Associated Disciplines
Urban Design Australia
Interior Architecture
Project Management
Arcform Pty Ltd

Practice

Hodgkison Matthews and Partners is an established and significant architectural practice with the capacity and expertise to satisfy briefs of any size, anywhere.

The partnership was established in Adelaide in 1975 and, to meet the needs of our national corporate clients, we also opened a Melbourne Office.

We have selected a team of professional, technical and administrative staff of varying backgrounds to ensure that we offer a wide range of skills through all facets of practice thus providing creative, cost-effective and practical solutions to all projects.

To complement these resources our offices are equipped with sophisticated design, documentation, communications and reprographic systems. Our computer aided design facility allows us to explore alternative solutions, providing to our clients walk through three dimensional models of their projects with full colour imaging, as well as an efficient and flexible documentation service. The system is undoubtedly one of the best available.

The practice is involved in commissions of all sizes up to $300 million, in all areas of development including office, education and health facilities, hotels, banks, shopping centres, public and private housing, industrial projects, defence establishments and recreational facilities. Projects have ranged from historic building restorations and the recycling of office buildings to multi storey constructions and major mixed use redevelopments.

Our client base includes Local, State and Federal Government Departments, Institutions, corporate and private developers.

Philosophy

The cornerstone of the Hodgkison Matthews philosophy is design challenge – to be mentally extended by every project, aspiring to the optimum solution.

The focus is on the end users and, by working closely with our clients and assisting them to develop their briefs, we ensure that the environment and the spaces created are appropriate to their needs. Human scale is of fundamental importance.

Our practice has achieved its success by providing what we believe to be the correct balance between:

– Total consideration for our clients' needs and their building environment in creating an architectural statement that is both stimulating and appropriate.

– Absolute professionalism and technical excellence, ensuring that all relevant architectural factors have been accounted for through all phases of projects.

– A sensible approach to design and documentation ensuring that time and budget constraints are met, providing value for money without compromise to the built form.

– A development awareness giving confidence to our clients that we understand marketability and profitability.

It is this communication and co-operation that has assisted in maintaining our long-standing relationships with our clients.

Hodgkison Matthews & Partners

Architects

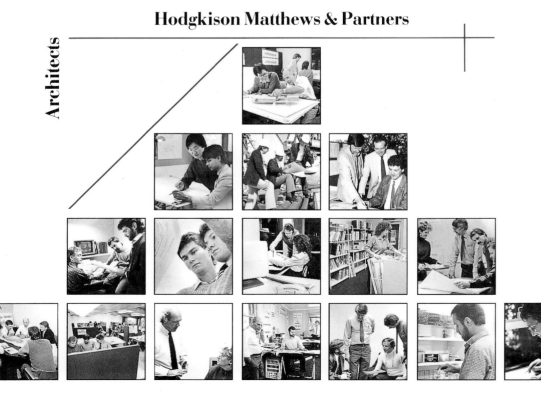

1

2

3

4

5

6

7

HOFFER REID AND COOMBS

Partners (left to right)
Frank Ernest Hoffer, B.Arch., F.R.A.I.A.
Bruce Reid, B.Arch., Dip. T. & C.P., F.R.A.I.A.
Darryl Ivan Coombs, B.Arch., F.R.A.I.A.
Philip J. Flook, B.Arch., A.R.A.I.A.

Established
1968

Address
175-183 Castlereagh Street
Sydney, N.S.W. 2000

Telephone
(02) 264 1571

Number of Employees
8 Qualified Architects
4 Under-graduates
and clerical staff, varying with workload

Current Projects
Total building cost $360M

Project Types	Percentage
Commercial	20%
Health	5%
Industrial	5%
Mixed Development	10%
Municipal	5%
Residential	35%
Retail	20%

Other Disciplines
Specialist skills in high rise and medium
density residential.
Shopping Centres.
Commercial, office, planning.
Building economy, feasibility studies,
financial advising.

Person to Contact
Enquiries to any partner

Current and Recent Projects
Commercial
'Daking House', Rawson Place & Pitt Street, Sydney
50 King Street, Sydney
Stockland House, Castlereagh Street, Sydney
Remington Centre, Liverpool Street, Sydney
Office for Legal Aid Commission, Sydney
Health
Nursing Home & Hostel for The Adult Deaf Society, Sydney
St. Elizabeth Nursing Home, Blacktown, Sydney
Medical Centre, Sydney
Medical Centre, Wyong
Industrial
Telecom Laboratories, Sydney
Industrial Estate, Sydney
Warehouses, Sydney
Mixed Development
Shopping, Medical Centre and Apartments, Bondi Junction, Sydney
Parking Station, Offices and Apartment Hotel, Melbourne
Municipal
Neighbourhood Centre, Newcastle
Community Centre, Library, Sydney
Residential
'Parkridge', Sydney
91 Darling Point Road, Sydney
Twin Towers, Bondi Junction, Sydney
Town House Projects, Sydney, Gosford, Jindabyne
Ski Resort Hotel, Jindabyne
'The Park Hotel', Sydney
Retail
Wetherill Park Town Centre, Sydney
Jesmond Regional Centre, Newcastle
Baulkham Hills Plaza, Sydney
Imperial Centre, Gosford
Merrylands Mall, Sydney
Maroubra Mall, Sydney
Wyong Plaza, Wyong
Retail Centre, Virginia, U.S.A.

History
The partnership was formed in 1968 by Frank Hoffer and not long after Bruce Reid and Darryl Coombs joined the partnership. Philip Flook has been an associate since 1975 and was made a Partner in 1987. All partners had considerable experience in other practices prior to the formation of this practice.

Frank Hoffer was trained originally in Europe and later in Australia and this early training is still reflected in the design work of the practice, particularly in the residential field. Bruce Reid, Darryl Coombs and Philip Flook all qualified from Sydney Universities, nevertheless, their work retains their individual styles.

The partnership believes that individual creativity should be encouraged and developed in all members of the staff while still retaining an overall design philosophy.

The partners designed the first 'Town Houses' in Sydney and were involved in originating the name for this type of residential development.

'Park Regis' was the first new high rise residential mixed development in Sydney for many years and the tallest residential concrete structure in the Southern Hemisphere when built.

'City Mews' was one of the earliest successful conversions of an old warehouse into residential apartments.

'The Park' was the first apartment hotel built in Sydney.

The practice advises shopping centre owners and managers on refurbishing and recycling existing centres so that they can improve their commercial viability.

In addition to conventional Architectural Services, the partnership is deeply involved in building economy, commercial feasibility study and advice, energy saving, finance and other aspects to achieve viable commercial ventures.

1   *Darling Harbour*

2   *Jesmond Shopping Centre*

3   *Town houses, Jindabyne*

4   *Harley Place, exterior*

5   *Harley Place, interior*

6   *Oxford Street, Bondi Junction*

7   *Eastgate Apartments*

HOFFER
REID and
COOMBS
ARCHITECTS

1 Government Offices, N.W. Corner, Forrest Place.
  Architects in association with B.A. Tomlinson
  Pty Ltd

2 Perth Concert Hall

3 Australian Institute of Management

4 Government Offices, East Perth

5 Government Offices, East Perth

6 Council House

7 Mount Newman House

Howlett & Bailey Architects

HOWLETT & BAILEY ARCHITECTS PTY LTD

Directors (left to right)
Jeffrey Howlett A.A. DIP (HONS) L.F.R.A.I.A.
Gregory Howlett B. Arch A.R.A.I.A.
Mark Howlett B. Arch A.R.A.I.A. DIP. Q.S.

Established
1960

Address
47 Havelock Street
West Perth, W.A. 6005

Telephone
(09) 321 6478

Facsimile
(09) 481 2415

Project Types
Commercial
Offices and Retail

Industrial
Factories and Warehouses

Civic/Recreational
Pools, Libraries and Malls

Educational Planning
Schools, Colleges and Universities

Health Planning
Hospitals and Research Laboratories

Resort Development
Hotels, Club Houses and Condominiums

Residential
Homes, Public Housing and Apartments

Other Disciplines
Project Management
Research and Planning
Urban Design
Restoration and Recycling
Interior Design

Person to Contact
Any Director

Profile

Jeffrey Howlett was trained at the Architectural Association School of Architecture in London from 1945 to 1950. He worked in the housing division of the Architects Department of the London County Council under the direction of Sir Leslie Martin, before establishing a partnership with D. Silver in Perth in 1953.

In 1956 he joined Bates Smart and McCutcheon and worked as senior design architect under the direction of Sir Osborne McCutcheon on a number of commercial offices and civic buildings, including buildings for the Universities of Melbourne, Monash and Adelaide, the Peninsula School at Frankston and Wesley College, Syndal. He established the present practice of Howlett & Bailey in conjunction with D.C.R. Bailey in 1960.

Donald Bailey retired from the partnership in 1973 to accept the executive directorship of the Royal Australian Institute of Architects in Canberra and subsequently, Gregory Howlett and Mark Howlett were admitted to the partnership.

The partnership was established with a successful submission for the Perth Town Hall competition, the first stage being the Council's administrative office building (known as Council House), which was constructed in time for the Commonwealth Games held in Perth in 1962. On its completion the Perth City Council and the Western Australian Government awarded the Perth Concert Hall complex to the firm.

Since its inception, the firm has been responsible either directly or in association, for the design, documentation and supervision of a number of additional major works including the Mount Newman House complex, the Law Chambers and Public Trust building and the Reserve Bank in Canberra. More recent projects are the State Government Office complexes, East Perth, and Forrest Place in conjunction with the Building Management Authority.

The firm was awarded First Prize in a National competition for the Reserve Bank of Australia and an office was opened in Canberra for the duration of the construction of this building of National importance.

Premiums were awarded in later architectural competitions for the design of the Western Australian Government Offices and Northpoint, a substantial office building in Victoria Park, Perth.

The office was commissioned to design and document the United States Navy support facilities and housing at North West Cape, being a joint venture with Macdonald Wagner and Priddle, Fraser Consultants Pty Ltd and W.E. Bassett and Partners Pty Ltd.

Similarly, the firm was involved with the design and documentation of a paper mill for Australian Paper Manufacturers at Spearwood, W.A., and industrial facilities for Mt Newman Mining Company in the North West, both projects in association with Fraser Consultants Pty Ltd, Consulting Engineers.

In addition, a number of high and low rise office buildings for commercial interests in Perth and several public buildings, including a number of retirement villages, have been designed, documented and constructed under the supervision of this firm.

In 1977 a new approach to allocating major school projects was adopted by the Public Works and the Education Departments.

The aim was to speed the buildings from documentation stage to occupancy within the year in which ear-marked funds remained available within departmental budgets.

Consortia of architects and builders were invited to make submissions on a design and construct basis. After departmental assessment within the framework of new design briefs, two finalists were awarded the jobs, the losing finalists were paid for their final submissions.

The commission for The Rockingham College of Technical and Further Education project and second place for the Nickol Bay Regional Hospital were awarded to this office for works allocated in this manner.

The architectural ability of Howlett & Bailey Architects has been acknowledged in national competitions and the following awards:

Award of Excellence 1973 for the Perth Concert Hall

Award of Excellence 1982 for Iona Convent. Performing Arts and Music Room from the Concrete Masonry Association of Australia

R.A.I.A. Commendation 1980 for a new Residence at 6 Riley Road, Claremont

Homes of the Year – 1965 and 1979

R.A.I.A. Architecture Design Award 1986 for Showroom/Warehouse, for Ceramic Tile Supplies, Perth

R.A.I.A. Architecture Design Award 1987 for the Australian Institute of Management

List of Major Commissions

Civic Projects
Reserve Bank, Canberra, A.C.T.
Council House, Perth, W.A., Perth City Council
Concert Hall, Perth, W.A., Perth City Council
Government Offices, East Perth, W.A.,
    Government of W.A.
State Government Offices, Forrest Place, W.A.,
    Architects in association with B.A. Tomlinson Pty Ltd
    Government of W.A.
Aquatic Centre, Armadale, W.A., Shire of Armadale
Aquatic Centre, Bentley, W.A., Shire of Bayswater
Police Stations, W.A., Public Works Department

Industrial and Commercial Projects
U.S. Naval Comm. Station Support Facilities,
    N.W. Cape, United States Navy
Mt. Newman Industrial Facilities, Port Hedland,
    Mt. Newman Mining Company
Paper Mill, Spearwood, W.A., Australian Paper Mills
Television Station, Perth, Swan T.V. Limited
H F Radio Station, Gnangara, W.A., O.T.C.
Coastal Radio Station, Broome, W.A., O.T.C.
Aircraft Hangar, Perth Airport, Murchison Air Charter
Restaurant, Belmont, W.A., Fabco Holdings
Tile Showroom, East Perth, Ceramic Tile Supplies

Shopping Centres
Claremont, W.A., Westlyn Investments Ltd
Fremantle, W.A., Diocesan Trustees
Falcon, W.A., Lacaze Pty Ltd

Hotels
Greenwood Forest Hotel, Swan Brewery Company
Kewdale Hotel, Hotel Developments Pty Ltd
South Hedland Tavern, Pennant Holdings
Ascot Tavern, Fabco Holdings

Institutional Projects
St Columba Residential College, University of W.A.,
All Saints College, Bullcreek, W.A.,
    Architects in association with Peter Hunt Architect
Primary Schools, (5 No.) W.A.,
    Building Management Authority
Rockingham Technical College, Rockingham, W.A.,
    Education Department
School of Mines, Collie, W.A. Institute of Technology
Australian Institute of Management, Floreat, W.A.
Convocation Pavilion, Nedlands, University of W.A.

Commercial Office Projects
Mt Newman House, Perth, W.A., Westgate Cloisters
Law Chambers, Perth, W.A., Diocesan Trustees
Public Trust Office, Perth, W.A., Public Trustees
Cable House, Perth, W.A., Producer's Properties Ltd
Savings House, Perth, W.A., Town and Country W.A.
Home Building Society, Head Office and Branches,
    Perth, W.A.
Professional Offices, West Perth, W.A., Israda, S.A.
Legal Offices and Chambers, Derinlea Holdings
Professional Offices, Collie, W.A., Western Collieries
Permanent Investment Building Society, Head Office

Group Housing
Family Housing, N.W. Cape, United States Navy
Retirement Village, 'Forrestfield Bible Fellowship'
Mt Newman Mining Company Housing, Port Hedland
Retirement Village, Shire of Mundaring
Shiloh Faith Centre, Wanneroo, W.A., Taylor Woodrow
Group Housing, Realty Development Corporation
Limited
Town Houses, Fremantle, W.A., Parry Corporation Ltd

Howlett & Bailey Architects

1 St Johns Church Renovations, Glenorchy, Tasmania

2 Proposed Development of a National Antarctic Museum

3 Proposed Crotty township, S.W. Tasmania

4 Low cost industrialised housing

5 Houses at the township of Shay Gap, N.W. of Western Australia

LAWRENCE H HOWROYD & ASSOCIATES

Architects, Engineers, Planners

Directors
Lawrence H. Howroyd A.H.T.C. F.R.A.I.A.
  (right)
Charles R. Howroyd B. Arch (Hons) (left)

Established
1961

Address
Kelly Steps
Battery Point, Tas. 7000

Telephone
(002) 23 7317

Facsimile
(002) 23 3910

Telex
58249

Associated Offices
Technic 10 Pty Ltd

Brian Howroyd Architect

Howroyd & Howroyd Architect

Number of Employees
15

Resources
Multiple purpose computers are installed
in the offices allowing a variety of
software, including Autocad, to be
available to clients.

Project Types
Commercial
Community/Recreational
Educational Planning
Civic Planning
Regional Planning
Feasibility Studies
Resort Development
Residential

Other Disciplines
Project Management
Town Planning
Engineering
Computer Programming
Cost Management
Environmental Studies

Persons to Contact
Lawrence H. Howroyd
Charles R. Howroyd

Current and Recent Projects

International Antarctic Centre, Hobart

State Government Information Centre, Hobart

A Centre for Cold & Remote Regions Technology,
Commonwealth Government

Salamanca Place,
Retirement Benefits Fund Investment Trust

Municipal Development Project,
Kingborough Municipality

Rosetta Primary School,
Department of Construction

Sandy Bay Branch,
ANZ Bank Ltd

Computer Design Services,
Department of Main Roads

Renovation of remote area housing,
Education Department

Elderly Persons Units,
Housing Department, Hobart

St Johns Church renovations,
St. Johns Church Presbytery

St. Brigids School additions,
St. Brigids School

Council Chambers,
Huon Municipality

Sports complex,
Spring Bay Municipality

Private residences,
Bruny Island, Howrah, Launceston, Hobart
(Tasmania)

Town planning, design and project management of
remote area townships and suburban residential
development in existing townships including economic
feasibility, environment and social impact studies.

Strathgordon, Hydro-Electric Commission of Tasmania

Roseberry, EZ Company

Shay Gap, Goldsworthy Mining

Laverton, Poseidon Ltd and Western Mining Ltd

Emerald, Gregory Coal Project and BHP

Leeman, Western Titanium

Eneabba, Joint enterprise mining venture

Alyangula, BHP

Darwin, Darwin Reconstruction Commission

Riverside, Beaconsfield Municipality

Pilbara Town Planning, Western Australian and
Commonwealth Governments

Packsaddle Townside Study, Goldsworthy Mining

Kingston Town Centre, Kingborough Municipality

Crotty, Hydro-Electric Commission of Tasmania

Queenstown, Hydro-Electric Commission of Tasmania

Waitangi Downs, Land development, New Zealand

Fremantle/Inner Urban Study, Local Authority

**National Estate Studies
(National Heritage Commission)**
Battery Point Slipyards (Tasmania),
Perth (Tasmania),
Gingin (Western Australia),
Cockburn (Western Australia)

The Architect who practises in the real world is
expected to be all things to all people – instantaneous
solver of immediate problems; artist; economist;
psychologist; builder; historian; writer; legal contract
writer and arbitrator. He is expected to translate dreams
into structures and provide leakproof roofs and
uncloggable drains. His competence is expected in
estimates, structural calculation, budgetary control and
in the choice of colour schemes, light shades and garden
plantings.

That our firm continues to exist after twenty seven years
practice in an increasingly complex world can be
attributed to a capacity to absorb detail and to
successfully identify with our clients' needs together
with the ability to combine design flair with a practical
approach to commercial realities. We continue to seek
for excellence in the processes under our control and to
obtain the best from the people we direct, whether
professional, technician or tradesman.

HOWROYD

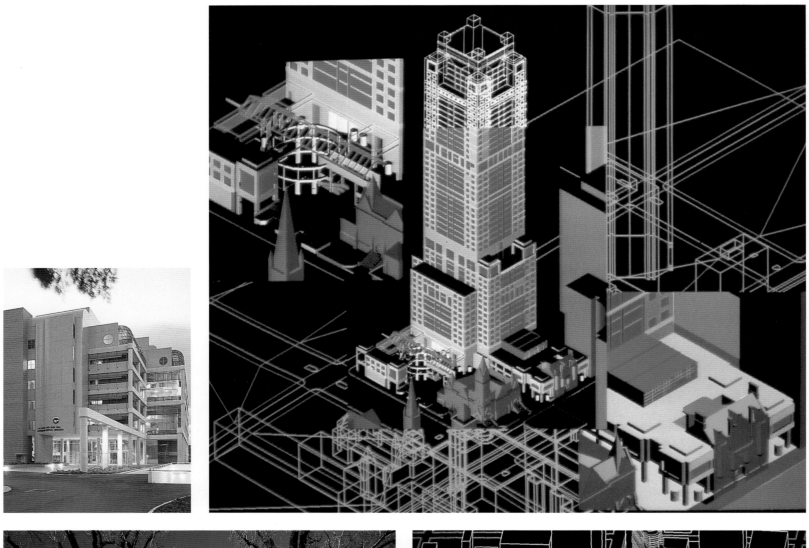

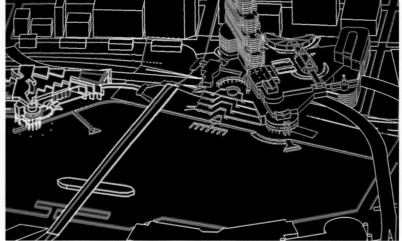

1 The Walter and Eliza Hall Institute of
  Medical Research, Melbourne

2 120 Collins Street, Melbourne

3 Graduate School of Management,
  University of Melbourne

4 Darling Harbour Casino Submission

5 National Sports Centre, Swimming
  Training Hall

DARYL JACKSON PTY LTD
Architects

Directors (left to right)
Daryl Jackson B.Arch Dip.Arch FRAIA RIBA
Bill Ryan Dip.Arch ARAIA
Ron Billard B.Arch (Hons) M.Arch ARAIA
Bob Sinclair Dip.Arch ARAIA
Robin Dyke B.Arch N.S.W.I.T. (Hons) ARAIA
Alastair Swayn Dip.Arch Dip.CABD ARAIA
RIBA

Established
1963

Address
35 Little Bourke Street
Melbourne, Vic. 3000
Telephone
(03) 662 3022
Facsimile
(03) 663 5239
Associated Offices
Daryl Jackson
Alastair Swayn Pty Ltd
49 Jardine Street
Kingston, A.C.T. 2604
Telephone
(062) 95 2000
Facsimile
(062) 95 0964
Daryl Jackson
Robin Dyke Pty Ltd
64 Rose Street
Chippendale, N.S.W. 2008
Telephone
(02) 319 2955
Facsimile
(02) 698 1116

Daryl Jackson
Robin Dyke
Interdesign Pty Ltd
2nd Floor
29 Elkhorn Avenue
Surfers Paradise
Qld 4217
Telephone
(075) 92 0214
Facsimile
(075) 39 0515

Number of Employees
95

Project Types
Commercial
Office/Retail

Community/Recreational
Pools, Libraries and Malls

Educational Planning
Schools, Colleges and Universities

Health Planning
Hospitals and Research Laboratories

Resort Development
Hotels, Club Houses and Condominiums

Residential
Homes, Public Housing and Apartments

Other Disciplines
Research and Planning
Urban Design
Facilities Programming
Interior Design

Person to Contact
Melbourne Daryl Jackson/Ron Billard
Canberra Alastair Swayn
Sydney Robin Dyke
Surfers Paradise Dan Callaghan

Current and Recent Projects
Commercial
90 Collins Street, Melbourne –
Lustig & Moar Group — $45M

Commercial Union Office Building,
La Trobe Street, Melbourne
Daryl Jackson/Peter Hunt Architects
in Association — $80M

120 Collins Street, Melbourne –
Essington/Grollo
Hassell Pty Ltd, Daryl Jackson Pty Ltd,
Architects in Association — $140M

McLachlan Offices, National Circuit, Canberra
Merit Award R.A.I.A. (ACT Chapter) 1982

Singapore High Commission, Canberra
Canberra Medallion R.A.I.A. (ACT Chapter) 1985

Esprit De Corp, Abbotsford, Victoria
R.A.I.A. National Presidents Award Citation 1985

Community/Recreational
National Sports Centre Swimming Training Halls,
Canberra
Sir Zelman Cowan National R.A.I.A. Award 1984

Australia Defence Force Academy, Canberra
Indoor Recreational Complex
Canberra Medallion R.A.I.A. 1987 — $6M

Ringwood Pool, Jubilee Park, Ringwood — $2.5M

Box Hill Indoor Recreational Centre,
Surrey Park — $3.2M

Western Australian Indoor Sports Centre, Perth
Architects in collaboration with
Peter Hunt and Robert Cann — $21M

High Street Mall, Penrith, Sydney — $1.3M

**Educational Planning, Schools, Colleges and
Universities**
Canberra School of Art, ACT
Sir Zelman Cowan National R.A.I.A. Award 1981

University of Melbourne Graduate School
of Management, Carlton — $8M

Ginninderra College, Belconnen, ACT — $13M

State Bank College, Baxter, Victoria
Bronze Medal R.A.I.A. (Vic. Chapter) 1978

Bond University, Queensland
Master Plan and Business, Maths, Computer,
Student Centre, Recreation and Student
Housing Buildings — $70M

Australian Film, Television & Radio School,
Sydney — $18M

Swinburne TAFE College, Melbourne,
Stage One — $8M

Health Planning, Hospitals
The Walter and Eliza Hall Institute
of Medical Research, Parkville, Vic.
Daryl Jackson and Godfrey & Spowers
Architects in Association — $36M

Eastern Suburbs Geriatric Centre,
East Burwood, Vic. — $11M

Southport Community Nursing Home,
Albert Park, Vic.

Resort Developments, Hotels
Cape Schanck National Golf Club and
Resort Development, Vic. 36 hole golf
course, club houses, condominiums and
resort hotel — $30M

The Hyatt Hotel, Canberra — $40M

Darling Harbour Casino/Hotel Development
Submission, Sydney
Lonrho Costain Kings — $300M

**Residential, Houses, Public Housing,
Apartments**
Abrahams House, Brighton, Vic.
Robert Haddon Award R.A.I.A.
(Vic. Chapter) 1982

Police Academy Residential Accommodation,
Goulburn, NSW — $3M

Camerons Cove Housing, Balmain, Sydney
Lend Lease Homes — $4M

Epsom Road Housing, Flemington, Vic.
Ministry of Housing — $2M

General
Australian Bicentennial Exhibition
A.B.A. Touring Exhibition
Australian Chancery Complex, Riyadh,
Saudi Arabia — $18M

Daryl Jackson Pty Ltd
Daryl Jackson Pty Ltd is an interdisciplinary design practice of architects, urban planners and interior designers. We seek creative solutions to opportunities and problems in the built environment. We are motivated by the desire to provide sensitive and stimulating environments for people which articulate and facilitate all aspects of human encounter and endeavour. Buildings must be usable, efficient and cost-effective.

Daryl Jackson has gained a national reputation for high quality consultation based on his ability to synthesise the conflicting demands of creativity, community planning, cost effectiveness and quality design. In 1987 the Royal Australian Institute of Architects has honoured Daryl Jackson with its highest award, the Gold Medal, for consistent architecture of excellence constituting a significant contribution to the development of architecture in Australia.

This has been achieved in close and co-operative relationships with our clients, through comprehensive (or selective) services tailored to meet specific demands: from initial feasibility studies to the hand-over of completed buildings. Our extensive range of services includes research and facilities programming; architectural, urban and interior planning and design; contract documentation and administration; and project and construction management.

Architectural Approach
In a democratic society we believe architecture is a social art. It must encompass and transcend aesthetic and formal concerns to reinforce, enhance and celebrate people's emotional, behavioural, and functional needs. Furthermore the architect has a visionary obligation to generate new ideas that facilitate cultural extension and anticipate future use.

Our process is one of leadership: we reveal, explore, conciliate and express the diverse and often contradictory demands of a project's client and user groups while considering community interests and statutory obligations. For us each project is unique and demands an exceptional response. The result is an architecture of many architectures, utilising functional and symbolic systems of expression to convey the idiosyncrasies of the complex parts through an ordered and synthesised whole.

The experience gained in solving diverse and complex design problems has highlighted three principal concerns in the design process.

Problem Understanding
We make a thorough analysis of a project's perceived objectives and causal relationships. Our briefing techniques draw from the client their expectations, understanding and knowledge, while research ensures that we engage in expertise available throughout the world. The knowledge of associated disciplines is evaluated, co-ordinated and incorporated.

Design Realisation
This is the imaginative and creative process by which our understanding of a project is transformed to an "idea". The "idea" serves to encapsulate our intent, structure the design process, and characterise the solution as a significant piece of architecture. The design process is iterative: ideas are constantly tested and reviewed against the physical, social, and economic constraints while exploring opportunities in composition, construction method, and materials.

Technological Authorization
Technical implementation requires the production of documents and the development of a construction programme. This is a demanding and time consuming endeavour in which the minutiae of each component must be identified and integrated within the design strategy.

In the design process the practice has an enviable reputation for maintaining a high level of performance, whether the project be educational, institutional, recreational, commercial or domestic.

1

5

2

3

4

JACKSON TEECE CHESTERMAN WILLIS & PARTNERS PTY LTD

Architecture Urban Design Interior Design Landscape Development Economics

Directors (left ro right)
David Jackson AA Dip LFRAIA FRIBA
Angus Teece B.Arch M.Bldg Sc FRAIA
David Chesterman B.Arch Dip T&CP FRAIA
    ARIBA MRAPI
David Willis ASTC (QS) Aff. RAIA AAIQS
Michael Bennett B.Arch Dip T&CP ARAIA
    MRAPI
Neville Thomas B.Arch

Philip Atkin B.Arch FRAIA
Ian Brodie B.Arch ARAIA
Bruce Fisher B.Arch
Nicholas Tesdorf B.Arch ARAIA ARIBA
Scott Wallace B.Arch FRAIA

Established
1971

Addresses
40 King Street
Sydney, N.S.W. 2000

Telephone
(02) 290 2722

Telex
ARCAD AA74462

Facsimile
(02) 290 1150

Associated Offices
Canberra
12 Thesiger Court
Deakin, A.C.T. 2600

Telephone
(062) 82 2061   (062) 82 3768

Facsimile
(062) 85 2564

Brisbane
Level 2
Rowes Arcade Building
235 Edward Street
Brisbane, Qld 4000

Telephone
(07) 229 5083

Facsimile
(07) 229 3323

Number of Employees
60

Project Types
Commercial
Office/Retail, Banking, Commerce,
Computer, Industrial, Institutional

Community/Recreational
Libraries, Malls

Sport/Recreational
Clubs, Theatres, Marinas, Playgrounds,
Sports, Swimming pools

Educational Planning
Schools, Colleges, Technical Training,
Conference Centres, Universities

Health Care Planning
Hospitals, Surgeries

Leisure/Hospitality
Hotels, Club Houses, Canteens,
Restaurants

Public Utilities
Bus Stations, Plazas

Residential
Apartments, Interior Design, Housing
Estates, Low Cost Housing, Senior
Citizens Housing

Specialist Skills
Research and Planning,
Urban Design,
Research Development (technical, social,
    health, economics, planning),
Interior Design,
Conservation,
Landscape Architecture,
Development Economics,
Development Feasibility Analysis

Person to Contact
Sydney
David Jackson
Angus Teece
David Chesterman
David Willis
Michael Bennett
Neville Thomas

Canberra
Bruce Fisher

Brisbane
Roger Hills

Current and Recent Projects
The Robert Garran Building for the Attorney General's
Department, Canberra

Sydney Stock Exchange

CSR Building, Brisbane

Thiess Contractors Regional Headquarters,
Taren Point, Sydney

Tomkins Nursery, Enfield, Sydney

Warehouse, Alexandria, Sydney for the State
Superannuation Board

Unisys Headquarters, Sydney

Centrepac Brewery, Sydney

Macquarie University Library, Sydney

New Teaching Building, Macquarie University

Dixson Library, University of New England

Parramatta Mall, Sydney

Birkenhead Point, Sydney

Orion Centre, Campsie

Tamworth Country Music Centre

Queanbeyan Community Centre

Sydney College of Advanced Education, North
Newtown, Campus

Sydney College of Advanced Education, Mallett Street,
Camperdown, Sydney (Institute of Nursing Studies,
Early Childhood Studies, College of Administration)
North Sydney Technical College

Ryde Medical Centre, Sydney

Kingsway Medical Centre, Dee Why, Sydney

Tuggeranong Bus Depot, A.C.T.

Circular Quay Plaza

Dalmar Retirement Village, Carlingford, Sydney

Housing Conversion, Crown Street Women's Hospital,
Sydney

Tyrrell House Residential Development, Newcastle

The Ferris House, Rose Bay, Sydney

Restoration Sandstone Facade, Sydney G.P.O.

Restoration Historic Terrace, Phillip Street, Sydney

Design Philosophy

The personnel of Jackson Teece Chesterman Willis &
Partners are design professionals; they have know-how
based on research and experience. The firm's aim is to
resolve problems before they are enshrined in brick,
steel, glass and concrete; its research is aimed at high
all-round performance of the firm's products and
services including such aspects as technical criteria,
building investment and social structures in planning
work.

JTCW aims for the ideal of buildings and places that
work properly. The firm believes that useful and lasting
buildings are the ones which are well-founded on an
understanding of society's needs and with a sound
relationship to the economics of the owner and the
community and their aesthetic values and spirit.
Such buildings last for a long time – they have an
intrinsic belonging.

JTCW seeks to identify strongly with the client's needs
in creating a building to do the things that are actually
needed now, and to adapt to future needs in this rapidly
changing world. Adaptability is considered to be of
tremendous importance; it makes sense for long term
investment whether for public or private purposes.
For example, a hospital planned with foresight can last
through many staffing and technological changes and
an adaptable office building will go on when others are
costing millions to refit. Buildings are built mainly as
an investment and, as such, those investments have to
stack up in every sense.

Everyone in the practice is encouraged to participate
in the design process. The result is that youthful design
ideas get the backing of years of experience.

Jackson Teece Chesterman Willis & Partners' constant
goal is the achievement of excellence in architecture,
interior, urban and landscape design: we achieve that
goal through the principle "sound research and get it
right".

JACKSON
TEECE
CHESTERMAN
WILLIS   PTY LIMITED
& PARTNERS

Technology West, Nth Strathfield, N.S.W.

Seaquester Quays, Qld

Tie Rack, Stores

289 Elizabeth St, Sydney, N.S.W.

Mariners' Village, Qld

Pittwater Palms, Avalon, N.S.W.

Fennell St, Nth Parramatta, N.S.W.

St Leonards Corporate Park, N.S.W.

Railway Pde, Burwood, N.S.W.

P.G.A. National Golf Course,
Riverside Oaks Corporate Training Centre, Cattai, N.S.W.

P.G.A. National Golf Clubhouse, Cattai, N.S.W.

JOHN BRUCE + PARTNERS PTY LIMITED

(Incorporated in N.S.W.)
Architects, Development Consultants, Project Managers, Interior Designers

Directors (left to right)
John Bruce ASTC (Arch) ARAIA
Dennis Rabinowitz B.Arch ARIBA MIA (SA)
Jeff Bennett B.Sc.(Arch) B.Arch
Paul Jeffery ACA
Mark Jackson B.Sc.(Arch) B.Arch.(Hons)
Jack Taylor B.Arch

Associate Directors (left to right)
Tom Cox B.Sc.(Arch) B.Arch (Hons) M.Sc.(Build)
Peter Fitzgerald
Marianne Halmos B.Sc.(Arch) B.Arch (Hons)
Peter Cotton B.Arch (Hons)
David Taylor B.Sc.(Arch) B.Arch
John Funston Dip.Arch ARAIA
Jos Agius ASTC (Arch) ARAIA
Martin O'Donoghue B.Arch Dip.Art ARAIA
Dennis Hubbard B.Sc (Arch) B.Arch (Hons)

Established
1979

Address
N.S.W. Office
551 Pacific Highway
St. Leonards, N.S.W. 2065

Telephone
(02) 439 2000

Facsimile
(02) 439 2312

Address
Queensland Office
19 Short Street
Southport, Qld 4215

Telephone
(075) 32 9106

Facsimile
(075) 51 0029

Number of Employees
45

Project Types
Commercial
Retail
Industrial/Warehouse
Ecclesiastical
Health/Medical
Recreation
Retirement Living
Residential

Other Disciplines
Development Consultancy
Project Control
Project Management
Interior Design

Current & Recent Projects

Commercial

Railway Parade, Burwood – AGC/Gordon/ Lucas Venture	$25M
Fennell Street, North Parramatta – IEL/ Areco Venture	$12M
Old Castle Hill Road, Castle Hill – Areco Group	$3M
Liverpool & Elizabeth Streets, City Gordon Pacific	$10M
Government Road, Hornsby – Caralis Group	$26M
Victoria Avenue, Chatswood – Girvan Bros	$5M
Pacific Highway, Gordon – K.B. Hutcherson	$2M
Bridge Road, Pymble – AFT Group	$4M
Unilever Building, Marrickville – J.P. Cordukes	$3M

Warehouse/High Technology

Herbert Street, St. Leonards – Leda Holdings	$25M
Talavera Road, North Ryde – Leda Holdings	$16M
Technology West, North Strathfield – Beachcorp	$75M
Bowman's Road, Blacktown – Greise Group	$3M
Hotham Parade, Artarmon – Leda Holdings	$6M
Mars Road, Lane Cove – National Mutual	$80M

Retail

Glenrose Shopping Centre – Lend Lease	$10M
Tie Rack Stores, Chatswood, Parramatta and Bondi Junction	

Health/Medical

Old Northern Road, Castle Hill – Medical Centre	$2M
Gold Coast Highway, Southport – Medical Centre	$2M
Hale Road, Mosman – Medical Centre	$2M

Recreation

'Riverside Oaks', Cattai, N.S.W. Corporate Training Lodges, Resort Hotel, 36-hole Golf Course, Condominiums	$60M
Windsor Road, Cattai, N.S.W. PGA National Golf Course and Clubhouse	$15M
Oxford Falls Road, Beacon Hill Tennis Centre	$2M
Muirfield Golf Course, Sydney 18-hole Golf Course and Fairway Housing	$40M
Island Resort, Yasawa Group, Fiji Bures, infrastructure	$5M
'Marlin Resort', Coffs Harbour Hotel, Golf Course, Fairway Housing	$20M

Retirement Living

'Pittwater Palms', Avalon – Leighton Group	$12M
'The Manors', Mosman – Leighton Group	$25M
'Fernbank', St. Ives – Hooker Group	$20M
'Swains County Manors', Killara – Nemeth	$4M

Residential

Mt. Alverna Estate, Wahroonga – IEL/Areco Venture	$10M
St. Ignatius College, Riverview	$0.5M
'Sanctuary Cove', Qld – Discovery Bay Developments	$35M
Panorama Estate, Gosford – Paul Ramsay Group	$70M
'Seaquester Quays' Runaway Bay, Qld – Burns Philp/Gordon Venture	$100M
'Mariners' Village', Runaway Bay, Qld – Burns Philp/Gordon Venture	$20M
Villas, Tallebudgera – Qld Hooker Rex	$3M
'Boronia Gardens' Carlingford Road, Epping – Hooker Group	$15M
'Linley Cove,' Stage IV, Sydney – Walker Group	$5M

Interior Design

Bruce Lyon Real Estate	Stanley Wines
Edgell/Bird's Eye	Netmap Computers
Westpac	Norwich Union
Hood Sails	Johnson & Johnson
Impact	Equitilink
Leda	Taylor Lauder

Furniture Design for AKAI sound componentry.

History

Founded in 1979, John Bruce + Partners is a vital and innovative Australian Company specialising in the fields of architecture, planning, development economics, project management and interior design. The Company believes that commercial reality and design excellence are inseparable and it has based its mode of operation and achieved its respected reputation on this philosophy.

The Company provides a comprehensive development evaluation and project consultancy service, where responsibilities are faced rather than by-passed and where, although incorporated, client relationships are maintained by individuals. It is a young Company, operated by interested and active professionals who have extended their knowledge and skills beyond the traditional confines of the practice of architecture.

John Bruce + Partners has 45 personnel in its Sydney and Southport offices who, collectively, have a wide range of professional architectural experience and business acumen. Drawing from this knowledge bank and the skills of an inter-related group of real estate and professional economic advisers, John Bruce + Partners is able to achieve commercially attuned architectural results.

The Company promotes the evaluation of innovative trends and continually seeks to improve its standards and levels of competence in the traditional facets of architecture, which remain its primary involvement. An extended range of services is available, however, beginning with the physical and commercial assessments of a site, through the preparation of computer-supported feasibility analyses into the traditional architectural area then into cost control and project management and finally into interior design. Clients are able to negotiate arrangements where a partial or total selection of these services is provided.

The Company has also developed expertise in new property evaluation and feasibility documentation areas so that, today, it operates in the commercial marketplace in a role where it instigates the bringing together of prospective projects with developers and financiers.

By understanding the importance of risk minimization and project control in the development process, by skilled practice in the negotiation and liaison with statutory authorities and by possessing the expertise to conceive and understand feasibility analyses and design within their confines, John Bruce + Partners produce more effective planning solutions which become the foundation for efficient and profitable architecture.

John Bruce + Partners has designed and completed a broad spectrum of projects in the retail, commercial, industrial, recreational, residential and retirement fields, in both high-rise and low-rise forms. It is currently involved in projects in Australia, USA and Fiji and its clients include Government entities, local councils, public and private companies and individuals. It enjoys continuing relationships with many substantial organisations including –

Capita, Amacon, Leightons, Lend Lease, Hooker Group, IEL, Gordon Pacific, Burns Philp, Norwich Union, Leda Holdings, Paul Ramsay Group, Equitilink, Beachcorp, National Mutual, Project Development Corporation, State Building Society, Australian Guarantee Corporation, AFT, Westpac, Landcom, Richard Crookes, Girvan Bros, J.P. Cordukes, CRI, Spectrum Golf, Akai.

The Directors and staff are problem solvers who generate alternative ideas and who approach each situation individually. They seek to achieve the best possible solutions for each client with functional, economic and buildable design concepts, that are responsive to commercial and marketing realities, excellent in resolution and aesthetically valid.

John Bruce + Partners is a closely knit, friendly and enthusiastic team keen to take responsibility and produce commercially viable solutions on time and to budget, whilst still producing fine architecture.

National Mutual Centre

Hotel Inter-Continental

Elcom Tower

Gateway Plaza, Completion 1988

Gateway Plaza (CAD)

Telecom Plaza (Model) Completion 1988

KANN FINCH + PARTNERS PTY LIMITED

Directors (left to right)
Alexander Kann ASTC, FRAIA
Raymond Chappelow B.Arch (Hons), FRAIA
Grahame Harris, B.Arch (Hons), FRAIA
Brian Kruger AASTC, FRAIA
Anthony Quigg, B.Arch (Hons), FRAIA

Associate Directors
Michael Gaston B.Arch (Hons), ARAIA
Donald Matthews B.Arch, ARAIA

Associates
Timothy Creer B.Arch, FRAIA, AAILA
Graham Swann B.Arch, ARAIA
Howard Moutrie B.Arch (Hons), ARAIA
Craig Hines B.Arch, ARAIA

Established
1963

Address
44 Market Street
Sydney, N.S.W. 2000

Telephone
(02) 20258

Facsimile
(02) 290 1481

Associated Companies
Sydney
Intergroup Interior Design
44 Market Street
Sydney, N.S.W. 2000
Telephone (02) 29 7035
Facsimile (02) 290 1481

KFP Services
44 Market Street
Sydney, N.S.W. 2000
Telephone (02) 20 258
Facsimile (02) 290 1481

Precinct Landscapes
44 Market Street
Sydney, N.S.W. 2000
Telephone (02) 29 7038
Facsimile (02) 290 1481

New Zealand
Kann Finch + Partners Pty. Ltd.
160 Beach Road
(P.O. Box 37007) Parnell
Auckland 1, New Zealand
Telephone (09) 39 6564
Facsimile (09) 37 6600

Number of Employees
80

Project Types
Commercial
Office/Retail

Community/Recreational
Parks, Malls, Community Centres

Resorts
Hotels, Island Resort Developments

Specialised Projects
Data/Computer Centres
Historical Refurbishments
Health Care Projects

Other Disciplines
Research & Planning
Project Management
Interior Design
Landscaping & Environmental
    Rehabilitation
Professional Support Services

Persons to Contact
Sydney
Raymond Chappelow
Grahame Harris

New Zealand
Michael Gaston

Current and Recent Projects
Commercial: Office/Retail
Telecom Plaza, 310-322 Pitt Street, Sydney
30 levels, gross area 42,000 sq. metres
Client: Telecom Australia
        Dept.|of Administrative Services

Gateway Plaza, Alfred, Loftus and Pitt Streets, Sydney
(A Kann Finch Peddle Thorp Joint Venture)
50 levels, gross area 65,000 sq. metres
Client: National Mutual Life Association

231 Elizabeth Street, Sydney
19 levels, 22,800 sq. metres
Client: O.T.C.
Project Administrators: KFP Consultants Group

Tower 2, Bondi Junction Plaza
18 levels, 16,000 sq. metres
Client: AMP Society

National Bank Centre
Queen Street, Auckland, New Zealand
26 levels, (twin towers) 30,000 sq. metres
Client: National Bank of New Zealand
        New Zealand Insurance
        Realty Development Corporation
In Association with Glossop Chan Partnership, Auckland

32 Martin Place, Sydney
16 levels, major refurbishment and reconstruction
Client: AMP Society

RDC House, Victoria Street, Auckland
Client: Realty Development Corporation

Resorts, Hotels
Hotel Inter-Continental, Sydney
554 rooms, restaurants, bars, convention rooms
Client: Aspley Park Hotels/Sir Robert McAlpine

Tiare Resort, New Caledonia
430 condominium apartments, 46 luxury villas
Client: Tiare Resort Ltd

Sheraton Wentworth Hotel, Sydney
Ballroom, function rooms and associated areas
Client: Sheraton Wentworth Hotel

Menzies Hotel, Sydney
Reconstruction of bedrooms, kitchens, coffee shops,
restaurants, cocktail bars, function rooms, reception
floor and associated areas
Client: Wynyard Holdings Ltd

Pokolbin International Resort, Hunter Valley, N.S.W.
230 bedrooms, function rooms, golf course and
associated resort facilities
Client: Leisure Corporation of Australia

Darling Harbour Casino (submission), Sydney
Client: HKMS Group, Hong Kong
In Association with Wong Tung and Partners, Hong Kong

Brooklyn Resort, Brooklyn, N.S.W.
Client: Brooklyn Resort Pty Ltd

Specialised Projects
Ryde Data Centre, North Ryde, N.S.W.
Regional Computer Centre for N.S.W.

Adelaide Data Centre
Regional Computer Centre for South Australia

Bondi Junction Data Centre
Regional Computer Centre
Client: AMP Society

Telecom Data Centre, St Leonards, N.S.W.
Client: Telecom Australia
        Department of Administrative Services

350 George Street, Sydney
Historic restoration 6 floor office building
Client: Leighton Properties Ltd

Profile
Established in Sydney in 1963, Kann Finch + Partners
is one of Australia's leading architecture practices
providing a comprehensive range of architectural,
project management, interior design, landscaping
and professional support services.

As the economic environment continues to place
increasing demands on efficiency and reliability,
the Firm draws on its 25 years of experience to provide
the expertise, professionalism and depth of management
to effectively service all its clients' needs. The Firm's
design, administration and co-ordination skills ensure
that the most advanced standards of design and technology are applied within the context of economically
effective solutions.

From multi-storey CBD buildings to hotels and island
resorts, data and computer centres, residential
complexes and the refurbishment of historical buildings
Kann Finch + Partners tailors all the highly sophisticated skills and services necessary to meet the specific
requirements of each project.

Kann Finch + Partners at Work
Kann Finch + Partners adopts a team approach on
every project undertaken. The Firm's diversity of
expertise is tailored to meet the needs of an increasingly
complex environment encompassing concept, design,
planning and administration, documentation and
execution to final completion.

Kann Finch + Partners' commitment to high standards
and quality is further enhanced by the Firm's extensive
involvement with Computer Aided Design (CAD)
technology. One of the first architects to explore the use
of CAD in Australia, Kann Finch + Partners is today the
largest user of this technology in the industry. Used in
the preparation of schematic design, 3-D perspectives,
detailed construction drawings, services and co-ordination
and as a marketing tool in combination with video, CAD
speeds up the documentation process, improves accuracy,
allows more modelling options to be analysed for project
efficiency and enhances cost efficiencies for the Firm's
clients.

An Expanding Involvement
KFP Consultants Group
Kann Finch + Partners draws both on the expertise
of this in-house division and its close association with
other leading consultants to meet the growing demand
for total project responsibility. This incorporates services
such as project planning, feasibility studies, design
development, cost planning and finance co-ordination
of consultants and project teams, tailoring or structuring
legal contracts, authority requirements and construction
management.

Using Kann Finch + Partners as Project Manager draws
together the specific expertise to ensure completion
dates, cost controls, and overall efficiency on even the
most complex of projects.

KFP Services Group
KFP Services is a specialised group committed to
improving standards within the industry and to ensuring
that the full spectrum of client needs is met for a wider
scope of professional independent and impartial
assessments, reports and professional advice across a
comprehensive range of disciplines including:

Building Inspection
Building and Structure Analysis
Dilapidation Surveys
Small Building/Emergency Works
Supervision Services
Clerk of Works Services

From inspections and problem diagnosis to supervision
and maximising standards of workmanship, KFP
Services provides the comprehensive attention to detail
that every project demands.

Intergroup Interior Design
Intergroup is a specialised service group providing
tenancy planning, interior design, decoration and
furnishing of commercial office and retail premises,
restaurants, hotels and showrooms. Among Intergroup's
range of services are the auditing of existing layouts,
analysis of fit-out requirements, establishment of trends
in future expansion in space, time and technology,
preparation of design philosophy, design implementation
and contract administration.

Working as part of Kann Finch + Partners' project team
or as an independent unit, Intergroup's design expertise
contributes to a fully integrated result.

Precinct Landscapes (Landscape Architects)
Precinct Landscapes is involved in varying scales of
work encompassing many aspects of landscaping and
environmental rehabilitation from building sites to civil
engineering projects including bridge works and major
roads. Precinct is acknowledged for its skills in adding
the final dimension in the creation of a 'total
environment'.

Since its formation in 1980, Precinct has been selected
by developers, government departments, public utilities
and architects for its expertise in design, landscape
restoration, civic area development and environmental
integration.

KEERS, BANKS AND MAITLAND
Architects

Address
Sydney
16 Leswell Street
Woollahra, N.S.W. 2025
Telephone
(02) 387 3077
Facsimile
(02) 387 3268

Project Types
Architecture
Interior Design
Space Planning
Refurbishment
Commercial
Hospitality
Retail
Industrial
Residential
Project Management
Fast Track
Industrial
Feasibility Studies

Persons to Contact
Gregory J. Banks
Jeffrey N. Maitland

Greg Banks Jeff Maitland Ron Keers

Directors
Greg Banks
Jeff Maitland

Principals
Gregory J Banks – Director
Diploma in Architecture 1966 (Sydney Technical College), F.R.A.I.A. Background expertise in retail and specialised buildings. Recent clients include the Spastic Association and the Public Works Department. Currently working in the hospitality sector on a convention centre with integrated accommodation facilities.

Jeffrey N Maitland – Director
Bachelor of Architecture (Honors), New South Wales Institute of Technology 1976, ARAIA, RIBA. Prior to joining Keers, Banks and Maitland in 1982, worked for Fry, Drew, Knight and Creamer in London, and Morrison Design Partnership in Kuwait. Particular expertise in refurbishment projects, commercial offices, the hospitality industry and all related interior fitout works. Recent clients include the Greater Union Organisation and the Government Insurance Office. Currently working on a large commercial office fitout and on a number of investment redevelopments.

Ronald B Keers – Consultant
Diploma in Architecture 1957 (Sydney Technical College), FRAIA. Involved in industrial and Public Authority works, has built up a vast expertise in contract administration and labour relations. Currently involved in a complex commercial renovation and redevelopment in the city.

Company Profile
Keers and Banks was established in 1973 by Ronald Keers and Gregory Banks. The company was renamed Keers, Banks and Maitland Pty Ltd when Jeff Maitland joined in 1982.

The practice has expanded from its original roots in industrial and retail projects to include commercial buildings and the attendant interior fitout works which project individual corporate identities.

Design Approach
Our belief is that a direct personal involvement with clients produces excellent results: by working closely with clients we can better interpret their unique needs, methods of operation, plans for future expansion and budget requirements.

In satisfying the client's brief we can provide innovative solutions which have integrity and are functional.

Our strength lies in our wide experience, our dynamic approach, our design flair and our ability to mobilise the best team to complete any project to budget and to programme.

Professional Services
Architectural Service
Analysis of clients requirements; concept planning; budgets; Council & Authority Approvals; working drawings, specifications and documents; site inspections through to the completed building handover; operating manual; post handover analysis.

Interior Design
We can co-ordinate all interior works to complement the architectural service, or provide an interior system for an existing building. This service should commence when you have first thought of moving or re-organising as we are able to provide cost-effective advice from the outset.

Investment and Development
We can offer an alternative to the design and construct package where we are on your side in a field full of risk. We have investment funds, a number of excellent building contractors and our own expertise and track record that enables us to offer you a wide variety of options. We can take the risks of finding the right property, developing it to your specification, funding it, building it and only then when you are completely satisfied you move-in on a lease or purchase basis.

Clients
Amev Insurance
Amacon Pty Ltd
Attorney-General's Department
Central Mapping Authority
Commonwealth Bank
Department of Motor Transport
Department of Housing & Construction
Flemings Food Stores
Greater Union Organisation
GIO
George Ward Distributors
Irvin & Johnson
Jove Industries
Lowes Menswear Stores
McGlynn & Co
NRMA
Noahs Ltd
NSW Police Force
Public Works Department
Qantas
State Superannuation Board
South Sydney Juniors
Spastic Centre of N.S.W.
Thredbo Alpine Centre
Traffic Authority of N.S.W.
University Chambers
Woolworths Ltd
Warringah Rugby Club
Wallaceway Shopping Centre

A Business-like approach to Architecture and Design

1 Overseas Passenger Terminal, Circular Quay, Sydney

2 Caroline Chisholm High School, Canberra

3 National Science and Technology Centre, Parliamentary Triangle, Canberra

4 Darling Harbour Casino/Hotel Development

5 Darling Harbour Casino Development, Sydney

6 Mount Druitt Hospital

LAWRENCE NIELD AND PARTNERS AUSTRALIA

Directors (left to right)
Lawrence Nield B Arch *Hons Syd* M Litt Cantab
FRAIA RIBA MSIA
Tony Fisher B Arch *NSW* FRAIA
Gary Leahey B Arch *Hons NSWIT* ARAIA
Keith Lapthorne B Arch *Hons NSW* PhD Cantab
FRAIA RIBA

Associates
Aladin Niazmand B.Arch *Hons Syd* ARAIA
Warwick Simmonds B.Arch *Hons NSWIT*
ARAIA
Dennis Small B.Arch *NSW* ARAIA
Robert Yuen B.Arch *Syd* ARAIA

Established
Lawrence Nield + Partners 1975

Address
88 Beattie Street
Balmain, N.S.W. 2041

Telephone
(02) 818 2833

Facsimile
(02) 818 5294

Associated Offices
Lawrence Nield and Partners
Australia Pty Ltd
35 Little Bourke Street
Melbourne, Vic. 3000

Telephone
(03) 662 2866

Suite 10, George Turner Offices
11 McKay Gardens
Turner, A.C.T. 2601

Telephone
(062) 47 3688

Facsimile
(062) 47 0142

Number of Employees
45

Project Types
Commercial
Office/Retail

Community
Libraries
Sporting Facilities

Transport
Airport Terminal Planning and Design

Theatre Design
Cinema and Lyric Theatre Design

Educational
Schools, Colleges, Universities, Museums
and Exhibition Centres

Health and Hospital Design
Private, Public
and Major Teaching Hospitals

Resort Development
Hotels

Residential
Public Housing, Apartments, Home Units

Other Disciplines
Research and Planning
Health Planning
Facilities Briefing
Urban Design
Heritage Studies

Current and Recent Projects
Commercial
Capitol Theatre Development, Sydney
with Travis Partners — $80M

Globe House, The Rocks, Sydney — $15M

509 Pitt Street, Sydney
Offices for State Rail Authority — $12M

NZI House, Canberra — $1M

Community
Wollongong Town Hall,
Art Gallery and Retail Submission — $18M

Transport
Qantas Temporary Terminal,
Sydney International Airport
with Ove Arup & Partners — $20M

Overseas Passenger Terminal,
Circular Quay, Sydney 1987
with Government Architect's Branch
of the Department of Public Works — $16M

Educational
National Science & Technology Centre,
Parliamentary Triangle, Canberra, for NCDC — $18M

David Maddison School of Clinical Sciences,
University of Newcastle
RAIA (N.S.W. Chapter) Merit Award 1982 — $12M

Caroline Chisholm High School, Canberra
RAIA (A.C.T. Chapter) Canberra Medallion 1986,
for NCDC — $7M

Wodonga College of TAFE Stage 1 for PWD Vic. — $8M

Life Education Centre, Colyton, N.S.W. — $1.5M

University of Queensland Clinical Sciences Building
Repatriation General Hospital, Greenslopes — $3M

Health and Hospital Design
Mt Druitt Hospital, Sydney
RAIA (N.S.W. Chapter) Merit Award 1983 200 beds $14M

New Fairfield Hospital, Sydney — 214 beds $30M

Greenslopes Repatriation General Hospital,
Brisbane — $20M

Launceston General Hospital,
with Woods Bagot — 380 beds $50M

St Vincent's Hospital, Melbourne
Masterplan — 600 beds $150M

Monash Medical Centre, Melbourne
Masterplan — 810 beds $120M

Bexley Private Hospital — $1.6M

University Hospital at
Royal Prince Alfred Hospital — $30M

Noarlunga Community Hospital, S.A.
with Woods Bagot — $26M

Noarlunga Health Village, S.A.
with Woods Bagot — $3M

Narrandera District Hospital — $3.5M

The Scottish Hospital — $1.5M

Lyell McEwin Hospital, S.A.
with Woods Bagot — $40M

Resort Development
Darling Harbour Casino/Hotel Development, Sydney
Submission Sheraton/Daikyo — $800M

Campbell's Cove Hotel, The Rocks 1986 — $40M

Holiday Inn Hotel, Wollongong, N.S.W. — $20M

Canberra Hotel, Canberra, A.C.T. — $46.3M

Housing
Town Houses, Port Moresby for Bodiam — $0.75M

Aged Persons Housing and Hostel, Deakin, A.C.T. $10M

Bridges
Belconnen Drive Footbridge,
with Ove Arup & Partners, for NCDC — $1.5M

Yamba Drive Footbridge,
with Ove Arup & Partners, for NCDC — $1.2M

Major Tuggeranong Highway Bridge,
with Maunsell Partners, for NCDC — $7M

General
User and Interaction Brief for New Parliament House,
Canberra

National Library Canberra, Strategy Plan

State Insurance Office, Melbourne, Brief

Masterplanning for Hospitals

Profile
Power
The architecture of Lawrence Nield and Partners
Australia's projects resist fashion and consumerism,
challenge mediocrity and have clear ideas at their
root. They have power, inventiveness and economy.

Lawrence Nield and Partners Australia is a design
practice that specialises in the most complex of
contemporary design problems such as hospitals and
airport terminals as well as the more direct problems
of office buildings and housing. The aim of the office's
design is to produce an innovative but practical solution
which will work in terms of the building's operations
and respond sensitively to its surroundings. In each
of the building types that have been carried out by
Lawrence Nield and Partners Australia new cost effective
solutions have been developed. In the case
of Mt Druitt Hospital, the David Maddison Clinical
Sciences Building and the Caroline Chisholm High
School this has been recognised in awards for
outstanding architecture by the Royal Australian
Institute of Architects.

Lawrence Nield and Partners Australia is involved from
the earliest stages of planning, research and the
development of briefs, analysis of movement and the
framing of feasibility studies through to design, interior
design, documentation and administration of the
construction process.

Inventiveness
In developing design, prototypes and models are critical
to the dialogue between client and architect. Models
often explain a building far more easily than drawings.
Prototypes allow appreciation of often full sized elements
of a building to be tested. The office has used prototypes
for building elements as diverse as handrails, sun control
systems and ward layouts in hospitals. In complex
building, prototypes are often the best way to test plans
and elements of the building.

Design quality, that is developing a building that both
works but at the same time gives enjoyment, is the
major aim of the practice. Architecture should give
a feeling of balance and reassurance of health and
appropriateness to its task. Architecture should proclaim
its self-sufficiency, substance and its craft. Furthermore
it should complement and enhance the city and the
activity of the cities in an urban location or interpret
and understand the natural setting. Good architecture
adds new texture to the life of the city.

Economy
Lawrence Nield and Partners Australia is known for its
systematic approach to building where it works through
research, brief, architectural intention to design and
documentation.

This approach has led to the successful design and
implementation of projects as varied as the Overseas
Passenger Terminal, Circular Quay, major exhibition
buildings such as the National Science and Technology
Centre in Canberra, commercial buildings and large
complex hospitals such as the Greenslopes Repatriation
Hospital, Brisbane and the New Fairfield Hospital in
Sydney. These projects have not only been realised as
effective and economic buildings but have responded to
the location and to the structure of the city. They have
developed a strong 'sense of place'.

LEIGHTON IRWIN – GARNET ALSOP (AUST) PTY LTD
LEIGHTON IRWIN PTY LTD

Leighton Irwin-Garnet Alsop (Aust) Pty Ltd

Directors
John Alsop
Alistair Stevenson
Ian Freeland
David Alsop
William Henning

Associate Directors
Michael Morriss
Mark Alsop
David Jackson
Manager, Engineering Services
Ron Dretzke

Address
114 Albert Road
South Melbourne, Vic. 3205

Telephone
(03) 690 6199

Facsimile
(03) 690 2317

Person to Contact
John Alsop
Alistair Stevenson

Irwin Alsop (Pacific)

9 Bau Street
Suva, Fiji

Telephone
(0011) 679 22825

Facsimile
(0011) 679 312737

Person to Contact
Michael Morriss (Manager)

Leighton Irwin Pty Ltd

Directors
Lindsay Skinner
Chris Vassiliou
Ferdinand Nolte
Ian Rungie
Donald Mills

Associate Directors
Graham Anderson
Michael Smithers

Address
33 Chandos Street
PO Box 107
St Leonards, N.S.W. 2065

Telephone
(02) 439 8388

Facsimile
(02) 439 3710

Person to Contact
Lindsay Skinner
Chris Vassiliou

Current and Recent Projects
Health Care
Repatriation General Hospital, Heidelberg
New 164 Bed Ward Block and Outpatient Department

St Vincent's Hospital, Melbourne
Redevelopment of various departments including
Pathologies, Pharmacy and Medical Imaging

St Andrew's Hospital, Melbourne
Redevelopment of entire Hospital

Box Hill Community Hospital, Melbourne
Upgrading of Engineering Services redevelopment

Diamond Valley Community Hospital, Melbourne
Continuous involvement with planning and
redevelopment of existing Hospital

Microsurgery Research Foundation, Melbourne
New multistorey training and research building

Birchip Bush Nursing Hospital, Vic.
Redevelopment of rural Hospital

Blue Mountains District ANZAC Memorial Hospital, N.S.W.
New Geriatric Rehabilitation unit, Central Energy
Building, Administration and Ward Block

Campbelltown Hospital, Stage 2 Development, N.S.W.
Alterations within existing Stage 1 building providing
new entrance and admissions office, Educational &
Conference facilities, Physiotherapy & Occupational
Therapy, Medical Records Departments, Pharmacy and
expanded Accident & Emergency Department

Gosford District Hospital, N.S.W.
Conversion of existing hospital to non-acute uses,
following the staged construction of a Major Extension to
accommodate Acute patient care functions

The Ryde Hospital, N.S.W.
Design of the Intensive & Coronary Care Unit

Royal Newcastle Hospital, N.S.W.
Planning and design of the development of the Hospital

Sydney Adventist Hospital, N.S.W.
New 300 bed Hospital and Radiotherapy Department

War Memorial Hospital, Waverley, N.S.W.
Conversion to a Geriatric Assessment and Rehabilitation
hospital and Day Care Centre

Recreational
Melbourne Zoological Gardens
Redevelopment plan, Hospitality Centre, Landscape
work and various exhibits

Melbourne Metropolitan Board of Works
Jells Park Interpretive Centre and its environs

Parkes Shire Council Administration & Library Building, N.S.W.
Design and construct new administration office and
library building

Enclosure of Olympic Pool, Blacktown, N.S.W.
Solar heated, computer controlled pool complex

Commercial & Industrial
180 Albert Road, South Melbourne
6 level office building development

471 Little Bourke Street, Melbourne
10 level office development

Ericssons Communications, Melbourne
Extensive building works including new Design Centre

Shepparton Preserving Company, Vic.
Warehouse Building

Eraring Power Station, Eraring, N.S.W.
Design and Construct Main Stores Building

Industrial Safety Centre, Londonderry, N.S.W.
Design Development and documentation of Fire Test
Control building

The Singleton Co-operative Society, Singleton, N.S.W.
Commissioned to increase floorspace and rationalise
various buildings into a sizeable "shopping complex" for
"The Store"

Educational
Pacific Adventist College, Port Moresby, P.N.G.
Complete campus masterplan and implementation

Korowa Anglican Girls School, Melbourne
Refurbishment of various classrooms and new
Gymnasium and indoor swimming pool

University of Melbourne
Architects for Veterinary and Agriculture faculty
buildings, both on and off campus

Presbyterian Theological College, Burwood, N.S.W.
Conversion of squash court complex to educational centre

Public Housing
Victorian Ministry of Housing, Melbourne
Housing projects for Estate improvement, medium
density and elderly persons housing

Aged Persons Care
Werribee District Hospital, Melbourne
Hostel and Day Centre

Mornington Bush Nursing Hospital
Nursing Home, Hostel and Day Centre

Port Fairy Hospital
Hostel and Day Centre

Nazareth House, Turramurra, N.S.W.
25 Bed Nursing Home

Adventist Nursing Home, Normanhurst, N.S.W.
Second stage of planned development of Adventist
Retirement Village

Avondale Retirement Village, Cooranbong, N.S.W.
Upgrading and expansion of retirement village

History Profile
Leighton Irwin-Garnet Alsop (Aust) Pty Ltd and
Leighton Irwin Pty Ltd are two affiliated practices, the
former located in Melbourne and the latter in Sydney
and offering a multidisciplined range of professional
services in Architecture, Engineering, Landscape
Architecture and Interior Design. Irwin Alsop (Pacific)
is a division of Leighton Irwin-Garnet Alsop (Aust)
Pty Ltd. The Leighton Irwin Company was founded in
1922 and incorporated in 1958 by the late Leighton
Irwin C.M.G. and Garnet Alsop and Partners Pty Ltd
founded in 1937 by H. Garnet Alsop. The two practices
merged in 1982, and were run as one National practice
until October 1984, when two separate entities were
formed, one located, owned and managed in Melbourne
and the other similarly in Sydney.

The group has expanded the scope of the professional
activities provided to include feasibility studies, master
planning, architectural design, energy studies,
engineering design, landscape design, interior design,
construction management and project management.
The in-house skills in these areas enables efficient design
and documentation of projects, the time and cost
savings being of benefit to our clients. Although usually
providing the total professional package, we are
frequently called upon to provide individual services,
often acting in a secondary consultant capacity,
particularly to major institutions and government
instrumentalities.

The firm has a commitment to the highest standards of
design, and the belief that it is of vital importance to
provide a service that enables projects to be monitored,
completed on schedule and within a pre-arranged
budget, and the client kept informed. It also believes
that the approach to every project may be different and
tailors the skills of the group to suit that project and
that situation.

The two principal offices are run independently,
however a conscious effort is made to develop different
and complementary skills. The implemented philosophy
of having every project the direct responsibility of a
principal of the firm, and the firm working along
partnership lines ensures every client and project
receives the very best attention. This system applies in
both offices.

The practice sees its market share as projects which
require a high standard of design and technical
requirement and where the multidisciplined nature of
the practice allows a tightly integrated, highly skilled
service. We have worked in every major city in
Australia, and in New Guinea, Malaysia and the South
Pacific, and enjoy substantial support from both the
Public and Private sectors.

Of particular relevance is a number of research projects
undertaken for Government departments, including a
solar air conditioned Hospital at Jerilderie, a study of
clean air systems in Operating Theatres and Health
Building Guideline studies for Hosplan. The continuing
policy of the group is to be involved in ongoing professional
development and research projects with our staff, and
to continue to attract new specialist skills through new,
younger members of staff. Our continued growth and
the quality of our projects attest to this philosophy.

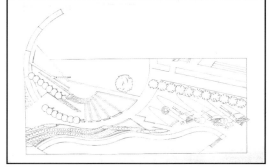

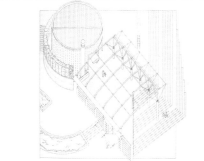

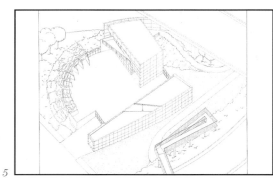

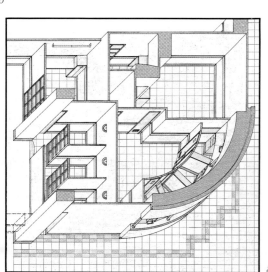

1   *Housing, Woolloomooloo*

2   *School of Military Engineering, Casula, N.S.W.*

3   *Urban Park, Darling Harbour*

4   *Kiosk, Darling Harbour*

5   *Maintenance Depot, Darling Harbour*

6   *Central Services Building, Darling Harbour*

7   *Hospital, Teluk Intan, Malaysia*

8   *MWSDB City Business Office*

McCONNEL SMITH & JOHNSON PTY LTD
Architects

Directors (left to right)
RN (Peter) Johnson AO BArch LFRAIA RIBA
  HonFRAIC HonFAIA
Peter Keys BArch DipTP LFRAIA RIBA
  MSIA MRAPI MRTPI
Bill Workman ASTC(Arch) FRAIA
Allan Maple BArch FRAIA
Louise Cox BArch DipTCP FRAIA RIBA
John Wyndham BArch Dip TCP
  FRAIA

Associates (left to right)
Mark Willett BArch ARAIA
Allan Rintoul BArch ARAIA
Simon Cundy BArch ARAIA
John Kornie BArch ARAIA

Established
1950

Address
35 Richards Avenue
Surry Hills, N.S.W. 2010

Telephone
(02) 33 4301

Telex
(02) 126613 MSJ

Facsimile
(02) 332 2402

Associated Offices
The MSJ Group
MSJ Keys Young Planners Pty Ltd
MSJ Design Consultants Pty Ltd

Number of Employees
68

Project Types
Commercial
Offices/retail (low and high storey)

Community/Recreational
Clubs, community centres, tourist
facilities, gymnasia, swimming pools,
laboratories

Education
Universities, colleges

Health/Welfare
Planning and design of hospitals and
clinics, feasibility studies and briefing

Public/Institutional
Courts, government offices, power
stations

Residential
Houses, homes, public housing

Restoration/Rehabilitation

Transport
Service facilities, underground stations,
signage, carparks

Other Disciplines
Research
Urban Design
Strategy Planning
Physical Planning
Regional Planning
Social Planning
Environmental Impact Analysis
Interior Design
Graphics

Persons to Contact
Bill Workman, Peter Keys or Matilde Busana

Current & Recent Projects
Commercial:
Water Board City Business Office, Sydney

N.S.W. Dairy Corporation Laboratories, Chippendale

Flight Operations Training Centre, Stages 1-5 for
Qantas Airways Ltd

Australian Dental Association, N.S.W. Branch Office,
Sydney

Educational:
School of Military Engineering, Casula, N.S.W.

Mechanical and Electrical Engineering Buildings for
Australian Defence Force Academy, Canberra

Law School for University of Sydney

Architecture School for University of Sydney
(in association with FMJM Partnership Pty Ltd)

Community/Recreational:
Urban Park, Darling Harbour

Childrens Playground, Darling Harbour

Kiosk, Darling Harbour

National Press Club, Canberra

Revolving Restaurant, Black Mountain, Canberra

Health/Welfare:
545-bed District Hospital at Teluk Intan, Malaysia
(in association with Philip Cox, Richardson,
Taylor & Partners Pty Ltd)

Repatriation General Hospital, Concord, Surgical and
Diagnostic Extension to National Estate post-war
hospital

Cooma District Hospital, NSW, New Main Block

Royal Prince Alfred Hospital, Camperdown,
336-bed ward and services block with Public Works
Department, N.S.W.

Restoration and Redevelopment of Sydney Hospital for
Public Works Department, N.S.W.

Master Development Plan for Ballina District Hospital

Darwin Private Hospital Submission
(in association with Philip Cox,
Richardson, Taylor & Partners Pty Ltd)

Public/Institutional:
Project Design Directorate for Darling Harbour
Development

Maintenance Depot, Darling Harbour

Central Services Building, Darling Harbour

Benjamin Offices, Belconnen, A.C.T., Office Complex
including Conference Centre, Gymnasium, Cafeteria and
Shops for National Capital Development Commission

Kenyir Power Station Building, Trengganau, Malaysia

Silverwater Gaol, Silverwater: Survey/Master Plan

Development Plan for Upgrading and Expansion of
existing Goulburn Gaol, N.S.W.

Law Courts, Queens Square, Sydney

Water Board Head Office, Sydney

Residential:
Pyrmont Point Housing

Cowper Wharf Road, Woolloomooloo Housing

North Ryde Housing

Various private houses

200 nurses and family residential
Teluk Intan, Malaysia

Restoration and Recycling:
Pitt Street Uniting Church

Pilgrim House

Old NSW Club

Horbury Terrace

Newcastle City Hall renovation
(as consultant to Suters & Busteed Architects)

Profile of the firm
McConnel Smith & Johnson Pty Ltd leads the MSJ Group
of companies with proven expertise in architecture,
planning and design. Experienced directors and staff
offer an unusually wide range of skills. Fields in which
the MSJ Group has worked successfully include:
- High-quality office buildings, including those designed
  for rapid construction at low cost
- Industrial and commercial structures – warehouses,
  laboratories, carparks and shops
- Recycling of buildings for new uses, from historic
  restoration to sympathetic renovation
- All aspects of planning from policy formulation, social
  planning and research to urban design
- Hospital and health care planning from earliest
  briefing and design to construction and fitting out
- Diverse interior design projects from offices to city
  halls and restaurants, including particular attention to
  the use of colour
- Master planning and design of specialised educational
  and institutional complexes

Professional Service
MSJ provides a service of the highest professional
standards tailored to a client's individual needs, whether
these call for buildings of special purpose and architectural character, or buildings which are straightforward,
economical and well-designed. The firm has been
credited with a number of RAIA Merit awards for its
design achievements.

Philosophy
MSJ accepts that serving society comes before the
pursuit of personal artistic goals. For us, architecture is a
social art in which we aim to meet the shelter needs of
the people who use the spaces we design in a way which
evokes a positive response. We believe that architects
must consider all the information available about the
needs of those for whom they design and, where
possible, share with them the experience of developing
the design.

Architecture takes place in an organisational context, a
physical context and a cultural context. It is the belief of
the firm that the inspiration for architectural form
should be drawn from the functional need for which the
building exists, from the physical location whether
natural or man-made and from the historical tradition of
the community.

Architecture is a social art in another sense – today it is
rarely the product of one person. We believe in working
together as a team so that not only those in the office
but also the specialist consultants and the builder and
his artisans, should have a sense of involvement and be
able to contribute actively to the nature and the quality
of the final work. As a consequence MSJ has always
thought of buildings as products of the firm as a whole
and not as the product of particular individuals.

1 Shopfronts, Errol Street, North Melbourne

2 Stables Interior, Canterbury Street

3 Tree Guard, Hardware Lane

4 Shop facades and verandahs, Victoria Market

5 Administration building model, Victoria Market

6 Conservation light, Parkville

Urban Design and Architecture
Technical Services Department
City of Melbourne
Urban Designers, Architects,
Landscape Architects,
Industrial Designers and
Major Project Co-Ordinators

Established
1870's Architecture
1985 Urban Design

Address
200 Little Collins Street
Melbourne, Vic. 3000

Telephone
(03) 658 9800

Facsimile
(03) 654 4854

**Chief Executive Officer
and Town Clerk**
D. N. Bethke

**General Manager –
Technical Services**
J. R. MacKenzie

**Manager – Urban Design &
Architecture**
R. J. Adams

Staff

P. Abraam	K. H. Loke
N. Alexander	V. Lopriore
A. J. Burnet	J. Noonan
C. Chin	M. O'Reilly
B. C. Credland	L. J. Parsons
I. S. Dryden	M. Paton
P. Eddleston	M. Playdon
T. Fitzell	M. Potocnik
A. Grant	C. Robertson
P. Hendry	J. Schnur
P. Hornidge	M. Terlikar
R. Jones	J. T. Tuang
B. Kent Hughes	J. Zorzi
G. B. Loader	

Key Staff
L. J. Parsons Head-Urban Design
G. B. Loader Head-Architecture
J. Noonan Head-Major Projects

Person to Contact
Rob Adams

Number of Employees
26

Project Types
Urban Design
Parks and Gardens
Streetscape Improvements
Street Furniture Design
Precinct Plans
Development Guidelines
Publications

Architecture
Retail
Commercial & Industrial
Recreational
Public
Community
Refurbishment
Conservation & Restoration
Interior Design
Furniture Design
Maintenance

History and Design Philosophy
Whilst Architecture has existed as a specialist service within the Council structure since the late 19th century, the recent addition of an Urban Design group marks a conscious recognition by Council of the importance of the overall design of the physical environment.

The City of Melbourne's 1985 Strategy Plan lead the way in this regard, with its emphasis on the city's distinctive physical characteristics as the basis for future action. The perceived need for major change has been replaced by a more pragmatic approach of gradually but consistently building upon Melbourne's existing strengths. A radical 1975 proposal to underground trams in Swanston Street should be compared with current moves to upgrade the same street by incremental change to furniture, lighting, verandahs and advertising.

The role of the Urban Design and Architecture Division is therefore one of providing an appropriate design framework within which the multitude of daily changes facing any city can take place. The Division has a broad range of projects, extending from the design of a tree guard to that of a large administrative building for the Queen Victoria Market. These projects are a means of reinforcing this framework and setting an example for others to follow.

Our approach to design, and the policies we have formulated, encourage greater attention to the physical context in which a development is set. The desire to create a unique and distinctive design must often be tempered by respect for the prevailing character of the area. As well as limiting development excesses, we aim to provide catalysts for future improvements through forward-looking frameworks, such as the Batman Park Master Plan.

A Council such as Melbourne obviously controls significant parts of the city in its own right. The City of Melbourne's property portfolio currently runs to some 700 buildings, ranging from small community centres to large office buildings. The Division is charged with the physical care and enhancement of all these assets of which many are historic structures. Through the design and maintenance of these buildings, the Division makes a direct and sizeable contribution to the appearance of the city and to the conservation of its heritage.

In order to provide these services, we have brought together a multi-disciplinary team of architects, urban designers, landscape architects, industrial designers and project co-ordinators. The Division operates on the basis of a small private practice charging out most of its time to various client departments. It is our intention to gradually extend our services to the private sector where there is an apparent need for the specialist consultancy we currently offer the Council.

Urban Design and Architecture Staff

Recent Projects
Urban Design
Gatehouse Street Improvements
Elgin Street Median
Hardware Street Tree Guards
Standard Seats
Parkville Conservation Lights
Fawkner Park Masterplan
Commonwealth Block Development Guidelines
Architecture
Canterbury Street Stables
Errol Street Shopfronts
Queen Victoria Market Shops and Verandahs
North and West Melbourne Community Centre

Current Projects
Urban Design
Batman Park Masterplan
Eight Hour Monument Reserve
Racecourse Road Shopping Centre
Block Place Upgrading
Various Street Furniture Designs
Greek Precinct Action Plan
Technical Note Series
Swanston Street Upgrading
Degraves Street
Publication, ''Grids and Greenery''
Architecture
Queen Victoria Market Administration Building
Council Accommodation Building
with Bates Smart and McCutcheon
Regent City Square Development
with Denton Corker Marshall
Council House Refurbishment
Nth. Carlton Community House
Extensions to Royal Park Golf Club
Extensions to East Melbourne Library
Development of Maintenance Programs
Interior and Furniture Design
Melbourne Town Hall Upgrading and
Exterior Stonework Repair
with Allom Lovell & Sanderson

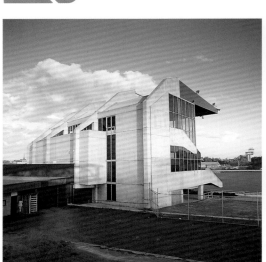

MELDRUM BURROWS & PARTNERS PTY LTD (Inc. Vic.)

Architects, Planners, Engineers, Landscape Architects, Interior Designers

Directors

R.J. Meldrum Dip Arch RMIT, BArch (Hons) Melb, FRAIA, FRIBA, Fellow Institute of Australian Directors, Fellow Royal Society of Arts, ARNZIA, Member Aust. Inst. of Landscape Architects, Ass. American Concrete Institute.

W.H.M. Barr Dip T&RP Melb, BT&RP Melb, FRAPI, FRTPI London, Member American Planning Ass.

J.H. McLuckie BArch Melb, Dip Arch RMIT, ARAIA

P.A. Edwards BArch NSW, ARAIA, Dip Business

G.V. Humphrey BArch NSW, ARAIA, Dip T&RP Syd

I.M. d'Oliveyra BT&RP Melb, Corporate Member RAPI

B.P. McNamara Bach. T&RP Melb, Grad. Dip Management RMIT, Corporate Member RAPI

R.J. Carrick BArch Adel, Grad Dip UR&R Qld, FRAIA, MRAPI

R.M. Drews BArch (Hons) Melb, Dip T&RP Melb, FRAIA, MRAPI

G.A. Fox BArch Melb, Dip Arch. RMIT, FRAIA

M.R. Hardman Assoc. (Architecture) P.T.C., M.A. (Urban & Regional Planning) NOTTS., FRAIA, FRAPI

L.D.I. Scott BArch (Hons) Heriot Watt University, Edinburgh, RIBA Registered Architect

D.P. Skues Dip. Arch (RMIT), ARAIA

Established

1938

Addresses

Melbourne
464 Collins Street
Melbourne, Vic. 3000

Telephone
(03) 62 5051, 62 3221

Facsimile
(03) 62 2965

Telex
EMPART AA38103

Sydney
281 Clarence Street
Sydney, N.S.W. 2000

Telephone
(02) 264 9705

Facsimile
(02) 264 6296

Telex
EMPART AA73826

Number of Employees

120

Project Types

Commercial, Ecclesiastical, Educational, Environmental, Health, Industrial, Interior Design, Landscape, Municipal, Recreational, Residential, Restoration, Retail, Town Planning

Person to Contact

Directors as listed

History

The firm of Meldrum Burrows & Partners was founded in 1938 by P.H. Meldrum with headquarters in Melbourne.

Since that time the practice has played a significant role in the development of the city and particularly the Central Business District. It has also diversified its activities both within Australia and externally in the regions of South East Asia and the Middle East.

In 1970 the firm of Meldrum & Partners amalgamated with the Sydney firm forming Meldrum Burrows & Partners with offices in Melbourne and Sydney.

In 1975 an office was opened in Riyadh, in Saudi Arabia and offices have since been established in Jeddah and in Dubai in the United Arab Emirates.

The firm has summoned up the 50 years experience of making major contributions to architecture, planning and engineering throughout Australia and overseas, and has combined this experience with newer disciplines and an ethos of innovation and high-tech capability to create a sophisticated multi-disciplinary practice. Our clients include major developers, corporations and government bodies.

Services include site selection, analysis of criteria and negotiation with controlling authorities. Clients are guided through the maze of bureaucratic regulations. State-of-the-art computer support is utilised for swift diagnosis of need and evaluation of design and documentation programmes.

Society is undergoing changes more rapidly than at any time in history. Different community and social needs and personal expectations of a fuller and more diverse life are all creating insistent pressures.

The Planning Group has special ability and experience in solving challenging planning problems with a professional, innovative and balanced approach.

Good architecture must be shaped with responsibility and foresight for it will be judged now and in the future. Practically it must meet the requirements of high durability and low maintenance costs. The Building Services Engineering group ensure that support infrastructures are of the highest quality and most advanced technical design.

The human factor too readily can be overlooked. Our Interior Design group has the skill to make reality of client needs and to create relevant places that are good to be in. Places that meet human needs and are of appropriate scale.

Harmony between architecture and its surroundings is a vital factor. We recognise we have a responsibility not only to our clients but to the community at large. Our Landscape Architecture group creates a subtle linkage between buildings and their environs so that each complements the other.

Architecture must create buildings and structures that withstand time both physically and conceptually.

Each commission has its own particular challenge and criteria. Our Melbourne and Sydney Architecture groups are committed to design excellence through systematic and multi-disciplinary procedures that satisfy all requirements.

Formalised thinking patterns and work structure have no place in contemporary and future professionalism. Now the very complexity of architecture, planning and allied disciplines requires innovative and constantly-renewed concepts.

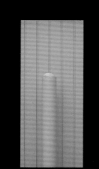
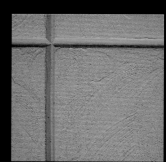

MILLAR SMITH PARTNERSHIP
Architects, Planners, Interior Designers

Principals (left to right)
James Millar B. Arch (RMIT), ARAIA
David Sainsbery Dip. Arch (RMIT), ARAIA
Michael Mulcair B. Arch (RMIT), ARAIA
Peter T Smith B. Arch (Melb), ARAIA, RIBA
Andrew Bunting M. Com, A.C.A., A.C.I.S.

Established
1978

Address
"Alma", Unit 16
663 Victoria Street
Abbotsford, Vic. 3067

P.O. Box 163
Abbotsford, Vic. 3067

Telephone
(03) 429 5733

Facsimile
(03) 429 8480

Number of Employees
25, plus support personnel

Consultant Services
Urban Planning, Master Planning,
Feasibility Studies, Interior Design,
Materials Storage and Handling

Contact
James Millar
David Sainsbery
Michael Mulcair

Project Types
Industrial
Commercial
Hotel/Hospitality
Retail
Civic
Educational
Recreation
Residential
Automotive

Photographer
Max Deliopoulos

Profile
The Practice
Millar Smith Partnership has attained an impressive
roster of commissions in a diversity of assignments.
Fresh, innovative solutions that have matched exacting
briefs and met the realities of budget parameters and
schedules.

Good credentials for a medium sized practice in
conservative Melbourne.

But the Partnership is not about to rest on past success
– to the contrary, this is a contemporary practice with
experience and reputation behind them, enthusiastic-
ally seeking new challenges in fields of their disciplines.
Millar Smith Partnership is not about to be catalogued or
labelled and has an enormous zest for architecture in all
its diverse expressions.

The Philosophy
Being able to listen and learn, not bringing any
preconceived solutions to a project are prerequisites
to understanding clients' needs and aspirations.
Only after absorbing the context of all myriad of issues
that impinge on the commission can optimum architectural solutions evolve.

For those who work or live within a finished building,
the architectural process provides performance and
style. But before the reality comes the disciplines
of detailed planning from design through contract
documentation, project management, interior design,
landscaping and signage.

The Partnership
As Architects, Planners and Interior Designers, the
Partnership can address the complete project cycle;
feasibility studies, master planning through to
completion.

What Millar Smith Partnership also brings to a
commission is that broader partnership between
the practitioner and the client that can turn good
architecture into an outstanding success.

Current and Recent Projects
Industrial Developments
Redwood Gardens Industrial Park, Dingley	$50M
Herald Street Industrial Estate, Moorabbin	$4.5M
Warrigal Road Estate, Moorabbin	$5.6M
Caribbean Gardens Industrial Park, Knox	$60M
Five Ways Business Park, Springvale	

Masterplans have been prepared for the following
additional major developments:

Latrobe University R & D Estate, Bundoora

Redwood Lakes Industrial Park, Braeside

Calder Technology Park, Calder

Manufacturing and Warehousing commissions have been
completed for the following clients:

Braemar Appliances, Email CRD Division,
SABA Furniture, G.J. Coles Distribution,
David's Holdings, Cadbury Schweppes, Remy-Blass

Commercial
Plumrose Corporation Headquarters	$2M
Office Development, Abbotsford	$3.5M
Shepparton Newspapers	$2M
Nepean Highway Offices	$4M
Carlton Wines and Spirits, National office	$2.5M

Hotel/Hospitality
Dingley International Hotel	$8M
Sherlock Holmes Tavern, Collins Street	
Cafe Alma, Alma Centre, Abbotsford	
Pioneer Hotel, Footscray	
Banana Alley Tavern, Melbourne	

Retail Centres
Gladstone Park Shopping Centre Extensions	$15M
Waverley Gardens Shopping Centre Extensions (feasibility)	
Parkmore Keysborough Shopping Centre Extensions (feasibility)	

Civic Offices
Hawthorn Civic and Office Development (Development Study)	$40M
City Square Redevelopment, Malvern (Development Study)	$8.3M
Dandenong Springvale Water Board	$2.2M

Recycled Buildings
Australian Fixed Trusts, 417 Collins Street	$1.8M
Alma Redevelopments, Abbotsford	$2.3M
Accountants Office, Queen Street	

Educational
Monterey High School Library	
Emerald Post Primary School, Stage 2	$2.5M
Eltham Primary School Masterplan and Multi Purpose Hall	
Research Primary School Masterplan and Multi Purpose Hall	

Recreation
Rosebud Pool and Bowl	$2.5M
Endeavour Hills Recreation Complex	$2.25M
Dingley Basketball and Squash Centre	$1.2M
Rules Leisure Complex, Keysborough	$10M

Residential
Davison Place Residential Apartments,
Melbourne CBD and various renovations,
restorations and new houses

Automotive
BMW Australian Dealer Development Program	
Trivett Classic BMW, Parramatta	$1.2M
Peter Menere BMW, Moorabbin	
Melbourne City Toyota, Elizabeth Street	

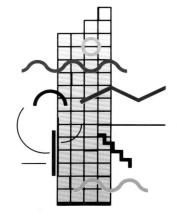

1

2

3

4

5

6

1 *Manufacturing Facility, Knoll International, Pennsylvania*

2 *Aviano Elementary School, Italy*

3 *Annenberg School of Communications, University of Pennsylvania*

4 *House of Representatives Courtyard, New Parliament House, Canberra*

5 *Entry Foyer, Volvo, Gothenberg, Sweden*

6 *Courtyard/Arcade, Cumberland Place, The Rocks, Sydney*

7 *New Parliament House, Canberra*

8 *Victorian State Library/Museum, Melbourne. Competition Entry*

9 *Music Auditorium, Swarthmore College, Pennsylvania*

7

8

9

MITCHELL/GIURGOLA & THORP ARCHITECTS

Partners (left to right)
Romaldo Giurgola B.Arch., M.Sc.Arch, FAIA, FRAIA
Richard G. Thorp B.Arch., AIA, ARIBA, ARAIA
Harold S. Guida M.Arch., AIA, ARAIA
Rollin R. La France B.Arch., AIA, ARAIA

Associates
Christopher Alcock B.Arch. (Hons.), ARAIA
Pamille Berg B.A., M.A.
Tim Halden Brown Dip.Arch., ARIBA, FRAIA
Andrew McKenna B.Arch.(Hons.)
Steve Moseley Dip.Arch., B.Sc.(Hons.)
Robert Pearce Dip.Arch., ARAIA
Phillip H. Walker B.Arch, ARAIA

Established
U.S.A. 1958
Australia 1980

Address
Endeavour House
Franklin Street
Manuka, A.C.T. 2603

Telephone
(062) 95 2211

Facsimile
(062) 95 3203

Affiliated Offices
Mitchell/Giurgola New York
170 West 97th Street
New York, New York 10025 USA

Telephone
(212) 663 4000

Facsimile
(212) 866 5006

Mitchell/Giurgola Philadelphia
6th Floor
414 Walnut Street
Philadelphia, P.A. 19106 USA

Telephone
(215) 925 0100

Facsimile
(215) 923 4258

Number of Employees
Australia 75
USA 60

Project Types
Commercial
Office, Retail, Parking, Urban Mixed Use,
Corporate and Industrial Parks

Community/Recreational
Museums, Art Galleries, Theatres,
Libraries, Precinct and City Master
Planning

Educational Planning
Campus Master Planning, Classrooms,
Libraries, Auditoria/Theatres,
Laboratories, Residential Accommodation,
Sports Facilities

Government
Administrative and
Civic/State Complexes

Health Planning
Laboratories, Health Care Facilities

Resort Development
Hotels and Urban Planning

Residential
Houses, Apartment Developments

Other Disciplines
Urban Design and Master Planning
Interior Design
Furniture Design
Office Planning
Art/Craft Planning and Co-ordination

Person to Contact
Australia
Richard Thorp/Harold Guida

New York
Paul Broches

Philadelphia
Fred Foote

Current and Recent Projects
Mitchell/Giurgola & Thorp Architects
Mitchell/Giurgola New York
Mitchell/Giurgola Philadelphia

Commercial
Volvo Corporation Headquarters Building, Gothenberg, Sweden	$18M
Office Building, The Rocks, Sydney	$12M
IBM Executive Education Centre, New York State, USA	$80M
Southbank Development Tender, Brisbane (In association Architects Cunnington McKerrell)	
Center West Office Tower, Los Angeles, USA	$80M
IBM Office Park, Texas, USA	$100M
Office Complex, Connecticut, USA	$10M

Community/Recreational
St. Thomas Aquinas Parish Church, Canberra	$0.5M
Anchorage Historical & Fine Arts Museum, Alaska	$9M
San Jose Convention Centre, California, USA	$80M
History Center, Virginia Air & Space Center, USA	$7.5M
Torslanda Museum, Gothenberg, Sweden	$7M

Educational Planning
Diamond Valley College of TAFE, Melbourne	$8.5M
Industrial Innovation Center, Rensselaer Polytechnic, New York, USA	$15M
University of North Carolina Art Museum, USA	$7.5M
Emerging Technologies Center, University of Vermont, USA	$6M
Fine & Performing Arts Center, University of West Florida, USA	$10M

Government
New Parliament House, Canberra	$894M
Courthouse Complex, Newport News, Virginia, USA	$5M
Foreign Service Institute, US Dept. of State, Virginia, USA	$125M
Suffolk County Courthouse Complex, New York State, USA	$80M

Health Planning
Outpatient Care Centre, UCLA, Los Angeles, USA	$15M

Hotels
Federal Hotels/Sabemo Hotel Casino
Development Tender, Darling Harbour, Sydney
Kern Corp. Hilton Hotel Development Tender, Canberra

Residential
Residence, Forrest, ACT	$0.35M
Westchester Housing Complexes, New York State, USA	$10M
Bayside Development Tender, Port Phillip Bay, Melbourne (In association Daryl Jackson Pty Ltd)	
Hudson View East Residential Development, Battery Park City, New York, USA	$7.5M

Urban Master Planning
Yerba Buena Esplanade Redevelopment,
San Francisco, USA

Free Harbour Redevelopment Plan for the City of
Gothenberg, Sweden

South East Victoria Square, Adelaide
Urban Design Study

Profile
Mitchell/Giurgola & Thorp Architects offers its clients resources which are unique among Australian architectural practices. Primary among these is the fusion of the maturity and depth of international experience of its partners and senior staff with the wide-ranging experience of its 55 Australian team architects in all building types in Australia.

The leadership provided by resident partners Harold Guida, Rollin La France, and Richard Thorp under the guidance and design direction of founding partner Romaldo Giurgola arises from their long association through years of work with the American practice and their developed Australian expertise afforded by seven years' practice from the firm's office in Canberra.

This leadership is complemented in the firm's project teams by Associates and staff architects drawn from practices throughout Australia. Their collective architectural experience ranges from design and documentation of houses, churches, and school or university buildings to major urban high-rise offices and retail developments in all of Australia's climatic zones from the Northern Territory to Australia's base camp in Antarctica.

The diverse resources provided by this staff make the practice one of the largest in Australia and afford great flexibility in the firm's ability to respond quickly and with an appropriately skilled team to new undertakings.

History
Founded as a partnership between Ehrman B. Mitchell Jr. and Romaldo Giurgola in 1958, the American practice has offices in New York and Philadelphia and has completed projects in over one hundred cities in the U.S., Europe and South America.

In 1976 the American practice was the recipient of the Firm Award of the American Institute of Architects, the highest award that organisation can bestow upon a practising group, and in 1981 Romaldo Giurgola was awarded the Institute's Gold Medal for his thirty years of leadership in design. Until his retirement from the firm in 1984, Ehrman Mitchell Jr. (FAIA) was a tireless campaigner on a national level for professionalism in the practice of architecture, and served as the AIA's national Vice President and President from 1976-1980.

Mitchell/Giurgola & Thorp Architects was formed in 1980 in response to the competition brief for Australia's New Parliament House and opened offices in Canberra later that year following the selection of the firm's design from over 300 entries. With the completion of the Parliament project, the firm now has a proven foundation for the continuation of its practice in Australia on a national basis.

Approach
Mitchell/Giurgola & Thorp Architects is consciously committed to the search for an architecture capable of enhancing life and of providing a sense of both inspiration and aspiration to those who participate in its presence.

The thirty years of combined architectural practice of the US and Australian offices have been characterised by a constant commitment to an architecture based on principles, balanced by a search for humane and life-enhancing solutions to built forms. The project-based design team approach utilised by the firm generates a fresh solution to each client's project rather than a pre-determined or predictable architectural solution. Equally important is the continuity of each architectural team from the early design phases through construction supervision, thereby ensuring that early conceptual development is not truncated during construction by unrelated field management solutions.

The Australian firm of Mitchell/Giurgola & Thorp Architects seeks to retain this method of practising architecture as a search for roots and linkages with cultural traditions, while at the same time allowing it to blossom in new ways through design of architectural forms determined by the vitality of Australia's rich and diverse identity.

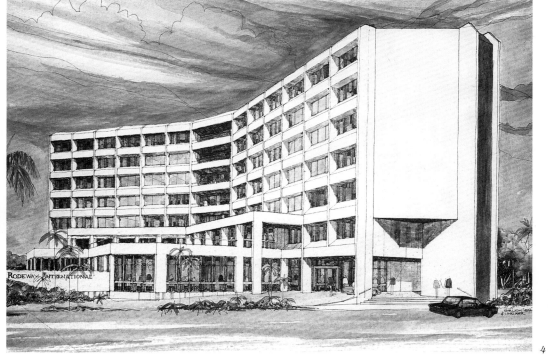

1 Residence, Nightcliff

2 Regional office, Palmerston

3 Residence, interior

4 160 bed hotel, Esplanade, Darwin

5 Coral Bay Resort

6 Sanderson High School

MLE ARCHITECTS

Directors (left to right)
Steven J. Ehrlich B.Arch., F.R.A.I.A.
Derek V. Moor B.Arch., F.R.A.I.A., A.I.Arb.A.
Roger G. Linklater B.Arch., F.R.A.I.A,
  A.I.Arb.A.

Established
1973 in Darwin

Address
6 Lindsay Street
Darwin, N.T. 5794

P.O. Box 715
Darwin, N.T. 5794

Telephone
(089) 81 7911

Facsimile
(089) 81 1510

Number of Employees
12

Project Types
Commercial
Industrial
Government
Hotel/Resort
Health
Education
Residential

Person to Contact
The Directors

Current and Recent Projects

Commercial

Woolworths Supermarket Complex Katherine	$6M
Coles Supermarket Complex Palmerston	$4M
Coles Refurbishment Casuarina	$6M
Karama Supermarket Complex	$5M
Territory Insurance Office	
Office Building – Palmerston	$3M
Offices Katherine – Stage I. & II.	$4M
Harbour View Plaza Office Building Darwin	$6M
Enterprise House Darwin	$2.5M
City Towers Project Darwin	$60M
Winnellie Home Retail Centre	$5M
Government Offices Jabiru	$1.5M
Twin Cinemas Casuarina	$1M
ANZ Banking Facilities (Various)	

Industrial

Channel Island Power Station	$225M
In association with G.H.D. – Black & Veatch	
Refit Armidale St. Power Station	
Skills and Training Centre	$0.6M
Telecom Installation & Operations Centres	$2M
In association with D.H.C.	
Industrial Laundry Facility	$0.6M
Roofing Centre Factory	$0.25M
O.S.S. Sample Preparation Laboratory and	
Admin. Offices and Workshops	$2.5M
In association with D.H.C.	

Local Government

Katherine Civic Centre	$2M
Malak Community Centre	$0.8M
Alawa Community Hall	$0.15M
Humpty Doo Child Care Centre	$0.3M

Education
In conjunction with Department of Transport
& Works

Sanderson High School	$12M
Katherine East Primary School	$8M
Katherine High School	$13M
In association with Architects Co-Partnership N.T. & Barclay Bros.	
Darwin Institute of Technology	
School of Business Administration Stage I.	$3.5M
School of Business Stage II.	$3M
Nightcliff Professional Services Centre	$1.8M

Health
In conjunction with Department of Transport
& Works

Katherine Hospital – 32 Bed Ward	$4M

Defence
Tindal Projects In conjunction with D.H.C.

Formation Base Squadron Headquarters	$2.3M
Central Equipment Stores	$1.7M
Motor Transport Buildings	$1M

Hotel/Resort
Rodeway International Darwin

Glynatsis-Sitzler Joint Venture	$20M
Coral Bay Resort	$6M

Television

N.T.D. Channel 8 Studio & Offices	$4M

Residential

Baddeley Residence Nightcliff	$0.3M
James Residence Humpty Doo	$0.25M
Residence Fannie Bay	$0.20M
Ranger Housing Project Jabiru	
Ranger Uranium Mines Pty. Ltd.	$2.5M
Various Medium Density Projects throughout Darwin	
Aboriginal Housing	
Narbalek, Jabiru and Kulaluk	

Project Range

As an established practice in a relatively remote community we have found it essential to involve ourselves in projects of all types, size and complexity. A review of our current and recent project list will indicate the breadth of the experience and expertise within the practice in terms of value, size of project complexity and type of construction.

This necessary flexibility and experience has meant that the practice is able to perform to a high standard whether the project be commercial, industrial, domestic, educational, institutional or recreational.

We have successfully developed projects from within our own resources and on behalf of our clients. We have been involved in joint project management of major projects.

A central core of the work of the practice is still concentrated on the traditional practice of Architecture where the clients' needs are professionally assessed, designed, documented and the contract administered. This traditional core of work assists in the retention of a high standard essential to success in these highly competitive times. We also have a group of traditional clients who are continually seeking our services.

The practice offers a successful record and stability in changing times. It offers the pursuit of excellence with flexibility and experience to ensure a high standard of service to its clients.

Profile

MLE Architects has evolved from the amalgamation of practices which have a long and successful history in the Northern Territory. The amalgamation of Moor & Associates and Roger Linklater & Associates to form Moor Linklater Perumal Architects in 1981 is the basis of the present practice of MLE Architects.

The Directors prior to establishing the practice in Darwin have had considerable experience in Sydney, Adelaide and Perth and combine that major city experience with extensive local knowledge of design and construction in the tropics.

The practice has achieved a consistent reputation for high standards in all respects of practice of architecture and seeks to maintain these standards in future work.

Architectural Approach

The basic Architectural Philosophy of this practice is to produce cost effective, practical, usable buildings of the highest standard, buildings which have straightforward construction, design, and also embody the best of contemporary technology.

The practice believes in excellence and therefore aims to provide sensitive tropical design solutions within the parameters of high standard and cost effective practical design.

On several occasions these design solutions have been recognised with Architectural Awards and commendations indicating the successful application of the design parameters.

1 Haileybury College, Assembly Hall

2 Trinity College Chapel, Restoration

3 Caulfield Grammar School, Wheeler's Hill Campus

4 Melbourne Grammar School, Rhoden Building

5 Royal Freemasons Homes of Victoria, Chapel

MOCKRIDGE STAHLE & MITCHELL PTY LTD

Directors (left to right)
Greville Gowty F.R.A.I.A.
George Mitchell L.F.R.A.I.A.
David Eyres B.Arch., F.R.A.I.A.

Associate
Robert Kranz

Consultant
John Mockridge L.F.R.A.I.A.

Established
1948

Address
82 Jolimont Street
Jolimont, Vic. 3002

Telephone
(03) 654 5544

Number of Employees
10

Project Types
Educational
Schools, Tertiary Colleges & Universities,
including specialist facilities.

Residential
Student Housing, Housing for the Aged,
Clubs.

Office Buildings

Religious Buildings

Other Disciplines
Brief Preparation
Master Planning
Restoration
Fire Protection

Person to Contact
Greville Gowty

Current and Recent Projects

Educational: Schools

Haileybury College
Assembly Hall, Music and Performing Arts Facilities, 1983.

Camberwell Church of England Girls' Grammar School
Ransom and Westcott Wings, comprising Gymnasium
and Swimming Pool, Art and Craft Centre and Home
Economics, 1983. Assembly Hall, Music and Performing
Arts Facilities, 1988.

Melbourne Church of England Grammar School
Physical Education Building, comprising Gymnasium
and Pool, 1983. Rhoden Building, comprising
Classrooms, Computer Facilities and Change Rooms,
1984. Grimwade House; Extensions to Classrooms, 1984.

Caulfield Grammar School – Wheeler's Hill Campus
Site planning and Landscaping, Classrooms, Science
Laboratories, Library, Physical Education and Performing
Arts Facilities, 1980-1987.

Caulfield Grammar School, Glen Eira Road
Creative Arts Centre, 1986-1987.

St. Joseph's School, Yarra Junction
Primary School Classrooms, 1986.

Brighton Grammar School
R. L. Rofe Creative Arts Centre, 1986.

Peninsula School
Year 10 Classrooms and Change Rooms, 1987.
Master Planning

Firbank Anglican School
Patricia Turner Creative Arts Centre, 1987.

Educational: Colleges

Bendigo College of Advanced Education
Arts and Ceramics, 1987. Health Sciences Building, 1987.

Dandenong College of T.A.F.E.
Plastics Building, Plumbing & Carpentry Building,
Gas Fitting Building, Art and Ceramics Building, 1985.

Whitley College, University of Melbourne
Theological Centre

Residential

Trinity College, University of Melbourne
Moorhouse Building, comprising Student Flats as
extension to residential building, 1981. Memorial
(Jeopardy) Building, Flats for Tutors, 1987.

Offices

A.C.I. Computer Services
Extensions, 1986

Accommodation for the Aged

Royal Freemasons' Homes of Victoria
Alterations to Hostel, 313 Punt Road, comprising a
Medical Clinic, Physiotherapy, etc., Occupational
Therapy and Staff facilities, 1987. Alterations to
Dining Hall and Bedrooms.

Ministry of Housing
Flats, Alma Road
Design Development and Documentation.

Religious

Ivanhoe Grammar School
Chapel, 1982

Royal Freemasons' Homes of Victoria
Chapel, 1983

St Paul's Cathedral
Consultancy

Wangaratta Cathedral
Bell Tower

Restoration

Trinity College, Melbourne
Chapel

Christ Church, South Yarra
Spire

Fire Protection

Melbourne Grammar School,
Melbourne Club
Royal Freemasons' Homes of Victoria
St Paul's Cathedral, Melbourne
Trinity College, Melbourne

History

Mockridge Stahle and Mitchell was founded in 1948 and
within a comparatively short time established a significant practice in Independent Schools, of which some
continue as clients today.

Early projects at Melbourne Church of England
Grammar School and St Catherine's School in Toorak,
designed by John Mockridge, set the firm's reputation
for buildings of quality and fine design, harmoniously
related to the best architectural components of the
existing buildings.

The practice developed into the design of buildings for
tertiary education and these included major buildings
for the University of Melbourne, among them, the
Completion of the Medical Centre in 1968, an appointment won in a limited competition. Considerable work
was completed in Colleges affiliated with the University,
including Trinity College, Janet Clarke Hall, Whitley
College and Ridley College, as well as International
House.

At the Australian National University the firm was
appointed architects for the H.C. Coombs Building,
following a limited competition and also designed
the Schools of Social Sciences and of Humanities at
La Trobe University.

With Government funding the firm designed many
science blocks and libraries for private schools in
Victoria. In 1960 the firm established an office in
Canberra and designed many primary and secondary
schools, including the award winning Downer Primary
School. Beryl Mann, Landscape Architect and an
Associate of the firm, took a major part in site planning
including the Lake Ginninderra project. Much of the
Canberra work was directed by Greville Gowty, who
became a partner in 1970.

The firm designed a considerable number of churches
including the Church of Mary Immaculate in Ivanhoe in
1962 and the Monash Religious Centre in 1967. A major
project in 1969 was the Camberwell Civic Centre and in
1978 the Municipal offices. John Mockridge's house was
given an R.A.I.A. Award in 1977. The firm was incorporated in 1975 and David Eyres became a director in 1986.

Philosophy

The aim of the practice is to provide beautiful and
practical buildings, answering the needs of our clients
and the wider community.

By 'beautiful' we mean buildings of grace and quality,
well built, well proportioned and fitting well into their
context. By 'practical' we mean buildings which fulfil
the basic needs of shelter and comfort with sensible
planning and appropriate use of materials, structure
and services.

A flexible and pragmatic approach is taken to design.
Rather than following fashionable trends, each project
is carefully assessed and designed to suit its unique
conditions and budgetry constraints. With experience
acquired in designing new buildings for existing
institutions, we design to suit the environment and are
responsive to the needs of the wider community as well
as our clients.

The Practice

A Director is responsible for each project in the office,
assisted by an experienced architect, well versed in the
design standards of the firm.

Close attention is given to site inspections and management of projects.

The office is large enough to cope with a wide variety
of work and small enough to encourage personal
involvement.

We work closely with our clients and specialist consultants and are able to provide the following services:

Advice on site selection:
Programming, scheduling and preparation of briefs,
Site Planning and Master Planning, Feasibility studies,
Schematic and sketch planning,
Negotiation with authorities,
Documentation, and
Contract Administration.

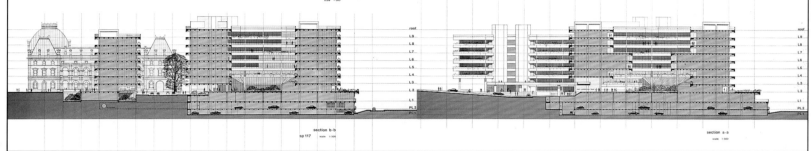

1 Redland Shire Offices and Library, Cleveland, Qld

2 Queensland Institute of Technology, Main Library

3 State Government Master Plan Development, Qld

4 Executive Annex, State Government Precinct, Brisbane

5 Proposed Commercial Office Development, Walker St, Sydney

6 Business and General Studies Building, T.A.F.E. College, Mount Gravatt, Brisbane

7 State Works Centre, Brisbane

JOHN M MORTON ARCHITECTS PTY LTD

Director
John Morton Dip. Arch (Manc), FRAIA

Established
This firm now incorporates the firm previously known as Lund Hutton Ryan Morton Pty. Ltd., whose origins go back to 1888.

Address
32 Little Edward Street
Spring Hill, Qld 4000

Telephone
(07) 832 1366

Facsimile
(07) 832 0128

Awards and Citations
Over the years the firm has received major awards and citations for excellence in architecture, and in 1977 received the RAIA Queensland Chapter Bronze Medal for the Townsville Civic Centre.

In 1987 the State Works Centre in Brisbane was joint winner in the Best Building category.

Other awards:

1960
Award for Meritorious Architecture
St. Matthews Church Townsville
1961
Award for Meritorious Architecture
The Shell Company Office Townsville
1963
Commendation for Meritorious Architecture
15 Storey Glenfalloch Home Units, New Farm Brisbane
1970
Citation for Meritorious Architecture
Lowths Hotel Townsville
1975
Citation for Meritorious Architecture
Mount Isa Civic Centre
1975
Concrete Institute of Australia Award
for Excellence in Concrete
Queensland Institute of Technology Main Library
1984
Meritorious Lighting Award
Jumbuck Productions Video Editing Studio Brisbane

Current and Recent Projects
The firm was successful in winning architectural competitions for the Mount Isa Civic Centre, Townsville Civic Centre, the Mackay Civic Centre, and was placed second in the Queensland State Art Gallery competition in 1973.

The Orange (NSW) Civic Centre was awarded to the firm after submissions were reviewed from Australia-wide.

In 1974 the firm was commissioned to prepare the Master Plan for the Queensland State Government Precinct, the first stage of which was implemented and completed in March 1986. The second stage, known as the Executive Annex, is currently under construction.

Projects have been carried out with several currently under development in the fields of:
commercial offices
community/recreational/resort development
university/college/school buildings
libraries
civic buildings
church buildings
laboratory/research buildings
residential
urban planning and design
housing studies

The firm's work is well known for its approach to climatic responsiveness, functional and technical solutions and cost effective implementation.

NAPIER THOMAS MANTESSO HEALEY PTY LTD
NTMH Group

Directors (left to right)
David Napier B. Arch ARAIA
John Thomas Dip. Arch ARAIA
Richard Healey B. Arch
John Mantesso B. Arch ARAIA

Associate Directors
Les Finnis B. Arch ARAIA
Patrick Ng B. Arch

Established
1986

Address
Southbank Corporate Centre
25 Haig Street
South Melbourne, Vic. 3205

Telephone
(03) 690 3700

Facsimile
(03) 690 6925

Number of Employees
28

Value of Commissions June 1987
Currently involved with works in excess
of $100 M

Project Types
Commercial
Office/Retail/Hotels

Community
Libraries, Art Galleries and
Child Minding Centres

Educational
Schools and University Projects

Industrial
High Tech Showroom/Warehouses

Residential
Individual Houses and Renovations

State Government
Multi Unit Housing and Boarding Houses

Tourism/Leisure
Multi-functional Aquatic Leisure
Centres, Country Clubs

Other Disciplines
Residential Interiors
Corporate Interiors

Person to Contact
David Napier/Richard Healey

Current and Recent Projects
Commercial
Corporate Headquarters, Palmer Corporation Limited, fashion house on the Yarra, Richmond.

Ocean Grove Country Pub Resort, Victoria.

Conversion of "Bakka" showroom High Street Armadale, to prestige shops.

Blackburn Hotel, Whitehorse Road, Blackburn.

Restoration of classified Tramway Engine House North Melbourne, to professional offices.

Redevelopment of island block City Road, South Melbourne, to Showroom/Offices.

New commercial office buildings
Market Street, South Melbourne
Bay Street, Brighton
Wellington Street, Windsor
Lava Street, Warrnambool

Warehouse conversion to commercial offices William Street, Melbourne.

Tisdall Winery/Restaurant Complex, Echuca Port, Victoria.

Community
South Melbourne Library Headquarters and Albert Park Branch Library.

Refurbishment of Malvern Central Library.

Shepparton Regional Library and Mechanics Institute.

Warrnambool Regional Art Gallery. Best Museum Category A – Museums Association of Australia Museum of the Year Awards 1987.

Child Care Centres at Chadstone and Blackburn.

Occasional Day Care Centre, Malvern.

Educational
Extensions to St Aloysius Primary School, North Caulfield.

Renovations and extensions to St Vincents Primary School, Strathmore.

Refurbishment of administration offices, Raymond Priestley Building, Melbourne University.

New experimental laboratories for Microbiology and Pharmacology, Melbourne University.

Industrial
High Tech, tilt slab factory/offices, Burwood.

Showroom/Warehouse development, Richmond.

Showrooms, constructed from precast concrete, Somerton.

Interiors
National Training Centre, Australian Directory Services, Box Hill.

Tenancy fitouts, Southbank Corporate Centre, South Melbourne.

Associated Retailers, Mensland Shops corporate design and shop fitouts throughout Australia.

Residential interiors for numerous renovation and individual house clients.

Residential
In addition to the successful completion of more than 200 residential renovations, the NTMH Group have been responsible for more than 25 new homes throughout Melbourne's suburbs and seaside resorts. Further, the Group is currently undertaking two of the 10 private residences to be constructed on Hamilton Island off the Queensland North Coast.

State Government
Ministry of Housing,
Rooming House, Port Melbourne.
Multi-unit Housing, North Melbourne.
Rooming House, Newport.
Elderly Persons Housing, Reservoir.

Public Works Department,
Police Station, Portland.

Tourism/Leisure
Aquatic Leisure and Entertainment Centre, Knox, Victoria.

Aquatic Leisure and Entertainment Centre, Noarlunga, South Australia.

Leisure Pool Complex, Camberwell, Victoria.

Strathbogie Country Club, Victoria.

History
Napier Thomas Mantesso Healey Pty Ltd, trading as the NTMH Group, was formed on the 1st of November 1986 from the merging of the two successful architectural practices of Napier Thomas Pty Ltd and Mantesso Healey & Associates Pty Ltd. Both companies were established in the early 1980's and had achieved a reputation for completing projects with a high level of design quality.

Since the formation of the NTMH Group the percentage of commercial and showroom projects has increased substantially with a necessary expansion in total staff numbers from 13 to 28.

Company Philosophy
Design
While quality and excellence of design are implicit in all our work, appropriate design is our cornerstone.

Permanence and longevity are prime considerations in the design of our buildings, with a preference for a style that reflects the requirements of our individual clients.

Service
The familiar adage "time is money" is particularly apt in the context of the building industry.

So while speed of turnaround remains one of our highest priorities, we take great care to ensure that it never compromises our standards.

We recognise that the progress of construction programs can be severely hampered by the participating parties. Therefore we make a firm commitment to our clients to maintain constant pressure on authorities and builders to ensure that our projects are kept on target and to a minimum cost.

Cost-Efficiency and Technology
Cost-efficient design and construction relies on several considerations, thorough and thoughtful planning, followed by careful selection of the most appropriate building technology and materials.

Change is such a constant in our industry, that it's essential to keep a monitor on advances in construction technology and building materials, as well as shifts and trends in the market place.

This, therefore, creates the need for flexibility.

Director Involvement
The NTMH Group brings a large degree of youthful energy to every project undertaken. Directors' involvement is very much "hands on" – from procurement and design, through to documentation and construction.

Each project is ultimately the responsibility of an individual director who maintains constant contact with the client – from project initiation to completion.

Each director is a designer with particular areas of expertise. Where possible, if an individual project requires specialist knowledge or skills, a specialist director will be assigned to that particular project.

Interior Design
While our major priority is the design and construction of each project, we are also vitally involved in the total co-ordination of each building, particularly its interior.

To this end, we employ fully qualified interior design staff to work in tandem with our own design team – thus achieving a totally unified package.

In conclusion, the NTMH Group has the necessary experience, expertise and resources to undertake successfully a broad range of building types. The total commitment of the Directors, Associates and Staff is to produce high quality, efficient and economic design within agreed time constraints for our Clients upon whom we depend for the continued growth and success of Napier Thomas Mantesso Healey Pty Ltd.

1 & 2 *Corporate Headquarters, Parramatta, N.S.W.*

3 *Tourist Information Centre, Scone, N.S.W.*

4 *Restaurant, Parramatta, N.S.W.*

5 *Swimming Pool Kiosk, Clubrooms and Facilities, Muswellbrook, N.S.W.*

6 & 7 *Senior Citizens and Community Health Facilities, Scone, N.S.W.*

8 *Child Care Centre, Muswellbrook, N.S.W.*

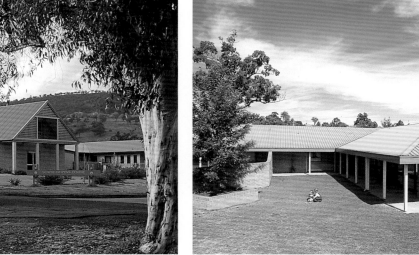

JOHN NICHOLAS & PARTNERS PTY LIMITED
Architects

Partners (left to right)
John Nicholas B. Arch (Hons), M.Sc (Build),
    A.R.A.I.A.
Robert Bittar B. Build (Hons), M.A.I.B.

Established
1974

Address
15 Boundary Street
Rushcutters Bay, N.S.W 2011

Telephone
(02) 332 4555

Facsimile
(02) 360 1009

Number of Employees
12

Project Types
Commercial
Industrial
Local Government & Municipal
Retail
Residential
Sports, Recreation & Tourism

Value of Commissions 1986-87
Currently involved with work in excess
of $30M

Other Disciplines
Interior Design
Building Surveys
Project & Construction Management
Building Programming
& Cost Control Management

Persons to Contact
John Nicholas and Robert Bittar

Current and Recent Projects
Commercial
Corporate Headquarters
Hunter Street, Parramatta, N.S.W.
– Neeta Homes Pty. Ltd.

Commercial Office Development, Penrith, N.S.W.

Office Building, Chullora, N.S.W. – S.R.A.

Commercial Office & Retail Complex, Liverpool, N.S.W.

Industrial
Workshop, Store & Office Complex,
Hunter Valley, N.S.W. – BP Coal Australia

Workshop, Hunter Valley, N.S.W. – ANI Komatsu

Amenities Facilities, Hunter Valley, N.S.W.
– BP Coal Australia

Workshop, Mortdale, N.S.W. – State Rail Authority

Amenities & Office Facilities, Hunter Valley, N.S.W.
– I.C.I. Australia Ltd

Local Government & Municipal
Senior Citizens & Community Centre
– Muswellbrook Shire Council, N.S.W.

Child Care Centres
– Muswellbrook & Scone Shire Councils, N.S.W.

Administration Offices & Library
– Scone Shire Council, N.S.W.

Restoration – Murrurundi Shire Council, N.S.W.

Senior Citizens & Community Health Centre
– Scone Shire Council, N.S.W.

Multipurpose Youth Resource Centre
– Canterbury Municipal Council, N.S.W.

Sports, Recreation & Tourism
Leisure Centre Facilities
– Muswellbrook Shire Council, N.S.W.

Tourist Information Centre
– Scone Shire Council, N.S.W.

Sports Fields & Stan Thiess Centre
– Muswellbrook Shire Council, N.S.W.

Tourist Information Centre
– Macarthur County Tourist Association, N.S.W.

Bay Village on Hastings St, Noosa Heads, Queensland

Retail
Shopping Complex, Richmond, N.S.W.

Regional Shopping Complex, Muswellbrook, N.S.W.

Shopping Complex, Fairfield, N.S.W.

Davids Restaurant, Parramatta, N.S.W.

History
John Nicholas & Partners Pty. Limited commenced
practice in 1974, and since its inception has serviced
a broad spectrum of clients, ranging from State and
Local Government Instrumentalities to Development
Enterprises.

On each commission a Partner is personally involved so
as to ensure that from the initial Schematic Design phase
through to the final completion phase, the project time
and cost objectives are monitored, managed and controlled.

In order to achieve a high design standard whilst still
maintaining optimal cost and time effectiveness, the
firm places strong emphasis on ensuring that the design
philosophy and construction techniques are compatible
and appropriate to the particular project.

The firm is conversant with the many varied methods
of building procurement used by today's building owners
and developers and offers a scope of services that is
innovative and flexible and suited to the particular role
and services required.

11-13 William Street Tower Development

St George's Square Office Tower Development

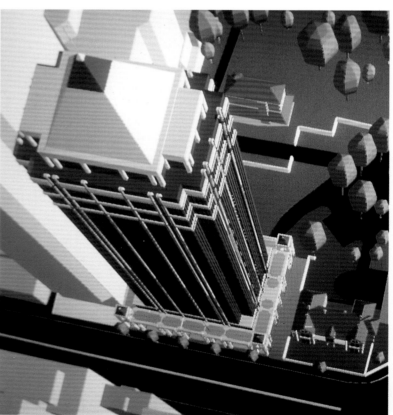

Computer Generated Perspective – St George's Square Office Tower Development

OLDHAM BOAS EDNIE-BROWN
Architects and Planners

Directors
Peter Arney F.R.A.I.A. F.R.A.P.I.
Tony Ednie-Brown F.R.A.I.A.
Lance Burton F.R.A.I.A.
Warren Jones F.R.A.I.A.
Neill Gardiner B.Arch., A.R.A.I.A.
Douglas Stafford A.A.S.A. C.P.A.
Ian Howell A.R.A.I.A.

Associate Directors
Peter Garvey A.R.A.I.A.
Ken Musto A.R.A.I.A.
Christopher Williams F.R.A.I.A.
Michael Zurzolo B.Arch. (Hons), A.R.A.I.A.

Consultants
Sydney Musto F.R.A.I.A.
Max Bevilaqua F.R.A.I.A. A.A.I.U.

Established
1896

Address
39 Labouchere Road
South Perth, W.A. 6151

Telephone
(09) 367 7766

Telex
93820

Facsimile
(09) 367 7976

Number of Employees
55

Value of Commissions
Currently involved in works in excess of
$150M

Project Types
Office Developments
Retail
Hotels and Residential
Government and Local Government
Industrial
Medical, Laboratories and Special Care
Educational
Planning, Environment and Tourist
Development

Other Disciplines
Research & Planning
Interior Design
Urban Planning
Landscape Design
Facilities Planning

Design Philosophy
To design buildings that achieve the goals of the client, with significant financial appreciation through excellence in design.

Applied Technology
The integration within the practice of computer technology and expertise comprising:
Rucaps Computer-Aided Design and Documentation
Computer-Aided Presentation, Natspec, Contract Management.
Computer Link-up to Consultants and Clients

The Future
A conviction to growth with increased technology, superior service to clients, and the design of high-quality buildings.

Current and Recent Projects
Commercial
St George's Square, Perth
11-13 William St Tower, Perth
London House, Perth
Australia Bank, Perth
Perpetual Trustees, Perth
Commonwealth Offices, Fremantle RAIA Award Commendation 1987
Capita Centre Stages I & II, Perth

Retail
London House, Perth
Centreways Arcade, Perth
Mirrabooka Shopping Centre
Kalgoorlie Markets and G J Coles Complex
Casuarina Shopping Centre, Darwin

Hotels and Residential
Parmelia Hilton Hotel, Perth
Roebuck Bay Hotel, Broome
Ocean Village, Perth
Strathearn Apartments, Perth

Government and Local Government
51st Supply Battalion Guildford
Airforce Base Derby
Perth Technical College Stages II & III
Roebourne Regional Prison
Broome Shire Council
Kalgoorlie Town Council
Perth City Council
City of Fremantle
City of Cockburn

Industrial
Bond Brewing Complex, Perth
Power Stations for SEC WA, Bunbury, Muja & Kwinana
Australian Airlines Services Buildings, Perth
Swan Brewery, Canning Plant, Perth

Medical Laboratories and Special Care
St John of God, Perth
Little Sisters of the Poor, Randwick N.S.W. and Perth
Kaleeya Hospital, Perth
Extensive State Government District Hospitals

Education
Lumen Christi College Perth Stages I, II & III
St Hilda's Anglican School for Girls (Inc)
Presbyterian Ladies College
Murdoch University West Academic II
Trinity College

Planning Environmental & Tourist Development
Melville City Council Regional Study
Shire of Mandurah – Marina Study
West Kambalda – New Townsite
Broome Resort Developments
Wildlife Park, Broome

1 St. George Building Society Ltd Head Office, Kogarah

2 AMP Place, Comalco Place, Central Plaza I, Brisbane skyline

3 Hyatt Hotel, Melbourne

4 Exchange Centre, Sydney

5 State Bank, Sydney

6 Harrington Park, N.S.W. Structure Plan

7 Maritime Services Board, Sydney

8 National Australia Bank House, Sydney

9 Central Plaza I, Brisbane

10 Mater Public Hospital, South Brisbane

11 Berry Street, North Sydney

12 Westpac Tower, Sydney

PEDDLE THORP PARTNERSHIPS IN AUSTRALIA
Architects Planners Designers

Partners
Graham M. Thorp M.C., M.Arch, F.R.A.I.A., F.R.I.B.A.
James F. Allchin F.R.A.I.A., A.R.I.B.A.
Peter Brook M.Arch (Urban Design), B.Arch.
Ron Burgess Dip.Arch., A.R.A.I.A.
Graham Ellwood Dip.Arch., A.R.A.I.A.
Glynne Fletcher A.R.I.B.A., A.R.A.I.A.
Peter G. Harvey B.Arch., F.R.A.I.A.
John Laird Dip.Arch., F.R.A.I.A.
James Learmonth B.Arch., Dip.TRP, F.R.A.I.A., R.I.B.A., H.K.I.A., H.K.I.P.
Rodney J. Pegus F.R.A.I.A., M.R.A.P.I.
Anthony Rossi B.Arch
Peter J. Watt B.Arch., F.R.A.I.A., R.I.B.A.
Mervyn Willoughby-Thomas F.R.A.I.A., F.I. Arb A., A.R.I.B.A.

Partnerships in Australia

Peddle Thorp & Walker
Architects, Planners
A.M.P. Centre
50 Bridge Street
Sydney, N.S.W. 2000
Telephone
(02) 232 5877
Facsimile
(02) 221 4139

Pegus & Peddle Thorp Pty Ltd
Urban Design Consultants
A.M.P. Centre
50 Bridge Street
Sydney, N.S.W. 2000
Telephone
(02) 232 5877
Facsimile
(02) 221 4139

David Hicks Peddle Thorp
Interior Design Consultants
56 Young Street
Sydney, N.S.W. 2000
Telephone
(02) 232 5100
Facsimile
(02) 233 4225

Peddle Thorp & Learmonth
Architects, Designers & Planners
394 Collins Street
Melbourne, Vic. 3000
Telephone
(03) 602 4766
Facsimile
(03) 670 4981

Peddle Thorp and Harvey Pty Ltd
Architects, Designers, Planners
Level 24
12 Creek Street
Brisbane, Qld 4000
Telephone
(07) 221 6249
Facsimile
(07) 229 3146

Peddle Thorp & Fletcher
Architects & Health Facility Planners
Level 24
12 Creek Street
Brisbane, Qld 4000
Telephone
(07) 221 6249
Facsimile
(07) 229 3146

Peddle Thorp & Harvey Pty Ltd
Architects, Planners
Centre Point Building
3290 Gold Coast Highway
Surfers Paradise, Qld 4217
Telephone
(075) 38 7122

Peddle Thorp & Willoughby-Thomas
Architects, Planners
10th Floor
Canberra House
Marcus Clarke Street
Canberra, A.C.T. 2601
Telephone
(062) 47 8428
Facsimile
(062) 57 2160

International Partnerships

Peddle Thorp & Aitken
Architects and Planners
Air New Zealand House
1 Queen Street
Auckland, 1 New Zealand
Telephone
79 9405
Facsimile
39 8443

Peddle Thorp & Montgomery
Architects and Planners
Local Government Building
Lambton Quay
Wellington, New Zealand
Telephone
721 666
Facsimile
781 606

Peddle Thorp Chapman Taylor
Architects and Planning Consultants
96 Kensington High Street
London W8 4SG U.K.
Telephone
01 938 3333
Facsimile
01 937 1391

Alfred Wong Peddle Thorp
Architects and Planning Consultants
111 North Bridge Road
12 02 Peninsula Plaza
Singapore, 0617
Telephone
337 6777
Facsimile
339 6956

Antara Alfred Wong Peddle Thorp
Architects, Engineers & Planning Consultants
6th Floor
Wisma Stephens
88 Jalan Raja Chulan
Kuala Lumpur, 05-12, Malaysia
Telephone
03 242 7566

P. T. Parama Consultants
Architects, Engineers, Planners
Jl. Asia Afrika No. 9A
Senayan
Jakarta, Indonesia
Telephone
58 1003-4
Facsimile
021 58 7708

Peddle Thorp & Harvey Pty Ltd
Architects, Planners
P.N.G. Development Bank Building
Somare Circuit
Waigani, Port Moresby
P.N.G.
Telephone
25 2182

Liang Peddle Thorp Architects & Planners Ltd.
2/F, New Henry House
10 Ice House Street
Central Hong Kong
Telephone
5-21 1199
Facsimile
5-8100195

Current and Recent Projects
Commercial, Office, Banking, Retail

Project	Value
State Bank Centre, Martin Place, Sydney — The State Bank of New South Wales	$115M
National Australia Bank House, George Street, Sydney AMP/NAB	$65M
St. George Head Office, Kogarah — Danaby Pty Ltd	$80M
530 Collins Street, Melbourne — ANZ Bank	$150M
Viewpoint, King Georges & Forest Roads, Hurstville — Adaston Pty Ltd	$16M
Central Plaza 1 & 2, Creek & Queen Streets, Brisbane — Avarton Pty Ltd	$190M
Gateway Plaza, Circular Quay, Sydney — National Mutual	$120M
MBF Centre, Bathurst Street, Sydney — Medical Benefit Fund of Australia	$25M
Maritime Centre, Kent Street, Sydney — Leighton Properties	$130M
Office Development, 1 O'Connell Street, Sydney — Northbourne Developments	$100M
Westpac Plaza, George Street, Sydney — CBA Properties Pty Ltd	$40M

Health Planning, Hospital

Project	Value
Mater Public Hospital, Mater Hill, Qld — Order of the Sisters of Mercy	$45M
Allamanda Private Hospital, Southport, Qld — Sukkah (Qld) Pty Ltd	$4.5M

Resort Development, Hotels

Project	Value
Hyatt Hotel, Collins Street, Melbourne — Lustig & Moar	$150M
Holiday City, Surfers Paradise, Qld — Leisure Developments (Qld) Pty Ltd	$59M
Sheraton Hotel, Symonds Street, Auckland, New Zealand	

Community, Recreational

Project	Value
National Tennis Centre, Melbourne — N.T.C. Trust	$55M

Industrial, Laboratories

Project	Value
Wine Bottling Plant, Chullora — McWilliams Wines	$7.5M
Repair & Overhaul Shop Complex and the Central Store Buildings, Mascot — Qantas Airways Limited	
RAAF Maintenance Hangar, Richmond — Department of Housing & Construction	$12M
RAAF 481 Squadron Maintenance Facility, Williamstown — Department of Housing & Construction	$20M
Tooths/Carlton Brewery, Broadway, Sydney	$30M

Residential, Houses, Public Housing etc
Staff Training College, St. Ives Commonwealth Bank
Riverpark Gardens, Liverpool Land Equity Group

Urban and Regional Planning
Rezoning Study of Northern Section Harrington Park
Rezoning Study, Campbelltown
Birkenhead Point Master Plan, Drummoyne
Rezoning of Pulpit Point, Hunters Hill
Land use study for air space development over Sydney Terminal Site for State Rail Authority

Authorities and Government

Project	Value
SEQEB Sub-Station South East Queensland Electricity Board	
Australia Post Office Centre, Brisbane — Department of Housing & Construction	$16M
Civic Centre, Moss Vale Wingecarribee Shire Council	
Australian Government Centre, Hobart — Department of Housing & Construction	
Woolloongabba Telecommunications Centre, Brisbane — Department of Housing & Construction	$19M
Peel Cunningham County Council, Head Office, Tamworth	

Peddle Thorp Partnerships
One of the largest architectural firms in Australia. Peddle Thorp Partnerships is an international organisation of architects and planners, with offices throughout Australia, New Zealand and Asia.

The Peddle Thorp Partnership provides clients with total capability in architecture, design and planning. Creativity in design is achieved through an architect's understanding of the technical requirements of buildings, of form, of planning, and through a sensitivity to the environment and a deep commitment to meeting customer requirements.

History
The practice was started in 1889 by James Peddle, and in its early days concentrated mainly on residential buildings – many of which are still in use today. In 1910, Samuel George Thorp became a partner in the firm. His achievements ranged from designing apartment blocks and office buildings to town planning. The third partner, W. Ernest Walker, who specialised in industrial projects, joined the firm in 1924.

The Peddle Thorp Partnership has been a leader in the profession since its early days. The firm won the first Sulman Prize for Science House in Sydney, and in 1938 won the biggest competition in Australia up to that time, for the Sydney Law Courts in Macquarie St, Sydney, a project which even then cost seven million pounds.

During the building boom of the 1960's, Peddle Thorp Partnerships continued to grow and expand, taking Sydney into a new era when it built the first modern office block in 1962 – The AMP Building in Sydney Cove.

Today the network of Peddle Thorp Partnerships is more than 500 people strong, with offices in Brisbane, Melbourne, Hong Kong, Auckland, Wellington, Canberra, Jakarta, Kuala Lumpur, Singapore, Port Moresby and London, as well as Sydney.

Recent Landmarks
The Peddle Thorp Partnership has been directly responsible for the design and construction of numerous multi-storeyed buildings and large scale projects throughout Australia and overseas.

In Australia the award winning National Australia Bank House in George Street and the State Bank Centre in Martin Place are just two of Sydney's landmarks designed by Peddle Thorp Partnerships.

Since the 1960's over 80 major office buildings throughout Australia, New Zealand and South-East Asia have been designed by the firm, with well over thirty major office buildings in the Sydney central business district alone.

Peddle Thorp Partnerships also have a solid reputation for the design and planning of major hospitals and health care centres, industrial facilities, retail establishments and residential buildings.

In Wellington, New Zealand, Peddle Thorp Partnerships have submitted a design proposal for a mammoth $500M redevelopment project covering more than 5.3 hectares in the city's business centre.

Services and Staff Resources
The firm's staff of over sixty qualified architects in Sydney alone, pride themselves on producing 'complete' buildings, through the co-ordination of a diverse range of skills. As well as architectural and planning, these skills include mechanical and electrical engineering, hydraulics, fire protection and prevention, acoustics, landscaping, wind analysis, and quantity surveying and programming.

In response to clients' requests, a Special Projects Group was set up recently to make available the firm's diverse range of architectural skills and services for smaller projects.

Technology, Research & Development
Peddle Thorp Partnerships make extensive use of computer-based technology, and have one of the most up-to-date CADD systems in the world.

The firm's advanced contract administration system provides clients with an accurate appraisal of any proposed development, allowing specific planning and design alternatives to be quickly evaluated. Architectural models are made in the firm's own model shop.

Local and international technical advances are evaluated by Peddle Thorp Partnerships to incorporate the latest materials and methods into projects, with prototypes thoroughly tested before use.

Conclusion Peddle Thorp Partnerships' resources extend beyond each individual office to form a network of local and international expertise. The Partnership's experience and organisational capability, acquired over nearly a century of practice, enable it to offer a comprehensive and dependable service to all its clients.

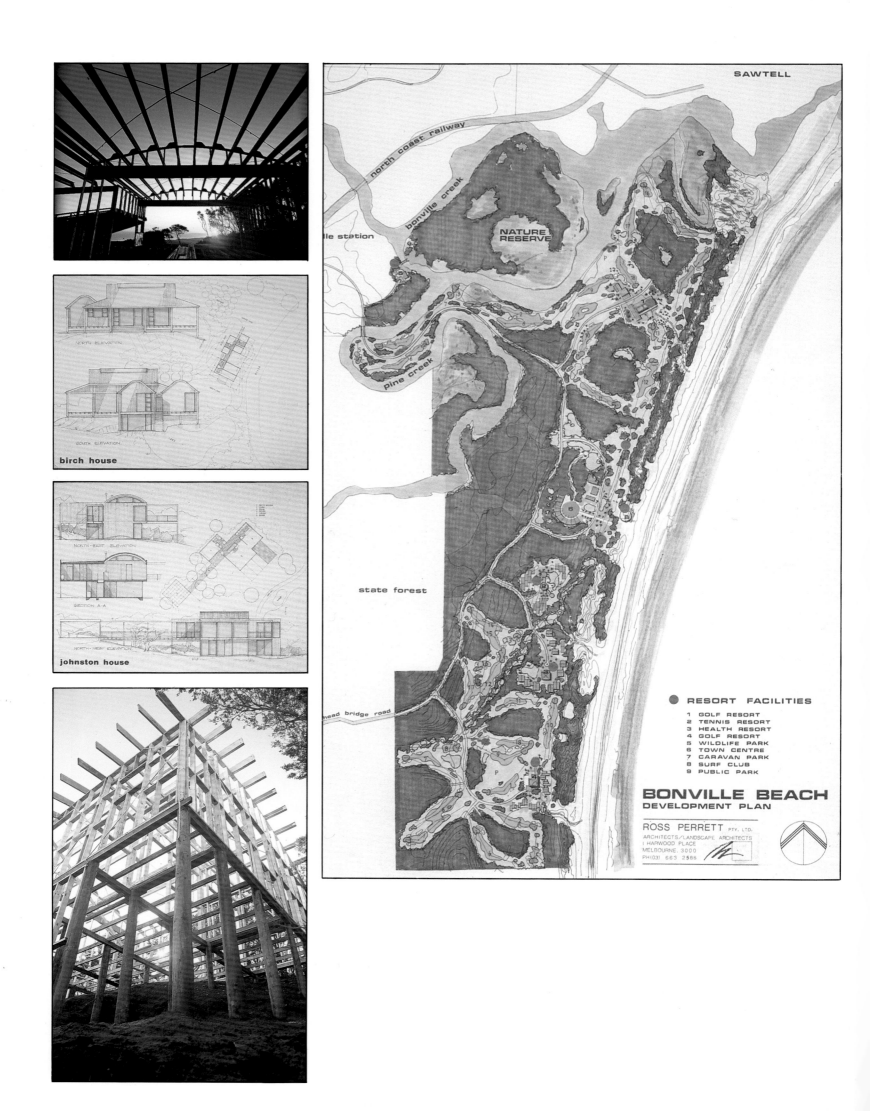

birch house

johnston house

● RESORT FACILITIES

1 GOLF RESORT
2 TENNIS RESORT
3 HEALTH RESORT
4 GOLF RESORT
5 WILDLIFE PARK
6 TOWN CENTRE
7 CARAVAN PARK
8 SURF CLUB
9 PUBLIC PARK

BONVILLE BEACH
DEVELOPMENT PLAN

ROSS PERRETT PTY. LTD.
ARCHITECTS/LANDSCAPE ARCHITECTS
1 HARWOOD PLACE
MELBOURNE, 3000
PH(03) 663 2588

SAWTELL

north coast railway

bonville creek

NATURE
RESERVE

pine creek

state forest

head bridge road

ROSS PERRETT PTY LTD

Directors
Ross Perrett A.R.A.I.A, A.A.I.L.A.
Victor Rule
Helen Perrett

Established
1984

Address
1 Harwood Place
Melbourne, Vic. 3000

Telephone
(03) 663 2588

Number of Employees
8

Project Types
Residential
Land Development
Educational
Recreational
Industrial

Other Disciplines
Landscape Architecture
Site Planning
Golf Course Design
Land Development

Persons to Contact
Ross Perrett
Ann Oldham

(left to right) Victor Rule, Les Watts, Ann Oldham, Sally Freeland, Y.C. Kan, Ross Perrett, Pat Ness, Danielle Plant

History and Philosophy

In 1984 Ross Perrett established the firm in recognition of the need for a practice that married the professional disciplines of architecture and landscape architecture – a practice committed to the principle that the environment and the built form are interwoven aesthetically and functionally.

The design group includes Architects, Landscape Architects, Site Planners and support staff who share an environmental awareness and a commitment to excellence in design.

An increasingly significant component of our work is large scale site planning involving the resolution of complex environmental, functional, aesthetic and economic factors. Here the interface between architecture and the landscape is critical.

The architectural solution emerges from an informed and sympathetic response to the client's needs, the building's function and its environmental context. Particular attention is given to the integration of internal and external space.

Our clients are from both the private and public sectors and projects range in scale from individual house sites to large residential, recreational and industrial developments.

Current and Recent Projects

Residential
Private Houses
Victoria & New South Wales

Land Development
Howqua Resort, Lake Eildon
Resort and Residential Site Planning

Bonville Beach, N.S.W.
Resort and Residential Site Planning and Golf Course Architecture

National Golf and Country Club, Cape Schanck
Resort and Residential Site Planning

Ministry of Housing, Burwood
Residential Site Planning

Educational
Deakin University, Waurn Ponds
Landscape Master Plan

Carey Grammar, Donvale
Landscape Master Plan

Swinburne TAFE, Hawthorn
Commons Area Landscaping

Recreational
Melbourne Country Club, Alphington
Architecture and Landscape Design

Promlee Resort, Barry's Beach
Golf Course Architecture

Hastings Development
Golf Course Architecture

Industrial
Croydon Technology Park, Croydon
Master Plan

1 Queensland Health Department Building

2 Arnott-Harper Pet Food Factory

3 The Brisbane Club Building

4 Civic Centre, Roma

5 Westpac Bank Chief Office, Brisbane

PERRY BLAND & PARTNERS PTY LTD
Architects and Town Planners

Directors (left to right)
N.C. Shrubsole ARAIA
T.A. Perry Dip. Arch. FRAIA
R.A. Bland B. Arch. FRAIA, MRAPI
P.J. Black Dip. Arch. ARAIA
L.W. McLennan Dip. Arch. ARAIA

Established
1864

Address
67 Lytton Road
East Brisbane, Qld 4169

Telephone
(07) 391 5600

Facsimile
(07) 891 5471

Project Types
Commercial
Office Buildings,
Insurance Company Offices, Banks

Branch Offices
Banks, Automobile Associations,
Societies, Insurance Offices

Industrial
Airline Facilities, Factories, Port Facilities

Community
Civic Centres, Libraries,
Sporting & Service Clubs,
Colleges and Schools, Courts of Law

Health
Hospitals, Clinics, Nursing Homes,
Housing for Aged

Resort Development
Hotels, Club Buildings

Residential
Homes, Home Units, Hostels

Educational
Seven Hills College
of Advanced Education

Interiors
Hotels, Offices, Residential

Town Planning
Town & Shire Planning

Other Disciplines
Town Planners registered in
the State of Queensland
Registered Builders
Interior Designers
Building Restoration Consultants

Number of Employees
20

Chronology of Practice
Founded by John Richard Hall
b. Chester-le-Flats, Eng. 1835, d. Brisbane 1883
Architect, Civil Engineer & Building Surveyor

1864-1866 John Hall
1866-1867 Chambers & Hall
1868-1882 John Hall
1882-1896 John Hall & Son
1896-1916 F.R. Hall & Dods
1916-1923 F.R. Hall
1923-1927 F.R. Hall & W.A. Devereux
1927-1929 F.R. Hall
1930-1939 F.R. Hall & H.M. Cook
1939-1962 Cook & Kerrison
1962-1978 Cook & Kerrison and Partners
1978-1981 Perry Bland Kennerson
          Loynes Pty Ltd
1981-1987 Perry Bland Kennerson Pty Ltd
1987-   Perry Bland & Partners Pty Ltd

Current and Recent Projects
Commercial
Westpac Bank – Chief Office, Brisbane

Brisbane Club Building

Queensland Health Department Building,
Twin Tower, Brisbane

Suncorp Plaza Building, Townsville

Offices – Moreton Tug & Barge Co. Pty Ltd

Administrative Office – Patrick Terminal
Fisherman Islands

Westpac E.D.P. Centre, Brisbane

Branch Offices
Commonwealth Banks
various Queensland areas

Westpac Banks
various Queensland areas

Suncorp Insurance and Finance, Queensland

Royal Automobile Club of Queensland
various Queensland areas

Medical Benefits Fund of Australia
various Queensland Branch Offices

Industrial
Tug Base, Whyte Island, Brisbane

Australian Airlines Support Facilities,
Cargo, Ground Equipment Maintenance,
Catering and Supply, Brisbane Airport

Arnott Harper Pty Ltd, Pet Food Factory, Brisbane

Arnott Morrow Biscuit Factory, Brisbane

Community
Shire Administrative Offices, Monto

Civic Centre, Roma

Courts of Law, Southport

Courts of Law, Beenleigh

Civic Centre, Laidley

Health
Wesley Private Hospital, Brisbane

New Medical Ward Block, Gladstone Hospital

Wongaburra Private Hospital, Beaudesert

Uniting Church Home for the Aged, Chermside

Freemasons Hospital, Sandgate, Brisbane

Medical Centre, Holland Park

Resort Development
Townsville International Hotel

Royal Queensland Yacht Squadron,
Additions, Manly, Brisbane

Mooloolaba Hotel, Refurbishment

Educational
Seven Hills College of Advanced Education, Brisbane

Interiors
Mayfair Crest International Hotel, Brisbane

Australian Airlines Guest Lounge, Rockhampton Airport

Australian Airlines, Guest Lounge and Offices,
Townsville International Airport

Australian Airlines, City Office, Townsville

Town Planning
Fitzroy Shire

Philosophy
A 123 year record of professional success and
experience, balanced with a progressive sense
of modernity and positive dedication – so vital
in today's volatile market place.

Our long standing roots have as their base,
the fundamental principles of Architecture:
Total Professionalism
Social Awareness
Environmental Responsibility
Client Service
Sound Business Practice
Positive Results

The diversity and collective experience of our team
provides a fully disciplined approach to any architectural
or allied project. Our highly creative talents span the
full range of applications, from town planning to interior
design.

Any project, large or small, is only successful when
it has been completed to the satisfaction of all parties
involved. That means the physical implementation
of that concept must be as meticulous as the initial
planning. This is the reason for Perry Bland & Partners'
distinguished track record – all our projects are well
conceptualized and soundly implemented.

To ensure that this philosophy is effective in every case,
we set stringent parameters: generate yield on clients'
capital expenditure; maintain architectural integrity;
provide effective and efficient interior design; meet
statutory authority requirements; satisfy economic
targets; accept environmental responsibility; and ensure
completion is truly complete.

The achievements of these results is a combination of
the following working disciplines.

Client Liaison
We believe this is a vitally important relationship.
It must be honest, professional, trusting and mutually
rewarding.

Preparation of the Brief
This function may take many forms and we are happy
to help in all aspects. Whether it's initial research,
preparation in conjunction with the client, or full
discussion and agreement of a prepared brief, Perry
Bland & Partners will ensure that the final commissioning document is complete in every detail.

Design
The ultimate design must obviously reflect the
objectives and requirements agreed in the brief.
It must be realistic, practical and on budget,
while still providing a high aesthetic end-result.

The Environment
We maintain a high level of dedication to ensure that
the environment, regardless of situation, is respected
and where possible, improved by the project at hand.

Lifestyle, traffic movement, access, public usage and
facilities are of course all carefully considered as an
integral part of the total plan.

Maintenance
Elimination of all unnecessary expense is a keystone to
Perry Bland & Partners' enduring practice. Maintenance
outlay must be kept to a minimum and all energy
resources must be maximized to provide the most
efficient, cost effective systems available.

Flexibility
The measure of good design is its ability to adapt.
Our planning when possible allows for flexibility of use
and the inevitable changes in user patterns.

Capital Yield
Maximum yield on expenditure for minimum capital
cost – a simple formula applied to every project, but one
which we hope has allowed our clients to prosper and
develop. This success has meant repeat business which
is the basis of our long history of practice.

Involvement
Our very nature will not allow us to be anything
but fully involved. Our client link is vital, selected
contractors must pass the most stringent scrutiny,
our control is rigid, and our contact with statutory
authorities is straight and thorough.

All these principles are not just theories, they represent
our fundamental operating procedures to ensure total
client satisfaction.

Services
Services rendered by the practice include:
The production or the assistance in production of
preliminary and final briefing; Planning activities in all
aspects, including regional, town, local and specifically
oriented areas; Research in all aspects of a commission,
and updating of previously fully studied activities;
The preparation of conceptual designs, together with
feasibility, viability, design and management studies;
The design and design development of all facets of
architecture; Advice on contract selection and
procedures; Tender and contract documentation;
Continuous cost control; Administration and management of construction services; The offer of services to
Engineering and other disciplines as consultants in a
secondary capacity where the alternate disciplines form
the major area of professional input and;
Consulting services to Developer/Builder companies and
the like where the Developer executes work on its own
behalf for third party sale or lease.

PETER HUNT ARCHITECT

1

2

3

4

5

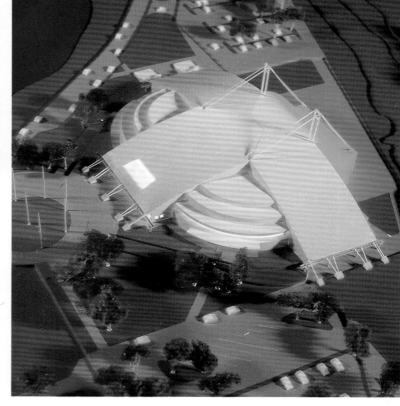

6

7

8

9

PETER HUNT PTY LTD
Architect

Principal
Peter Hunt A.A.P.T.C. F.R.A.I.A.

Directors
Geoff Clough A.R.A.I.A.
Ron Edenburg A.A.W.A.I.T. A.R.A.I.A.
Con Lampropoulos A.A.W.A.I.T. A.R.A.I.A.

Established
Perth
1970
Sydney
1982

Addresses
Perth
8 Colin Grove
West Perth, W.A. 6005

Telephone
(09) 322 6033

Facsimile
(09) 324 1691

Sydney
Suite 15
283 Penshurst Street
Willoughby, N.S.W. 2068

Telephone
(02) 407 1736

Facsimile
(02) 406 4359

Number of Employees
20

Project Types
Commercial/Retail
Community/Recreational
Educational
Residential
Religious
Institutional

Ron Edenburg, Con Lampropoulos, Peter Hunt, Geoff Clough

History and Design Philosophy

Peter Hunt Architect has grown from a Perth based architectural practice into an interstate organisation with a client base in Sydney, Melbourne, Hobart and Adelaide.

The firm's design philosophy being client orientated, coupled with a proven record of completing challenging projects within tight time and cost constraints, has led to this growth.

Peter Hunt, as principal of the practice, demands a high level of performance and enthusiasm from his dynamic team ensuring repeat commissions from this growing number of valued clients.

Every project the firm undertakes is treated as a singular design exercise specific to each client's needs and aspirations, technically implemented to ensure a functional and satisfying architectural solution. Client participation is considered essential in achieving this primary objective.

Although design innovation and flair are fundamental skills of this practice, Peter Hunt's multi-disciplinary team has gathered a resource of expertise encompassing the broadest parameters for the built environment. This enables Peter Hunt Architect to provide professional services in research, feasibility studies, design and planning, interior design, project documentation, administration and project management.

Current and Recent Projects
Commercial: Office/Retail
Australian Fixed Trust High Rise Office Redevelopment, St. George's Terrace, Perth, W.A.

Commercial Union Office Building, La Trobe Street, Melbourne, Vic. in collaboration with Daryl Jackson Pty. Ltd.

Chatswood Offices (Monitor Money), Pacific Highway, Sydney, N.S.W.

Frenchs Forest Business Park, Warringah Road, Sydney, N.S.W.

Techway Office Building Rodborough Road, Frenchs Forest, Sydney, N.S.W.

Solomons Commercial Developments, Nunawading, Melbourne, Vic.; Victoria Park, Perth, W.A.; Gouger Street, Adelaide, S.A.

National Australia Bank Premises, W.A.

Civil Servants Association Office Building, Hay Street, Perth, W.A.

Community/Recreational
Derwent Entertainment Centre, Hobart, Tas. in collaboration with Blythe Yeung & Menzies.

Western Australian Sports Centre ('Superdrome'), Graylands, W.A. in collaboration with Cann Architects and Daryl Jackson Pty. Ltd.

Indoor State Equestrian Centre, Brigadoon, W.A.

Indoor Aquatic and Recreational Centre, Mandurah, W.A.

Busselton Beach Timeshare Resort, Busselton, W.A.

Kwinana Recreation Centre, Kwinana, W.A.

Educational
Western Australian International College, Joondalup, W.A.

Mandurah High School, Mandurah, W.A.

All Saints College, Bullcreek, W.A. in collaboration with Howlett & Bailey Architects.

St Josephs College, Albany, W.A.

Mercedes College, Perth, W.A.

Mercy College, Koondoola, W.A.

Residential
National Australia Bank Staff Quarters, Wickham, W.A.

Group Housing for Hamersley Iron at Dampier, Paraburdoo and Tom Price, W.A.

Individual houses for specific clients.

Religious
Roman Catholic Churches, Newman, South Hedland, Karratha and Wickham, W.A.

Anglican Church, Greenwood, W.A.

Institutional
Retirement resident funded units and nursing home, Ray Village, Busselton, W.A.

Kwinana Nursing Home and Hostel, Kwinana, W.A.

1 *Australian Fixed Trusts High Rise Office Redevelopment, Perth, W.A.*

2 *Frenchs Forest Business Park, Warringah Road, Sydney, N.S.W.*

3 *National Australia Bank, Cottesloe, W.A.*

4 *Ray Village, Busselton, W.A.*

5 *Chatswood Offices (Monitor Money), Pacific Highway, Sydney, N.S.W.*

6 *Commercial Union Office Building, La Trobe Street, Melbourne, Vic.*

7 *Western Australian Sports Centre ('Superdrome') Graylands, W.A. (Pool Hall)*

8 *Derwent Entertainment Centre, Hobart, Tas.*

9 *Western Australian Sports Centre ('Superdrome') Graylands, W.A.*

PHILIP FOLLENT ARCHITECT

Director
Philip Follent B.Arch ARAIA

Associate
Greg Mulheran Dip. Arch ARAIA

Established
1982

Address
38 Durran Street
Tugun, Qld 4224

Telephone
(075) 344 873

Facsimile
(075) 345 316

Number of Employees
3

Project Types	Percentage
Commercial	15%
Governmental	10%
Educational	5%
Recreational	25%
Residential	45%

Other Disciplines
Specialist Playground &
Play Equipment Design,
Landscape & Interior Design

Person to Contact
Philip Follent
Greg Mulheran

History

The Practice was established by Philip Follent in 1982 after leaving the Gold Coast Firm known as the Davis Heather Group. Philip's earlier architectural experience was gained in the Brisbane office of James Birrell Architect & Town Planner and later at Geoffrey Pie Architects, Planners Pty Ltd.

The small practice has earned an enviable reputation within the profession as one which consistently devotes time and energy to design solutions and details that are fresh and ingenious.

The Architectural Profession has indeed acknowledged the practice with Architectural Awards for very diverse projects.

The office is run as a design studio with each project being directly under the design control of Philip Follent.

The range of projects vary considerably and each design solution is tailored to suit the needs of site and the client. Consequently no one visual style is in evidence in the variety of work produced by the practice. More important is the observation that planning and detailing have been executed with a vital and enthusiastic commitment.

The human involvement with each project is supplemented with modern electronic tools of architecture and it is through this availability of advanced technology that the practice is able to take on larger scale projects and in some cases harness the skills and man-power of architectural colleagues where specific projects so demand.

The practice is committed to maintaining a small scale operation in order to retain a close involvement with clients and also to enhance the practice's efficient operation.

Involvement with building companies enables Philip Follent Architects to offer a Design and Construct package on specific projects. This service along with the ability to link up with other skills and expertise enables the office to vary its scale of projects from the small domestic types to larger commercial and high rise work.

Every project is undertaken with care and respect for client and environment and the practice continues to strive for design solutions that are not only economically and environmentally responsible but also capable of stirring and delighting all those who come in contact with the built result.

Prizes & Awards

1984
RAIA Qld. House of Year Award.
RAIA Qld. Gold Coast Division, Citation. (Housing)
RAIA National Awards Finalist, Robin Boyd Award. (Housing)

1986
RAIA Qld. Gold Coast Division, Citation – Currumbin Sanctuary Playpark. (Recreational)

1987
RAIA/MONIER DESIGN COMMISSION – Expression of Interest – Finalist. (Site Development).
RAIA/MONIER DESIGN COMMISSION – Australian House Design – Winner.

PhilipFollent

ARCHITECT

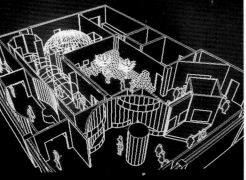

1 'The Pines' Shopping Centre, Elanora, Qld.

2 Workers Compensation Building, Brisbane

3 'Garden Square', Mt. Gravatt, Brisbane

4 TVO, Channel O, Expo 88 Studio

5 Regent Theatre, Brisbane

6 'Univations', Expo 88 (Combined Universities)

POWELL, DODS AND THORPE
Architects

Partners (left to right)
Robin E. Dods F.R.A.I.A.
Stewart T. Thorpe F.R.A.I.A.

Frederick N. Winter F.R.A.I.A.
Graham C. Hobbs F.R.A.I.A.
John H. Blake F.R.A.I.A.

Kenneth L. Alexander A.R.A.I.A.
David J. Matthews A.R.A.I.A.
John McL. Stirling A.R.A.I.A.
Michael M. Strazds A.R.A.I.A.

Established
1938

Address
24 McDougall Street
Milton, Qld 4064

Telephone
(07) 369 1222

Facsimile
(07) 368 2832

Number of Employees
20

Project Types
Commercial
Office Developments
Cinemas
Medical Facilities
Television Stations
Retail/Shopping Centres
Hotels
Specialty Shop Fitouts

Education/Recreation
Schools
Library, Resource Centres
Laboratories
Swimming Pools
Gymnasiums
Residential Accommodation
Sports Fields/Bowls Greens

Residential

Industrial

Recycling/Restoration

Interiors

Other Disciplines
'In-house' computer aided drafting
   and graphic drawing facility
Research, Planning and Feasibilities
Environmental and Economic Studies
Authority Approvals
Project Programming,
   Analysis and Management
Construction Research
Submissions for Grants and Fundraising
Historic Research
Maintenance Programming
Project Inspections and Reports

Persons to Contact
Fred Winter
Graham Hobbs
John Blake

Current and Recent Projects
Commercial
420 George Street, Brisbane
National Australia Bank
(In association with Hassell and Partners)

270-280 Adelaide Street, Brisbane
F.A. Pidgeon & Son Pty. Ltd.

Queensland Police Headquarters
Makerston Street, Brisbane

'Garden Square', Upper Mt. Gravatt
(Coles Myer Queensland State Office)
F.A. Pidgeon & Son Pty. Ltd.

Various Commercial Premises
A.M.P. Society
Australia and New Zealand Banking Group
Colonial Mutual Life Association Limited
National Australia Bank
Westpac Banking Corporation

Regent Theatre Reconstruction
The Mayne Estates and Hoyts Theatres Limited

Albert Cinemas Redevelopment Proposals
Greater Union Organisation

Television Studios, Mount Coot-tha
Universal Telecasters Limited (Channel O)

Television Studios, Expo 88
Universal Telecasters Limited (Channel O)

'Pacific Fair' Extensions, 1982
A.M.P. Society

'Tweed Mall' Refurbishment
A.M.P. Society

'Redbank Plaza' Documentation
Jennings Industries Limited
(In association with Buchan Laird & Bawden)

'The Pines' Shopping Centre, Elanora
Carringbush Pty. Ltd.

'Garden City' Shopping Centre
Tenancy Co-ordination

Super K-Mart Conversion, Chermside
Coles Myer Ltd.

Bob Jane T-MARTS

Various Shopping Centres
A.M.P. Society
Coles Myer Ltd.
Trevor Davies and Associates
Jennings Industries Limited
F.A. Pidgeon & Son Pty. Ltd.
Restifa and Partners
Stockland Trust

'Brisbane City Travelodge'
Brisbane Transit Centre
Pidgeon/Southern Pacific Hotels

Site Agency Services – Expo 88
I.B.M. Pavilion
French Pavilion
(In association with Span Design Group)
Idemitsu Exhibition

Education/Recreation
S. Margaret's School
Sisters of the Society of the Sacred Advent

The Toowoomba Grammar School
Library and Resources Centre
(In association with Durak, Brammer and Stekhoven)

University of Queensland Sports Association
Tennis Centre
Swimming Pool Restoration
Gymnasium and Sports Testing Centre

Queensland Police Youth Clubs
New Sports Centres

Queensland Gymnastics Association
New State Centre

Girls' Schools' Sports Association
New Sports Fields Complex

Industrial
New Industrial Centre, Acacia Ridge
Bond Corporation

Warehouse, Acacia Ridge
Coles Myer Ltd

CAD/CAM Centre, Mt. Gravatt
Department of Industry Development

Stewarts Warehouses

Recycling Restoration
'The Brisbane Arcade'
The Mayne Estates

'The Regent Theatre'
The Mayne Estate/Hoyts Theatres Limited

St. Paul's Presbyterian Church
St. Paul's Terrace

Fire Restoration – Dods' Chapel
Sisters of the Society of the Sacred Advent

Interiors
A.M.P. Society
Sales Offices' Fitouts

Telecom Australia Chief State Engineer
'Brisbane Transit Centre'

Coles Myer State Office – Upper Mt. Gravatt

Deloitte Haskins and Sells

Elders Lensworth Finance

Inspection Services
Australian Guarantee Corporation
Department of Industry Development

Our Office provides a complete range of Architectural
and Building Procurement Services to a diversified and
increasing Clientele which continues to require our
services on successive Projects.

Our success, over 50 years, continues to be in the
provision of a personalised quality service.

POWELL, DODS & THORPE
Professional Architecture

1 Zenith Centre, Chatswood N.S.W.

2 141 Walker Street, North Sydney

3 The Pavilion, 580 George Street, Sydney (Model)

4 110 Walker Street, North Sydney (New Head Office for Rice Daubney)

5 Charter Grove Commercial Complex, St Leonards, N.S.W. (Office Development)

6 Queen Victoria Building refurbishment, George Street, Sydney

RICE DAUBNEY
Architects

Corporate Board (left to right)
Kevin Rice B Arch (Hons) MBA LFRAIA ARIBA
Ross Gardner B Arch (Hons) ARAIA
John Daubney B Arch ARAIA Dip TCP

Operating Directors
Kevin Riggs B Arch (Hons)
John Rayner Dip Arch ARAIA ARIBA
Tim Alexander B Arch ARAIA
Rod Groom B Arch ARAIA

Tony Simmons Dip Arch ARAIA FRIBA
Tony Oliver Dip Tech (Arch) ARAIA
Paul Frischknecht Dip Arch ARAIA
Lewis Stenson B Arch ARAIA
Ian Parker B Arch FRAIA

Established
1976

Address
97 Pacific Highway
North Sydney, N.S.W. 2060

Telephone
(02) 929 0577

Facsimile
(02) 959 3015

Associated Offices
Rice Daubney
Level 1
Cnr Beach Road & Parnell Rise
Auckland 1, New Zealand

Telephone
(09) 37 8848

Facsimile
(09) 37 6600

Number of Employees
145

Project Types
Commercial/Office
Educational
Health
Hotel & Leisure
Retail
Medium Density Housing

Other Disciplines
Urban Planning
Interior Architecture
Building Diagnostics
Landscape Architects
Health Systems

Person to Contact
Sydney Ross Gardner
New Zealand Warren Dixon

Current and Recent Projects
Commercial Office Developments
Carringbush Tower and Pavilion,
George & Bathurst Streets Sydney, N.S.W.
for Carringbush Pty Ltd $90.0M

Zenith Centre, Pacific Highway, Chatswood, N.S.W.
for Zenith Development Corporation $90.0M

Office Building,
141 Walker Street, North Sydney, N.S.W.
for Public Authorities Superannuation Board $33.0M

The Interchange, Commercial/Retail Development
Chatswood, N.S.W. for Mirvac Pty Ltd $80.0M

Macquarie Tower, Office Development, Parramatta
for Girvan Corporation $20.0M

The Foreshore Abbotsford
for Jennings Industries Ltd $140.0M

The Capita Building and Chatswood Club
for Paynter Dixon Pty Ltd $13.0M

Office Development,
5-11 Wentworth Street, Parramatta
for Girvan Corporation $12.0M

Prince Albert Centre, Auckland
Office/Hotel/Retail Development
for Realty Development Corporation Ltd $80.0M

Christie Street, St Leonards
Commercial Office Development
for Quotidian No. 15 Pty Ltd $60.0M

Retail Projects
Queen Victoria Building
Conversion/restoration to retail and public uses
for Ipoh Garden Berhad $65.0M

Bay Village N.S.W. for Hooker Corporation $15.0M

Stafford City Retail Centre, Qld
for Allen Holdings/Hooker Corporation $11.0M

Chatswood Chase, Interior design all public areas
Chatswood, N.S.W.
for Lustig Moar and Multiplex (interior work) $5.8M

Neutral Bay Village Shopping Centre
for Hooker Retail Developments Pty Ltd $2.5M

Retail Centre, Jindabyne, N.S.W.
for Diverse Development Corporation $2.0M

Neutral Bay Circle Shopping Centre
for Comcican Pty Ltd & Moonmerra Pty Ltd $1.1M

Riverside Plaza Shopping Centre, Queanbeyan
for Government Insurance Office
of New South Wales $13.5M

Hotel and Leisure Projects
Regent Hotel, Sydney
Consultant Architects
to Lend Lease Corporation $75.0M

Gazebo Hotel, Sydney
Consultant Architects to
Australian Development Corporation $15.0M

Bondi Plaza Hotel, Sydney
for Leisure Lea Limited $75.0M

Hotel, Motel and Conference Centre, Merimbula
for Diverse Development Corporation $8.0M

Thredbo Village Master Plan
for Greenfield Development Co Pty Ltd

Merritts Base Station, Thredbo Stage I and II
for Greenfield Development Co Pty Ltd $8.0M

Australia's Wonderland
Theme Park, Minchinbury, N.S.W.
for Leighton Contractors Pty Ltd $10.0M

Residential
Medium Density Housing, Perisher Valley Resort
for Diverse Development Corporation $3.0M

Multi-Storey Residential Flat Building
Chatswood, N.S.W.
for Tingha Street Developments $5.0M

Residential Accommodation and Chapel
Darlinghurst, N.S.W, for The Sisters of Charity $0.75M

Glebe Estate Rehabilitation of Housing
for N.S.W. Department of Housing $4.0M

Health Buildings
St Vincents Hospital, Darlinghurst, N.S.W.
New Department of Immunology
for St Vincents Hospital $3.5M

St Vincents Hospital, Darlinghurst, N.S.W., Hospice
for Sisters of Charity and the
N.S.W. Department of Health $12.0M

Institute of Medical Research, Darlinghurst, N.S.W.
for The Garvan Institute of Medical Research $70.0M

Research Laboratories, Rushcutters Bay, N.S.W.
for Pac Bio Pty Ltd $5.0M

History
Architects Kevin Rice and John Daubney founded Rice Daubney more than twelve years ago. Since then the company has expanded rapidly – the team now includes ten additional working Directors and the business encompasses not only the traditional architectural services but an increasingly important variety of skills in Urban and Environmental Planning, Interior Architecture, Building Diagnostics, Landscape Architecture and Health Systems.

The establishment of these independent consultancies allows Rice Daubney clients to select, on either an independent or an integrated full service basis, the services designed specifically to fulfil their development needs.

Capabilities
Rice Daubney capabilities are strongly related to large and complex projects and the capacity to carry out such work is clearly demonstrated by projects such as the Zenith Centre, the Prince Albert Centre in Auckland, Carringbush Tower and The Pavilion, the Queen Victoria Building and the Interchange.

Commitment to architectural and technological excellence is allied to the development of cost efficient design solutions. Working closely and creatively with clients to provide them with buildings which work in the best possible way, Rice Daubney

– Design and documentation processes are fully aided and closely monitored by computer technology

– Quality is pursued by an innovative use of methods and materials which enhance the building's life cycle

By investing heavily in the design and development of appropriate internal computer technology, by supporting research and development of building technology, by innovative use of materials and by encouraging an environment in which young professionals can work creatively and effectively, Rice Daubney is prepared for the future. The Company will continue to grow and together with their clients will deliver work of the highest architectural and technological excellence.

1 The Connaught, Sydney

2 M.M.I.C.L. Office, Chatswood

3 N.A.B. Building, Sydney

4 M.W.S. and D.B. Offices, Blacktown

5 Churchill and Brewongle Stands, S.C.G., Sydney

6 J.R. Fleming Stand, Rosehill

ROBERTSON & MARKS ARCHITECTS PTY LTD and GUY FULLER COOK PTY LTD
In Association

Fuller   Mayes   Guy   Ryan   Cook

Directors
John Trevor Guy A.S.T.C. F.R.A.I.A.
Robert Peter Fuller B.Arch. F.R.A.I.A.
 A.R.I.B.A.
Robert William Cook B.Arch. F.R.A.I.A.
David Graham Mayes B.Arch. F.R.A.I.A.
John William Ryan B. Arch. A.R.A.I.A.

Associate Directors
Geoffrey S. Crocker B.E. M.I.E. Aust.
Peter Agnew
Graeme J. Scott B.Arch. (Hon.) A.R.A.I.A.
Wing K. Wong B.Arch A.R.A.I.A.

Associates
Brian J. Carrigan
Christopher G. Chalmers

Established
1892

Address
52 Clarence Street
Sydney, N.S.W. 2000

Telephone
(02) 2 0267

Telex
AA 176093 GFC

Facsimile
(02) 262 2989

Number of Employees
35

Project Types
Commercial
Banks
Office Buildings
Retail Shopping
Recreational
Racecourses
Sporting Arenas
Swimming Pools
Schools
Residential
High Rise Apartments
Industrial
Factories
Laboratories
Educational
Universities

Other Disciplines
Project Administration
Research – Planning
Interior Design

Person to Contact
Any Director

Current and Recent Projects

Commercial

New Office Block, 1-7 Bligh Street	$11M
National Australia Bank, Branch Offices	Varying
National Australia Bank, 343 George Street, Sydney Maintenance and Restoration of Heritage Building	$3M
Hooker Projects, Blacktown, New Building	$7M
James Hardie Building, York Street, Sydney Recycling	$10M
Westpac Banking Corporation, 341 George Street, Sydney Maintenance and Restoration of Heritage Building	Varying

Recreational

Canterbury Racecourse	$20M
Rosehill Racecourse	$24M
Canberra Racecourse	$5M
Sydney Cricket Ground	$20M

Educational

Government Schools	Varying

Residential

The Connaught, Liverpool Street, Sydney	$48M

Industrial

Blackmores Laboratories, Roseberry Street, Balgowlah	$2.5M
Arnotts Biscuits Limited Various ongoing projects	Varying

Other Disciplines

Parramatta Stadium Consultant Architect Superintendent	$16M
Sydney Football Stadium Consultant Architect Superintendent	$62M
Aquatic Centre – Homebush Preparation of Design Tender Brief	$28.5M
Racecourse Consultants Auckland Racing Club Federal Government	$15M

Profile

History
Robertson & Marks Pty. Ltd. is one of Australia's oldest Architectural Firms, having been in continuous practice in Sydney since 1892, and was initially involved in residential, commercial and industrial projects, many of which are recorded in the Royal Australian Institute of Architects' list of Twentieth Century Buildings of Significance.

The original practice was founded by George Birrell Robertson and Theodore John Marks and was continued after their deaths in 1913 and 1941 respectively, by Struan Robertson, Kelvin Robertson, Frederick J.N. Turner, Don Robertson and Trevor Guy.

The present practice was changed to a Company in 1971 when Trevor Guy was joined by Peter Fuller and Robert Cook, and was augmented in 1972 by the formation of Guy Fuller Cook Pty. Ltd., Engineers, Architects and Planners, as a parallel and complementary practice.

Recently two new Directors were appointed to the practices; David Mayes in 1984 and John Ryan in 1987.

Architectural Approach
The Practice has produced an extensive record of successful and significant buildings throughout its long history and continues today with enthusiasm and current skills to contribute to the architectural environment and service the demands of our Clients' functional and economic needs.

The Practice has had considerable experience in all types of projects and in a diversity of roles to suit our Clients' requirements.

A full range of architectural and related services are provided with in-house staff and include the following:

Site inspections and reports
Feasibility studies
Cost programming
Analysis of contractual and construction programmes
 and procedures
Full or partial architectural design and documentation
Interior design
Furniture and fitting design
Project administration
Project supervision
Co-ordination of specialist consultants

The success of the Practice can be attributed to the loyalty and experience of the staff and the personal and continuing service and responsibility to each individual Client.

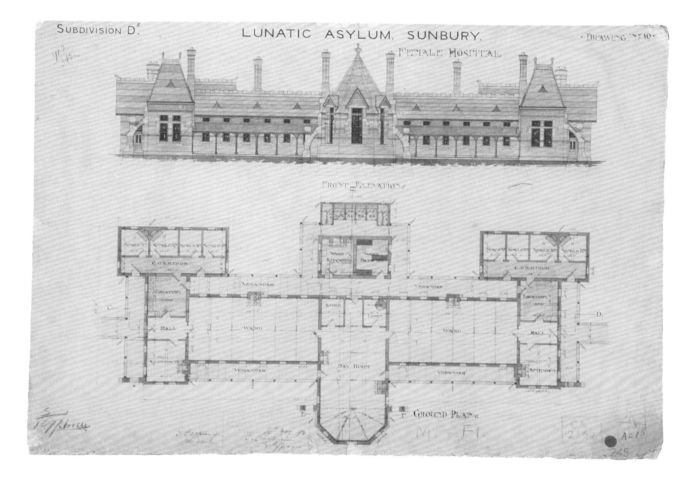

Lunatic Asylum, Sunbury, circa 1892.

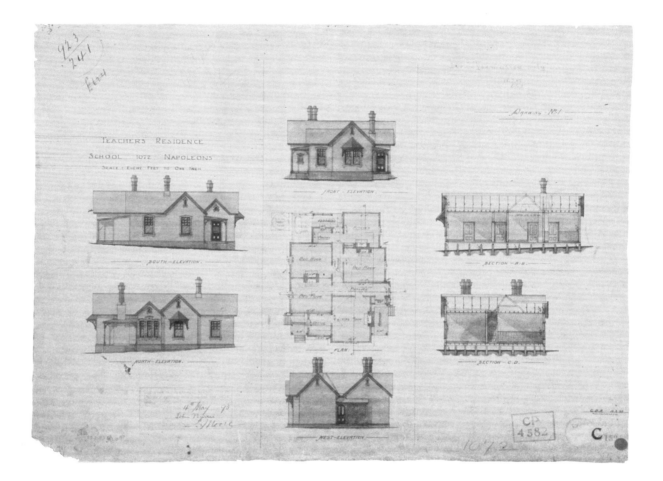

Teachers' Residence, School 1072, Napoleons, circa 1893.

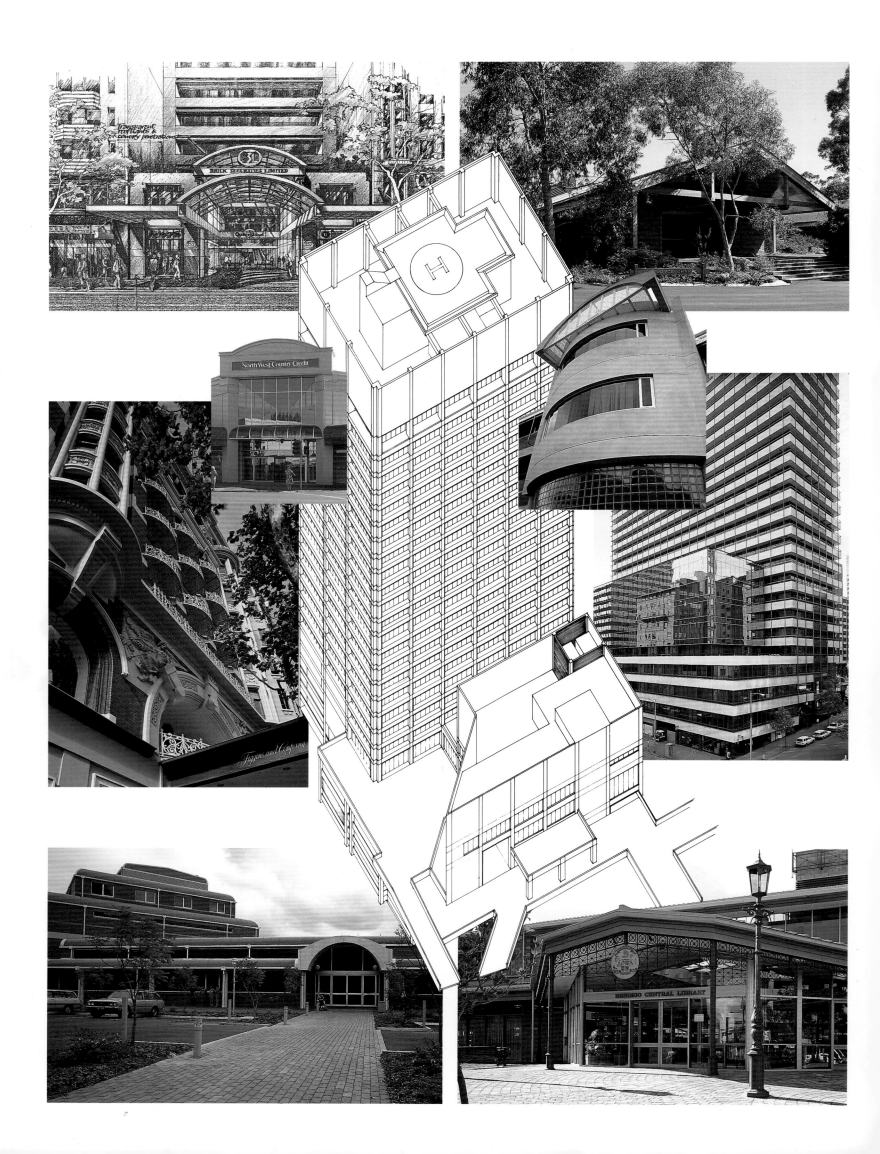

ROBINSON LOO WYSS & SCHNEIDER PTY LTD
Architects and Interior Designers

Directors
Peter K. Loo B Arch, FRAIA
Peter A. Wyss ARAIA
Desmond G. Schneider ARAIA

Associate Directors
Lindsay J. Calvert Dip Arch, ARAIA
James R. Hart B Arch

Consultant
Bruce H. Robinson Dip Arch, FRAIA, ARIBA

Established
Melbourne 1975

Address
2 Market Street
Melbourne, Vic 3000

Telephone
(03) 62 5243

Facsimile
(03) 62 5595

No. of Employees
20 to 25

Value of Commissions
Currently involved in work in excess of
$40 M

Project Types
Commercial
Educational
Industrial
Health
Community Services and Leisure
Retail

Other Disciplines
Interior Design

Person to Contact
Peter K. Loo

Practice Profile

Robinson Loo Wyss & Schneider Pty Ltd was formed in 1975 by its Directors, all of whom had been involved in large architectural practices in senior executive positions and were personally responsible for projects of considerable size and variety.

With the combined architectural skills in design documentation and administration of projects, Robinson Loo Wyss & Schneider Pty Ltd provides individual attention to the needs of clients, a service often lacking in larger organisations. The application of these skills to achieve economical concepts and practical solutions to problems has been the principal aim of this practice. Since its formation the practice has expanded to include two Associate Directors and employs some twenty to twenty-five staff. In the continuation of this principle an extension of services now includes an interior design section to ensure that a full range of skills is available in the execution of a total architectural commission.

In line with this progression, documentation has been enhanced by the introduction of Computer Aided Drafting with the specific aim of increasing and improving flexibility and accuracy with reduced production time.

The practice is currently involved in a wide variety of projects with Directors closely involved in all aspects of the works with considerable importance placed on the teamwork approach to the execution of commissions.

Current and Recent Projects

Commercial
410 Collins Street
14 Level Office Redevelopment
for Sun Alliance Insurance Limited

National Mutual Life Association of Australia Limited
Head Office Extension and Refurbishment

NM Computer Services Pty Ltd, Computer Centre

Refurbishment of 14 Level Office Building
for 155 Queen Street Pty Ltd

Cheltenham, 6 Level Office Development
for Rathmines Investments Pty Ltd

Headquarters for North West Country Credit, Bendigo

Carlton, 4 Level Office Building for
Williams the Shoemen Pty Ltd

Ground Floor Extension, 34 Queen Street
for Sun Alliance Insurance Limited

28 Level Office Development for Pernas International
Hotels & Properties Bhd, Kuala Lumpur, Malaysia

Municipal Offices, City of Sunshine

Proposal for Broadmeadows Railway Station
Redevelopment

Proposal for redevelopment of Ground Floor
257 Collins Street for Brick Securities Limited

Retail
The Shop of Shops, Collins Street

Figgins Diorama, Collins Street

Williams the Shoemen, Randy River and
Livewire Shops throughout Australia

New World Shopping Centre, Bendigo

Extension to Target Store, Bendigo

Alterations and Restoration of Bourke Street
Chinese Emporium for David Wang Nominees Pty Ltd

Community Services and Leisure
Regional Library and Senior Citizens Club
for the City of Bendigo

Marie Mill Community Centre and Senior Citizens
Complex for the City of Sunshine

Tallintyre Reserve Community Centre and Sporting
Complex for the City of Sunshine

Project for Cultural Centre
for the Chinese Association of Victoria

Crematorium and Chapel Complex
for Fawkner Crematorium and Memorial Park

Health
Military Hospital, Kapooka, New South Wales
for the Department of Housing and Construction

Industrial
Factory Extensions and Amenities Building
for Blythe Colours

Automatic Stacking Warehouse
for Vulcan Australia Limited

Steel Preparation and Storage Building
for Vulcan Australia Limited

Educational
Teaching Facilities, Student Amenities and
Learning Resources Centre, TAFE College, Wangaratta
for the Public Works Department of Victoria

Trades Buildings TAFE College, Wangaratta
for the Public Works Department of Victoria

Masterplanning and Initial Stages of Holmesglen
College of TAFE for the Public Works Department of
Victoria, in association with EFPAC Pty Ltd

North Albion Pre-School for the City of Sunshine

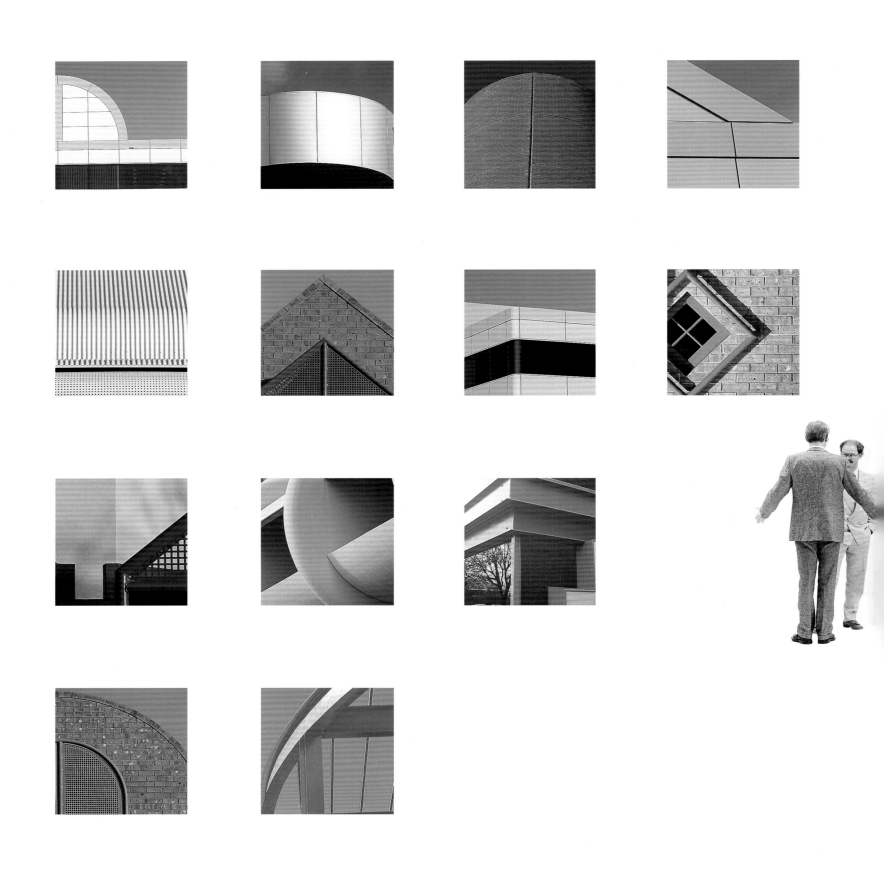

ROD ROACH ARCHITECTURE PTY LTD

Address
328 The Parade
Kensington, S.A. 5068

Telephone
(08) 31 2888

Facsimile
(08) 332 1597

Asked about his design philosophy, Rod Roach carefully avoids the word 'vision': "it sounds a bit pretentious". Instead he talks about attention to and delight in detail and achieving the most satisfying overall design within the constraints of a particular brief. "It's obvious but it can't be too highly stressed. Good detail is intrinsic, not an optional extra. It emerges from relationships in proportion. I aim for clarity and strong, simple statements in buildings."

He sees himself as a flexible architect – a problem-solver: "I don't believe in being dictatorial with clients for its own sake. I'm a commercial architect. People use me to get the highest return on their investment. I work with a lot of developers, but most of them these days don't need to have the economic advantages of good design explained to them."

Rod Roach's early training as a quantity surveyor has left him with a passion for hands-on involvement in construction. "Building buildings excites me and understanding the nuts and bolts helps make for better design. As well, we regard the builder as a specialist member in the team because recognising and harnessing that expertise achieves better results."

If the design is a product of team work, what part does the head of the practice play in it? "I'm a benevolent autocrat to some extent; the first among equals in a fairly young office. We're all aware of the dangers of 'architecture-by-committee', which tends to bland out the character of the end result. There is always, finally, a fairly distinctive character to our work."

On a major scale, The Fire Brigade Headquarters, which he designed in conjunction with Woodhead Hall, is a good example of his collaborative work. As Peter Ward recently observed, "It's one of the four or five best modern buildings in the city."

On a smaller scale, but just as distinctive, is Roach's office on The Parade, Kensington. His fondness and respect for vernacular is apparent in the form itself – a steel variation on the tin shed – in the penchant for the curvilinear and in the understated brilliance of its detail.

ROGERS & CO.

ROGERS & CO PTY LTD
Architects and Planning Consultants

Principal
Robert S. Rogers B. Arch. FRAIA

Established
1978

Address
30 Peel Street,
Collingwood, Vic. 3066

Telephone
(03) 419 8955

Facsimile
(03) 419 7805

Mobile
(007) 335 893

Contact Name
Robert S. Rogers B. Arch. FRAIA

A selection of Current and Recent Projects

Commercial
David Wang & Co., Bourke Street, Melbourne

MPW Offices, Lt. Lonsdale Street, Melbourne

Mt Buller Bus Terminal, Mansfield

Industrial
Arlec Soanar Warehouse, Box Hill

Greythorn Timber Co

GAAM Pumps

Government
Daylesford & Hepburn, Mineral Springs Study

Shire Offices, Daylesford

Hepburn Springs Bathhouse

Educational
Frankston Tafe College

VCAH Lecture Theatres, Country Victoria

Licenced Lounge, Dookie

Tenancy
Edgley, Mutual & General, Melbourne

Chapman Solicitors, Melbourne

Gargaro Accountants, Melbourne

Recreation
Billabong Sports Stadium Proposal, Bulleen

Squash Courts, Horsham

Tourism
Bellinzona Guesthouse, Daylesford

Marylands Guesthouse, Marysville

Tawonga Holiday Village

Pretty Valley Ski Lounge, Falls Creek

Residential
Lansell Road, Toorak

Monaro Road, Kooyong

Honybun Court, Donvale

Illawong Drive, Donvale

Licenced Premises
Bogong Hotel, Tawonga

Sawasdee Thai Restaurant, Melbourne

Doncaster Tower Restaurant, Doncaster

Health
Prince Henry's Hospital

Collagen Clinique, South Yarra

Consulting Rooms, Kew

Unit Development
Abercarn, South Yarra

Dover Street, Flemington

Profile

When you consult Rogers & Co., you have the advantages of dealing with the Principal of the firm and have access to a broad range of specialist consultants built-up over the years.

Our firm is a Consulting practice servicing the needs of clients by preparing reports, assisting in establishing a proper brief and achieving that brief within realistic design, cost and time constraints.

We search beyond design and documentation solutions to ensure we understand the commercial as well as the planning and architectural requirements of our client.

We work with builders, consultants and Construction Managers to secure the best results for our clients.

Robert Rogers has a sound background in the field of architecture including experience as a senior architect with the Department of Constructions, and later in private practice working with builders and developers on commercial projects and as a consultant both in the Private and Government sectors.

The firm has experience in planning, development and renovation work, particularly in the Commercial and Tourism areas, and to keep abreast of ideas and new horizons, study tours have been made around Australia, Asia and America.

Past and present clients

MPW Australia

Edgley, Mutual & General Pty Ltd

Coca Cola – Beverage Division

David Wang & Company

Greythorn Timber Company

Glenbervie Timber Company

Arlec Soanar Electronics Group

Victorian Colleges of Agriculture and Horticulture

Ministry of Education

Ormond College

Mineral Springs Advisory Council

Shire of Daylesford and Glenlyon

City of Box Hill

Gargaro Accountants

Chapman Solicitors

Huntingford Homes

Billabong Hotel Group

Doncaster Tower Restaurants

Bogong Hotel, Tawonga

Marylands Guesthouse

1

2

1 Major refurbishment to an exclusive shopping arcade

2 Redevelopment of historical buildings into a new hotel

3 Retail/warehouse development

4 Sophisticated CAD systems are used in the production of working drawings

5 Proposed development incorporating retail, commercial, residential and medical facilities

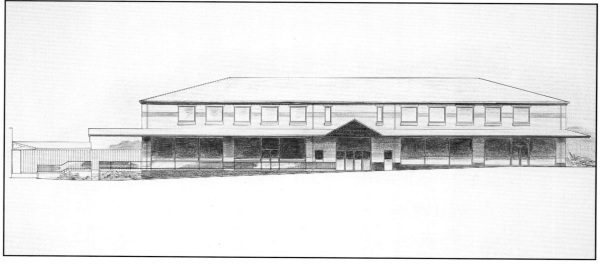

3

SHK ARCHITECTS (NSW) PTY LTD

Directors
Henry Hayes Arch FRAIA
Ian Hayes

Established
1987

Address
157-159 Harris Street
Pyrmont, N.S.W. 2009

Telephone
(02) 692 9144

Facsimile
(02) 660 0640

Number of Employees
14

Project Types
Commercial
Office blocks
Retail centres

Resort Development
Hotels

Industrial
Warehouses
Factories
Industrial estates

Other Disciplines
Interior Design

Person to Contact
Henry Hayes

SHK Architects (NSW) Pty Ltd

SHK Architects (NSW) Pty Ltd was formed in 1987 by Henry Hayes. During the previous 25 years, Henry Hayes was a Principal with Stokes Hayes & Kanas Pty Ltd, which ceased trading earlier this year.

SHK Architects has as its main client base the commercial and corporate sectors, although a significant number of commissions involving retail, hospitality and industrial developments as well as refurbishments are currently being undertaken.

The Principal of the firm is personally involved with each project, from the early stages of the design brief through to its final completion. The firm maintains a close working relationship with its clients in order to fully understand their requirements, and thus ensure that these are interpreted correctly and incorporated into the design.

As designers of the built environment, SHK's primary objectives are:

(1) to tailor each project to the individual organisation concerned;

(2) to design buildings that are aesthetically pleasing, commercially successful, and sympathetic to the end user's expectations.

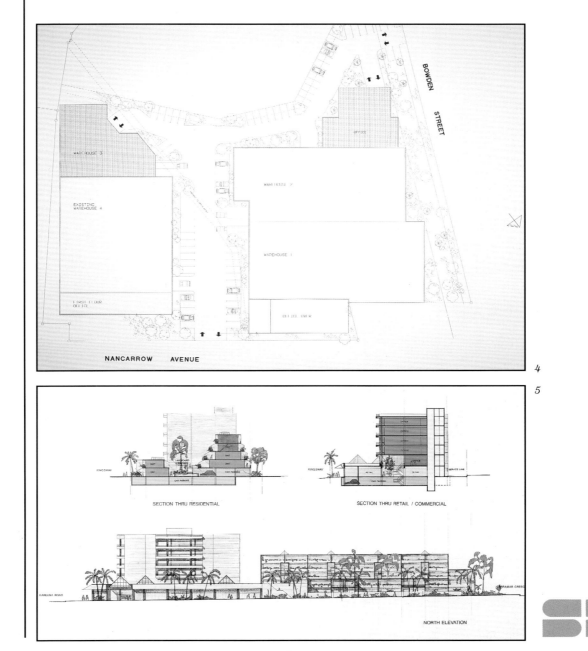

4

5

E. SMREKAR PTY LTD

Established
1969

Address
35 Dryburgh Street
West Melbourne, Vic. 3003

Telephone
(03) 329 0399

Facsimile
(03) 326 5473

Person to Contact
Mr Ermin Smrekar F.R.A.I.A.

Current Value of Work in Progress
In excess of $40M

Project Types	Percentage
Commercial Offices	45 %
Ecclesiastical/Community	5 %
Educational	10 %
Retail	15 %
Entertainment	10 %
Residential	15 %

History

E. Smrekar Pty. Ltd. is a progressive Architectural practice whose performance and design skills have allowed the office to expand and undertake major projects because of the consistent standard of professionalism and efficiency shown throughout the life of the practice.

The office, led by its Principal, Ermin Smrekar, has developed a reputation for approaching every commission with inspired energy, dynamism and strong commercial attitude towards development.

Philosophy

The Practice has enjoyed a very wide range of commissions and accordingly has produced a design philosophy that is based strongly on flexibility of thought, and originality of ideas, thus creating the ideal conditions for innovative, intelligent and inspired alternatives.

The basic belief is that the requirements for each building are various and different from other buildings and the final design should address all the perceived issues; consequently each building should express a unique personality.

The practice has been producing Architecture that is both distinctive and functional.

The approach to design is based on wide experience, technical data and respecting Clients' needs.

The greatest concern expressed in the design is for people; those who use, visit or maintain the buildings.

The major commitment is to create quality projects of appropriate scale and character, buildings that are human and enjoyable, Architecture that is not only functional but can be admired and enjoyed.

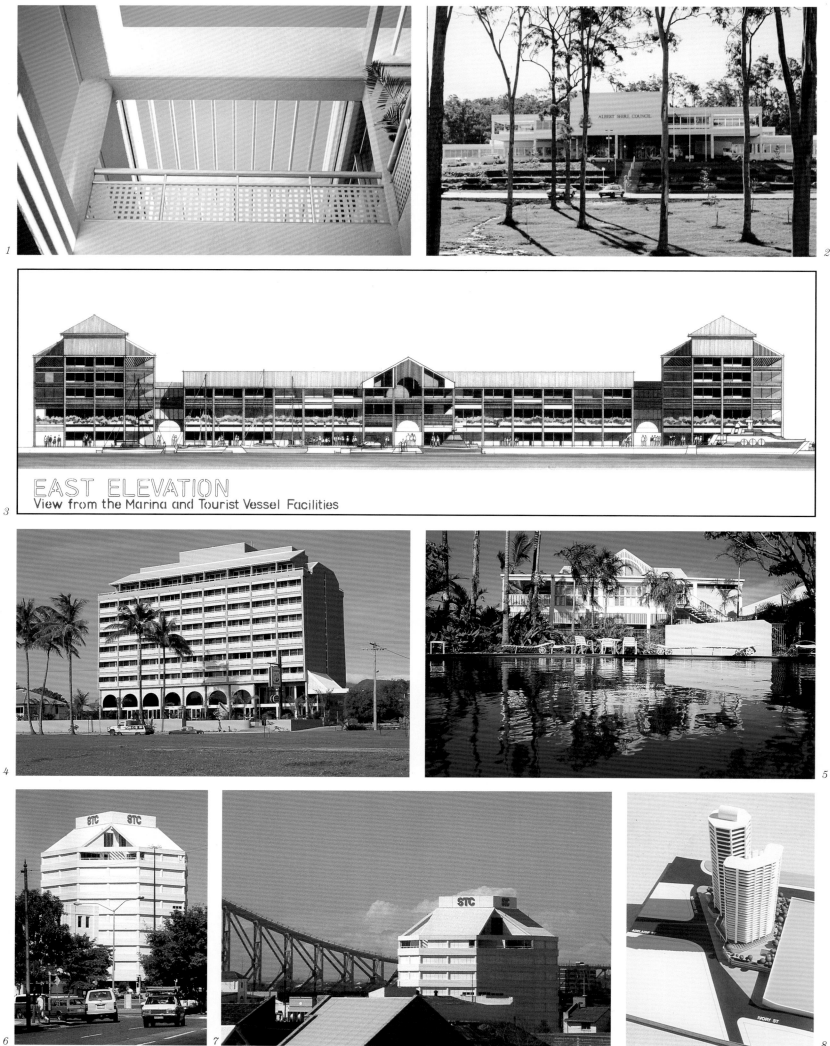

EAST ELEVATION
View from the Marina and Tourist Vessel Facilities

STENDERS + PARTNERS
Architects, Urban Designers, Town Planners

Professional Activities
Architecture
Urban Design
Town Planning

Addresses
Brisbane
165 Gregory Terrace
Spring Hill, Qld 4000
Telephone
(07) 832 4172
Facsimile
(07) 832 1286
Cairns
206 Grafton Street
Cairns, Nth Qld 4870
Telephone
(070) 51 5289
Facsimile
(070) 52 1363

1 Verandah and shade cover – Albert Shire Administration Building

2 Approach view – Albert Shire Administration Building

3 Sketch elevation – The Pier Hotel and Festival Market, Cairns Waterfront

4 "Harbourside" Hotel, The Esplanade, Cairns

5 "Tradewinds Outrigger" Tourist Hotel, Cairns

6 STC House, Commercial Development, Queen Street, Brisbane, illustrating system of external sun-control blinds

7 STC House, Commercial Development, Queen Street, Brisbane, illustrating rooftop office penthouse suites

8 Project Design – "Boundary Place", Hotel and Commercial Development proposal, Ann Street, Brisbane

The Firm: Overview
Stenders & Partners is a Queensland based architectural, urban design and town planning consultancy practice with offices in Brisbane and Cairns. The principal, Andris Stenders is a graduate of the University of Queensland (B.Arch. – 1st Cl. Hons) and of the University of Liverpool U.K. (Master of Civic Design). The Cairns practice, Stenders, Morris & Partners is directed by Mr Stenders and the Cairns partner, Mr Barry Morris, Architect, who is resident in Cairns.

The practice is essentially a design-orientated one and operates on a studio basis with the partners being directly involved in all major work undertaken. The majority of the firm's work is derived from the private development sector and consequently the practice has adopted a market-sensitive approach to its consultancy activities. The principal and senior personnel have a working knowledge of urban land economics and can apply analytical techniques to projects undertaken. Through its urban design and town planning consultancy activities the practice has a background of experience with statutory controls and a thorough understanding of the systems of approval necessary for successful project implementation.

Philosophy of Approach
Through its ten years of operation, the practice has developed its own architectural language of expression. Within the confines of development feasibility, requiring a cost-effective approach, the firm has sought to achieve the quality of "timelessness" in its buildings.

It endeavours to produce buildings and local environments that eschew fashion, but reflect design principles of a fundamental and lasting quality. This approach, together with continuing close attention to building functional and construction systems, has produced viable and attractive solutions within the built environment.

In addition to a systematic, managed design process, closely monitored through progressive feasibility analyses, the firm undertakes all of its own project documentation and contract management.

This integrated approach has been effective in both cost and time control during project realisation and in the production of results consistent with client expectations. Because of its size and method of operation the practice is able to operate almost as an "in-house" design and development team in particular instances. This obviates the inefficiencies of liaison and allows full harnessing of the skills and techniques often available within a client company.

Areas of Particular Expertise
The effective combination of disciplines and principles involved in town planning with the more specific design and implementation skills inherent in architectural practice has fostered the development of a comprehensive approach. Equal emphasis is placed upon and attention given to the context or location of a building or grouping of buildings as to the planning and resultant character of the structures. Skills applied and services provided are not limited to architectural expertise but cover the fields of physical, biological and community environmental analyses, urban land economics and statutory control systems.

Through its development of appropriate methodologies, the firm has changed from a general architectural and town planning consultancy practice into one providing highly developed skills in particular areas of endeavour. Broadly grouped these are:
Tourism development;
Commercial and retail architecture;
Housing; and
Urban Design.

Tourism Development
The basic philosophy adopted by the practice has been the development of resort environments and architecture that reflect an Australian character and provide a visual experience differing from that encountered in the "international" style hotels available at tourist destinations all over the world. The architecture produced by the practice is not based on replication of historic forms but rather draws on the somewhat fragile aesthetic of traditional Australian buildings, using various elements such as sun-control, breeze channeling,

weather protection etc. in a practical way to produce buildings sensitive to the environment of their location. The resort buildings produced by the practice reflect relevant user requirements and standards of accommodation expected by the market at which they are aimed, but endeavour to achieve this within a built environment that provides an "Australian" experience.

The practice is familiar with hotel operational systems and the requirements of a diverse range of operator groups. It has a record of being able to provide buildings that satisfy these requirements within project packages attractive to the investment sector. Currently it is engaged in four major Queensland tourist hotel projects totalling some 1200 bedrooms.

Commercial and Retail Development
Projects in this grouping range from city centre offices, through regional shopping centres to fringe and suburban area, small scale development. Again particular emphasis has been placed upon functionality, financial competitiveness and aesthetic quality.

The firm has a deliberate policy of continuous upgrading of knowledge and expertise in component aspects such as services technology, product science and operations planning. Its architecture recognises climatic and locational aspects and tends to be more a reflection of characteristics induced by such considerations and building performance requirements than the more universal formalist approach. Particular expertise has been developed in strata or group-title commercial development where savings in operational costs through proper environmentally based design are a major consideration.

In addition to a capability to determine retail catchment areas, expenditures and supportable floorspace, the practice is currently developing expertise in new forms of retailing. It is active in the design of retail or "festival" market type shopping and in the development of specialised, tourist-orientated retail facilities.

Housing
A number of tract housing schemes and apartment developments have been successfully completed. Such developments range from low-cost attached housing sold in group-title form, to up-market apartment and serviced apartment developments.

Emphasis is given to the design of not only the built space and form of the buildings but also to the use of site space, indoor-outdoor relationships and the consequent maximisation of overall attractiveness and livability. Particular expertise has been developed in the concepts of "add-on" and "adaptable" housing, i.e. provision of basic units capable of owner expansion and apartments suitable for sectionalisation to facilitate multiple letting.

Urban Design
The principal and senior personnel have an extensive history of involvement in town planning practice in Australia and Europe. Significant achievements include the introduction of policy, strategic and "action" or development planning to Australian practice. The current town planning system of Development Control Plans in Queensland is based on 1970's work done by A. Stenders in consultancy to the Gold Coast City Council.

The firm undertakes commissions for the development of residential, leisure and resort communities as well as regulatory exercises for local authorities. During the last five years it has deliberately moved from statutory planning into areas of innovative planning design.

New techniques of "image creation" and development of visually and functionally attractive urban environments, reliant on modelling and illustration for ready assimilation of proposals have been developed. This field of work has been regarded as supportive of and complementary to the firm's philosophy of comprehensive design.

**STENDERS+
PARTNERS**
architects
urban designers
town planners

STEPHENSON & TURNER SYDNEY PTY LTD

Directors (left to right)
Robert Cleland B.Arch.(Hons), M.Arch.Harvard,
North London Dip.Health Facility Planning,
F.R.I.A., N.Z.I.A., R.I.B.A., A.A.C.A.,
Chartered Architect
Richard Mainwaring Dip.Arch., F.R.A.I.A.,
H.K.I.A., R.I.B.A., A.A.C.A.,
Chartered Architect
Bruno Gallacé B.Sc.Arch., A.R.A.I.A.,
Chartered Architect
David Turner B.Arch., A.R.A.I.A.,
Chartered Architect
Alan Thomas A.S.T.C.Arch., A.R.A.I.A.,
Chartered Architect
Don Tailby University N.S.W.,
Dip.Airconditioning, I.C.C.

Established
1920

Address
Stephenson & Turner Sydney Pty Ltd
77 Berry Street
North Sydney, N.S.W. 2060

Telephone
(02) 957 5500

Telex
127110

Facsimile
(02) 957 5521

Stephenson & Turner Hong Kong
Level 17 Fairmont House
8 Cotton Tree Drive
Central Hong Kong

Telephone
(0011) 852 5 241125

Telex
(020) 80265709

Facsimile
(0011) 852 5 297830

**Stephenson & Turner Canberra
Architects**
6 Geiles Court
Deakin, A.C.T. 2600

Telephone
(062) 95 7632

Stephenson & Turner Cairns
36 Grafton Street
Cairns, Qld 4870

Telephone
(070) 52 1131

Person to Contact
Bruno Gallacé Sydney
Garry Bray Hong Kong
Trevor Vivian Canberra
Max Clark Cairns

Project Types
Specialist health facility planning
All aspects of the design, and development of hospitals and related health care facilities. Stephenson & Turner Sydney Group are a major exporter of health facility related services.

Hospitality Industry
Full range of services including specialist teams for both the Central Business District, hotels and destination and resort/destination facilities.

Commercial
A specialist in the particular problems related to Town Planning, Urban Design and management of major commercial enterprises of an international scale.

Restoration
The firm has specialist expertise at historic restoration and commercial recycling of older properties.

Other Disciplines
Town Planning
Urban Design
Interior Design
Building Services Engineering
Health Facility Planning
Hospitality Industry Analysis
Computer Services
Project Management

Stephenson & Turner Sydney Pty Ltd is the key architectural member of the Cleland Mainwaring Group. As such it is a member of a multi-disciplinary professional group offering a complete range of services to the building industry throughout Australia, Asia, Europe and North America. Other members of the group include interior designers, building service engineers, retail planning, computer applications and specialist services.

Stephenson & Turner Sydney is structured as an autonomous, corporate body with its own vigorous management structure and design objectives. This structure allows the firm not only to be a specialist architectural practice, but also gives it access to the inter-related disciplines enabling the firm to offer a service at the cutting edge of the industry. As one of the firms which emerged from the original Stephenson & Turner partnership, Stephenson & Turner Sydney draws on nearly seventy years of experience in all areas of design. This heritage, together with the scale of the new firm gives the practice the capacity to provide skills of the highest standard to both developers and institutional owners.

Design Philosophy
The underlying philosophy of the firm is, together with other members of the group, to provide services related to the transition from the client's liquid assets (money) to fixed assets (buildings). This philosophy provides the framework for the development of a high quality cost-effective architectural product.

Current and Recent Projects
The Restoration of the Queen Victoria Building
(in association with Rice Daubney)

Refurbishment of No. 1 Chifley Square, Sydney

Commonwealth Offices, Wollongong, N.S.W.

Ramada Renaissance Hotel, Pitt Street, Sydney

Peppers on Sea, Terrigal

1 NMRB Burns Philp Building, Sydney

2 Counter details NMRB

3 NZI Securities Australia Limited
   Boardroom, Sydney

4 NZI Reception area

5 Custom made Light NZI

6 Foyer refurbish CML Building,
   Martin Place, Sydney

7 NZI Securities Reception area

TASMAN STOREY & ASSOCIATES PTY LTD
Architects & Interior Designers

Principal
Tasman Storey, F.R.A.I.A.
Bach. Architecture (Hons) UNSW

Established
1983

Address
Suite 803
47 York Street
Sydney, N.S.W. 2000

Telephone
(02) 29 6398
(02) 29 6108

Facsimile
(02) 29 6416

Project Types
Commercial
Institutional
Heritage
Industrial
Retail
Domestic

Other Disciplines
Interior Design
Graphic Design
Furniture Design

Person to Contact
Tasman Storey

Current and Recent Projects
Financial Institutions
Australian Bank Limited
Sydney offices and Money Market
Brisbane office and Retail Banking Chamber
Continuing Consultancy
Bank of New Zealand
Offices and Computer Room
Continuing Consultancy
National Mutual Royal Bank
Offices and Retail Banking Chamber
P.N.C. International Services Pty. Ltd.
Offices and Money Market
Capel Court
Offices and Computer Room
NZI Securities Australia Limited
Offices and Money Market
Colonial Mutual Life
Parramatta Offices
Hurstville Offices
Head Office Foyer and Lift Cars
Growth Equities Corporation

Commercial Offices
Reckitt and Colman
Head Office
P.H. Cary – Accountants
Peter Wallman – Stockbrokers
Egon Zehnder – Executive Recruiters
Syrinx Research – Industrial Equipment
KKL Kangaroo Lines

Industrial
Lincoln Contractors – Cold Store Layouts

Project Management Teams
Concrete Constructions
Lend Lease Interiors

History and Design Philosophy

Tasman Storey & Associates Pty. Ltd. was founded in 1983 to provide a specific and personalised service, in the central business district of Sydney.

Tasman Storey, the Company Principal, after some years as Director of a large city firm of architects saw the opportunity to commence an architectural practice, related to the technical intricacies of modern commercial entities.

From a one client practice serving the Australian Bank Limited, the Company has grown to service a number of banks and financial institutions as well as handling other commercial, institutional and domestic clients.

The offices of Tasman Storey & Associates Pty. Ltd. are located in the centre of Sydney, sharing a group base with other architects and designers who, from time to time, are able to augment the production of documentation.

Emphasis is placed on efficient production by the use of computer aided draughting and advanced reprographic techniques. Close liaison with key contractors has ensured the completion of projects to tight programmed schedules.

For the detailed functions of electronic services Tasman Storey & Associates Pty. Ltd. can provide an overview and broad ranging experience which is of benefit to the co-ordination of the varied services necessary in areas such as money markets and computer rooms.

Detailed and customised furniture receives special consideration and economic solutions to dealers' desks, board tables and reception areas have been produced for satisfied clients.

Recent works have ranged from large scale housing projects to terrace house restorations. Specialist skills are offered in heritage projects, based on experience gained on a number of significant historic buildings.

Philosophy
Each project is treated as an individual assignment and has the personal involvement of the Principal from the collection of the brief to final completion. Tasman Storey & Associates Pty. Ltd. will strive to find that balance between the technical requirements, the economic constraints and aesthetics which produce a unique and satisfying space as a base for the clients efficient operation.

83 York Street, Building Refurbishment, Sydney

Shopping Arcade, Port Macquarie

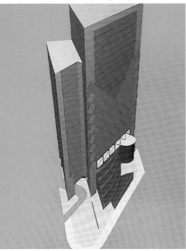

Office Tower concept, C.B.D. Sydney

Residence, Sydney

Interior, Staff Training College

Cinema Shopping Complex, Port Macquarie

State Rail Authority Staff Training College, Sydney

STRAESSER POLI LITTLE & ASSOCIATES PTY LTD

Architects
A division of the E.G.O. Group

Established
1971

Address
'E.G.O. House'
304 Kent Street
Sydney, N.S.W. 2000

Telephone
(02) 267 7522

Facsimile
(02) 262 1906

Directors
Georg E. Straesser
Carlo A. Poli
Stephen P. Little

Number of Employees
30

Project Types
Commercial
Leisure
Refurbishment
Retail
Residential
Restoration
Educational

Other Disciplines
Architecture
Interior Design
Landscape Design
Space Planning
Refurbishment Feasibilities
Residential
Urban Design
Hotels/Resorts

Persons to Contact
Russell H. Nichols
Georg E. Straesser
Carlo A. Poli

Company Profile

Straesser Poli Little & Associates was founded in 1971 as part of the E.G.O. Group, Architects and Interior Designers.

Over the past 16 years Straesser Poli Little & Associates, under the leadership of Georg Straesser, Carlo Poli and Stephen Little, expanded rapidly with its corporate and institutional clients.

The philosophy of the firm has its basis in the creation of an Australian style of architecture. The style and experience of the company is backed up by a professional team which has carried out a number of important projects within a controlled cost environment.

From the outset Straesser Poli Little & Associates' approach has been based on the quality of communication. Close involvement is maintained between the Group's principals and the client throughout every project. The ability to understand client's needs, the skills to create innovative design solutions and the resources to implement them effectively remain the cornerstone of Straesser Poli Little & Associates' design service.

Current and Recent Projects

Office Building
Pymble, N.S.W.

International Hotel
Rosehill, N.S.W.

International Hotel
Port Macquarie, N.S.W.

State Rail Authority of N.S.W.
Training School, Petersham

State Rail, Authority of N.S.W.
Residential Hostel

The Ritz Centre
Cinema & Shopping Complex
Port Macquarie, N.S.W.

Gateway Motor Inn
Devonport, Tasmania

Building Refurbishment
Arunta House – Sydney

Linkside Retirement Village
Bundanoon, N.S.W.

Regents Park Industrial Estate
Regents Park, Sydney

Building Refurbishment
261 George Street, Sydney

THE E.G.O. GROUP

TASARC PTY LTD

Directors (left to right)
John H. Blythe F.R.A.I.A., F.I. Arb. A.
Glenn W. Smith A.R.A.I.A., Dip. Arch., D.I.P. U.P.
Patrick Y. F. Yeung F.R.A.I.A., F.I. Arb. A.
Carol M. Smith B.A. Env. Des., Grad. Dip. Arch.

Associate Directors (left to right)
David N. Menzies B.A., A.R.A.I.A.
Eric D. Richardson A.R.A.I.A., B. Arch.
Prudence L. Cotton L.D.A.D. (Lon.),
   S.I.A.D. (Lon.)

Established
1987

Addresses
Hobart
17 Morrison Street
Hobart, Tas. 7000

Telephone
(002) 23 4011

Facsimile
(002) 23 2582

Launceston
16 Paterson Street
Launceston, Tas. 7250

Telephone
(003) 31 3466

Facsimile
(003) 34 0215

Melbourne
65 Smith Street
Fitzroy, Vic. 3065

Telephone
(03) 417 6853

Facsimile
(03) 417 7919

Number of Staff
35

People to Contact
Hobart
John Blythe

Launceston
Glenn Smith

Melbourne
Glenn Smith

Tasarc

Tasarc has been formed in direct response to Tasmania's requirements for a local architectural practice with the talent, size and resources to handle the state's biggest and most complex projects.

Tasarc meets these requirements by combining, in a proprietary company, two of the state's most innovative and successful firms, both with a distinguished history of major public projects.

Tasarc comprises
Blythe Yeung & Menzies, of Hobart
Glenn Smith Associates, of Launceston

This formidable combination has created an interdisciplinary design practice with a depth not previously available in Tasmania. Its disciplines include
Architecture
Interior Design
Planning
Landscape Architecture
Project Management
Arbitration

Major, recent, projects carried out individually by Blythe Yeung and Menzies and Glenn Smith Associates include

Executive Building, Hobart	$13.0M
International Velodrome, Launceston	$6.5M
Mines Department Complex, Hobart	$5.5M
Community College, Launceston	$3.2M
Burnie Technical College, Phase II	$6.0M
TSIT Nursing School	$1.5M
Commonwealth Offices	$5.5M
Derwent Entertainment Centre	$11.6M

Horsham Plaza Shopping Centre, Horsham

Australian Gallery of Sport, Jolimont

Champagne Store, Chateau Remy, Avoca

Offices, Lincoln Square North, Carlton

Fountain Gate Shopping Centre, Berwick

Myer City Stores and Myer House, Melbourne

TOMPKINS, SHAW & EVANS PTY LTD
Architects

(left to right)
John Taylor, Ron Bourier,
Brian Smith, Bill Woodburn,
James Woodburn

Directors
Bill Woodburn B.Arch., F.R.A.I.A
Brian Smith B.Arch., F.R.A.I.A., M.A.A.S.
Ron Bourier F.R.A.I.A., M.A.A.S.

Associates
John Taylor Dip.Arch., A.R.A.I.A.
James Woodburn M.B.A., B.Arch.(Hons),
    A.R.A.I.A.

Established
1891

Address
14 Grey Street
East Melbourne, Vic. 3002

Telephone
(03) 419 2522

Facsimile
(03) 419 6284

Number of Employees
15 Technical Staff
3 Support Staff

Project Types
Retail
Industrial
Commercial
Recreational

Other Disciplines
Architecture
Interior Design

People to Contact
The Directors

Current and Recent Projects
Retail
Fountain Gate Shopping Centre, Berwick

Brandon Park Shopping Centre, Waverley

Myer, Melbourne

District Centre Redevelopment, Frankston

Cranbourne Park Shopping Centre, Cranbourne

Tok H Centre, Toorak

Parkmore Keysborough Shopping Centre, Keysborough

Southland Shopping Centre (1968), Cheltenham

Horsham Plaza Shopping Centre, Horsham

Super K Mart, Shepparton

Wodonga Plaza Shopping Centre, Wodonga

Marong Village Shopping Centre, Bendigo

Industrial
The Herald and Weekly Times Limited, Melbourne

Remy & Associates, Blackburn

William Adams, Clayton

Castrol Australia, Brooklyn

Robert Bosch (Aust) Auto Test Centre, Clayton
in association with Stanley McConnell & Associates

Ford Motor Company, Broadmeadows
in association with Stanley McConnell & Associates

Commercial
Office, 52 Albert Road, South Melbourne

Office, Lincoln Square North, Carlton

Myer House, Elizabeth Street, Melbourne

The "Pub" Development, Scott Street, Dandenong

HSV7 Colour Nucleus Building, South Melbourne

Telecom House, Dandenong

Recreational
Olympic Dining Rooms, Sponsors' Boxes
and Western Stand, Melbourne Cricket Club, Jolimont

Australian Gallery of Sport, Jolimont

Fountain Gate Hotel, Berwick

Toorak Hotel, Toorak

History and Philosophy
This practice has been around for a long time. So have many of its clients. They like responsiveness to their requirements, creative but sensible solutions, and easy personal contact at any level within the firm. They also like projects that are built on time, within budget, and with a minimum of fuss.

T.S. & E. has developed skills in "fast tracking" projects by rapid generation of feasibilities, early negotiation with authorities and builders, and maintenance of pressure on projects throughout their duration.

The majority of the firm's works are in the retail, commercial and industrial areas. T.S. & E. has particular expertise in the shopping centre field and is able to offer clients the benefit of experience gained in the production of many landmark centres. Planning for the commercial success of these projects, while maintaining high functional and aesthetic standards, are key priorities, the achievement of which was recognised by the R.A.I.A. Victorian Chapter in awarding its 1969 Bronze medal to the firm for the design of Southland Shopping Centre, Cheltenham.

Computerization of many T.S. & E. office functions including drafting, data recording and specification writing, augment the personal inputs of management skills and professional expertise which have always been available from the firm.

The practice provides architectural and interior design services and can assemble and lead a team of outside specialist consultants most appropriate for any client or project.

By using these methods, T.S. & E. fulfils its aim to provide high levels of service and design quality, and above all, client satisfaction.

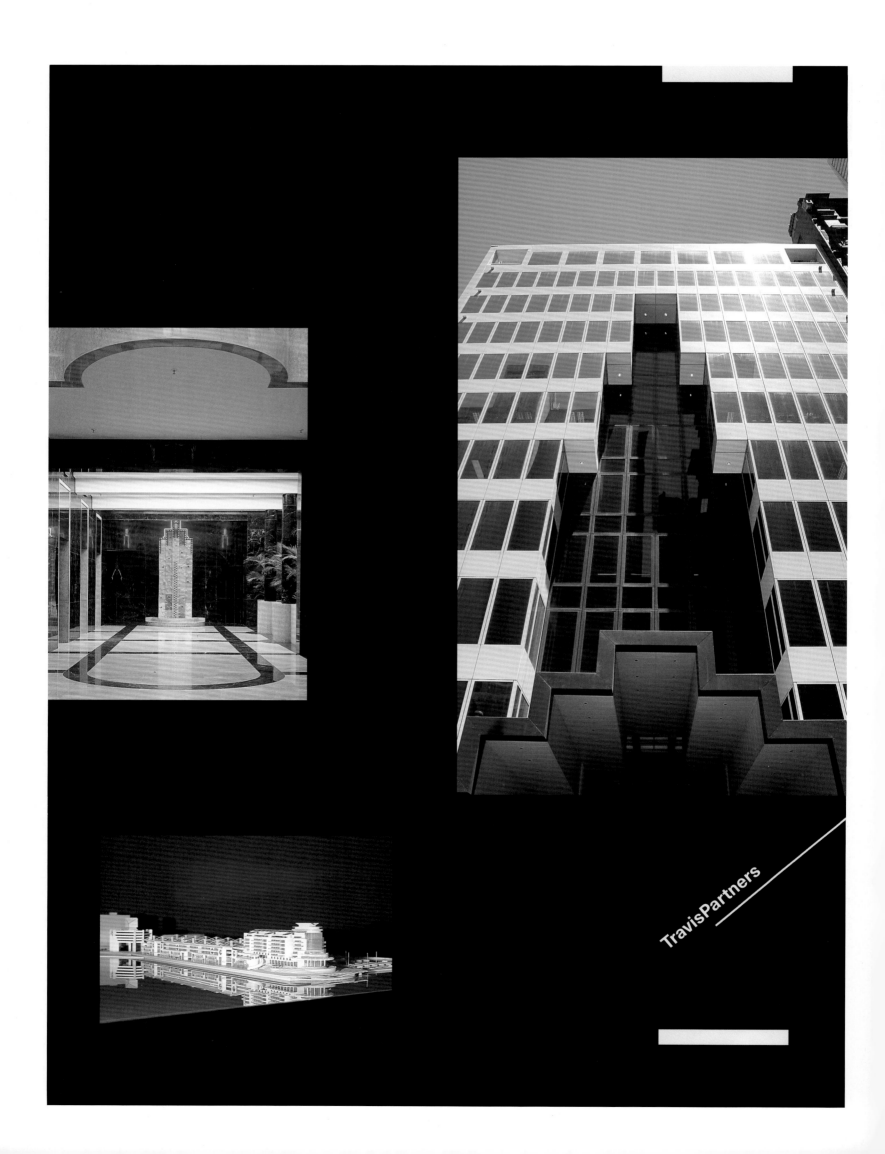

TravisPartners

TRAVIS PARTNERS PTY LTD

Directors (left to right)
Richard Travis BArch ASTC Design FRAIA
  ADIA, Managing Director
Richard McEwen BArch (Hon) ARAIA
Michael Harrison MArch City Plng
  ARAIA MRAPI
Keith Franklin BArch(Hon) ARAIA RIBA

Associate Directors
John Humphreys ASTC(QS) AAIQS
Bruce Ramsay BArch (Hon) ARAIA
Keith White BSc(Arch)

Associates
Robert Stephenson BArch MArch UD ARAIA
Wal Richardson
Garry Booth
Peter Scott BL/Arch AAILA
Grahame Fuller DipArch FRAIA
Gregory Loomes BArch

Established
1973

Address
41 McLaren Street
North Sydney, N.S.W. 2060

Telephone
(02) 929 0522

Facsimile
(02) 959 5765

Associated Offices
Travis Partners Avery Leuschke
Architects in Association
17 South Street
Auckland, New Zealand

Telephone
64 9 370966

Facsimile
64 9 371712

Number of Employees
90

Project Types
Commercial
Municipal
Tourism/Leisure
Residential
Adaptive Re-Use/Refurbishment
Conservation/Restoration

Other Disciplines
Urban and Regional Planning
Landscape Architecture
Interior Architecture
Cost Planning
Quantity Surveying

Persons to Contact
Australia
Richard Travis

New Zealand
Bruce Ramsay

Current and Recent Projects

Commercial
28 Margaret Street, Sydney

The Mayfair Offices
73-75 Castlereagh Street, Sydney

Chubb House
64 Clarence Street, Sydney

George Patterson House
Cnr Arthur & Mount Streets, North Sydney

Cnr Miller & Berry Streets, North Sydney

33 Argyle Street, Parramatta

91 Phillip Street, Parramatta

Dow Chemicals (Australia)
Head Office, Frenchs Forest, N.S.W.

Municipal
Shortland Electricity Administration Centre,
Wallsend, N.S.W.

Joint Coal Board Administration Centre,
Singleton, N.S.W.

Civic Centre, Singleton, N.S.W.

Civic Administration Building, Armidale, N.S.W.

Mosman Square, Mosman, N.S.W.

Council Chambers & Administration Building,
Narrabri, N.S.W.

Council Chambers & Administration Building,
Inverell, N.S.W.

Council Chambers & Administration Building,
Eurobodalla Shire, N.S.W.

Council Chambers & Administration Building,
Shoalhaven, N.S.W.

Council Chambers & Administration Building,
Lake Macquarie, N.S.W.

Tourism/Leisure
Darling Harbour Hotels, Sydney
Two hotels with a total of 900 rooms
Travis Partners Hoffer Reid & Coombs
Architects in Association

Princes Wharf, Auckland, New Zealand
225 room hotel, Festival Market in major mixed use
development

Fairmont Hotel and Tourist Resort, Leura, N.S.W.
350 room tourist resort

Korolevu Beach Resort, Fiji
300 room tourist resort

Dunedin Rail Land Redevelopment, New Zealand
11.5 ha mixed tourism/leisure and retail

Walsh Bay Redevelopment Plan, Sydney
Master plan for re-use of historic wharf precinct

Singleton Leisure Centre, N.S.W.

Residential
Alexandria Housing Project
Department of Housing, 264 dwellings

Dougherty Centre Retirement Complex, Chatswood
Department of Housing, Willoughby Municipal
Council and Uniting Church, 136 units

Waterloo Housing Rehabilitation, Sydney
Department of Housing, 150 Victorian terraces

Jesmond Housing, Newcastle, N.S.W.
Department of Housing, 84 dwellings

Kenilworth Retirement Village, Bowral, N.S.W.

Adaptive Re-Use/Refurbishment
4-16 Dowling Street, Woolloomooloo
Department of Housing
RAIA Merit Award, 1984

''The Vintage'' Apartments, Sydney
Conversion of warehouses to apartments

Pier One, Walsh Bay, N.S.W.
Conversion of wharf for leisure/retail uses

Wynyard House, 301 George Street, Sydney

287-289 Clarence Street, Sydney
Conservation analysis and refurbishment
of classified building.

Conservation
Quarantine Station Conservation Plan, Sydney

Darlinghurst Courthouse Conservation Plan, Sydney

Phillip Street Police and Justice Museum, Sydney

Heritage Study, Mosman, N.S.W.

Observatory Hill Conservation Plan, The Rocks, Sydney

City Mutual Building, Hunter Street, Sydney

Richmond Main Colliery Industrial Park

St Johns Church Hall, Newcastle

45 Lower Fort Street, The Rocks

Profile
Travis Partners Pty Ltd is a multi-discipline practice
dedicated to excellence in design and successful project
delivery.

We offer professional consulting services in:
Architecture
Conservation Architecture
Urban and Regional Planning
Interior Architecture
Landscape Architecture
Cost Planning
Quantity Surveying

Whilst each discipline may provide services independently of other groups within the firm, any project
undertaken by Travis Partners benefits from the full
range of services available in-house.

In fact, this diversity of in-house capabilities allows us
to offer a total service, from a project's early planning
stages right through to its successful development and
realisation.

Architecture nevertheless remains the major focus
of the firm's professional activity. Travis Partners has
achieved an enviable record of producing aesthetic
and functional architecture within cost and programme
controls. By assembling a broadly-based group of
architectural and project control staff we are able to
give a targetted response to the various needs and
interests of each particular client.

The Sydney office employs over 90 professional and
technical personnel working in teams under the
guidance of Directors, Associate Directors and Associates.

An office in New Zealand has also been established
to serve our growing number of clients in that country.
Through our association with Auckland Architects
Avery Leuschke, Travis Partners are providing to
New Zealand clients the same range of services currently
offered by the Sydney Office.

The firm is poised to further expand into New Zealand
and the Pacific Rim area as a result of our recent
commissions on major commercial, hotel and resort
projects in those areas.

TravisPartners

Architects
Urban Designers/Planners
Interior Architects
Landscape Architects
Conservation Architects
Cost Planners
Quantity Surveyors

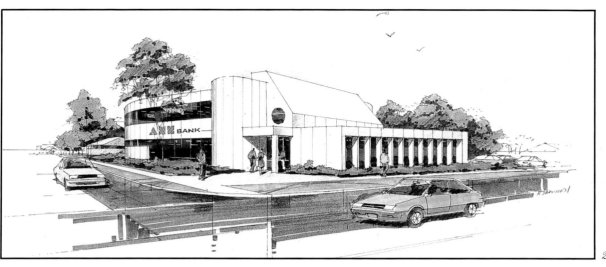

1 *Silver Sands Resort, Mandurah*

2 *Office Development*

3 *Silver Sands Resort, Mandurah*

4 *Silver Sands Resort, Mandurah*

5 *St. Stephens School, Duncraig*

6 *St. Stephens School, Duncraig*

TSIGULIS & ZUVELA PTY LTD
Architects Planners

Directors
John Tsigulis Ass.Arch (P.T.C.), F.R.A.I.A.
(bottom centre)
Max Zuvela Ass.Arch (P.T.C.), Dip.T.R.P. (P.T.C.),
F.R.A.I.A., M.R.A.P.I. (bottom left)

Established
1965

Address
16 Kings Park Road
West Perth, W.A. 6005

Telephone
(09) 481 0685

Facsimile
(09) 481 4983

Number of Employees
12

Project Types
Commercial
Offices, Retail premises

Industrial
Warehouses, factories, workshops

Residential
Group housing, flats, motels, home units

Health
Hospitals, medical facilities

Educational
Schools, training centres

Recreational
Resorts, sporting facilities, motels, hotels

Community
Civic centres, libraries,
aged persons facilities

Planning
Urban design, recreational planning

Other Disciplines
Research and Planning
Urban design
Interior design

Person to Contact
Max Zuvela

Current and Recent Projects
Commercial
Bullcreek District Shopping Centre
Office Building, Kings Park Road, West Perth
Chamberlain John Deere Administration Centre

Industrial
Warehouse and office, Kewdale Road, Kewdale
Graylands Workshop and Stores

Residential
Bullcreek Aged Persons Housing
Smiths Lake Group Housing
Nor West Towers, Tuart Hill

Health
Psychogeriatric Extended Care Units at Bentley,
Midland, Osborne Park, Lemnos and Armadale
Armadale Permanent Care Unit

Educational
St. Stephen's High School, Duncraig
Training Centres at Fremantle, Geraldton and
Bayswater
Water Training Facility, Garden Island

Recreational
Silver Sands Resort
Cottlesloe Beach Resort Hotel

Community
Esperance Civic and Cultural Centre
Indoor Pool, Len Shearer Aquatic Centre
Northam Recreation Centre
Blue Gum Recreation Centre
W.A. Deaf Centre
Bullcreek Library and Hall

Interior Design
National Acoustic Laboratories Hearing Centre,
Balcatta

Planning
Master Planning, Bullcreek District Centre
Wongan Hills Parking Precinct Study
Shire of Peppermint Grove Town Planning Scheme

Profile
John Tsigulis and Max Zuvela founded the firm in
1964 as the partnership Tsigulis & Zuvela. In 1979
the partnership became Tsigulis and Zuvela Pty. Ltd.

The practice has gained a reputation for providing a
high standard of professional design and service.

The firm has a strong organisational core which is
structured to enable expansion to meet specific task
requirements.

The firm undertakes intensive research and analysis
of a given problem and where appropriate will provide
innovative solutions.

The strongly analytical approach enables the achievement of an appropriate response to unique briefs.

All stages of services are seen by the firm as a team
effort. Consequently team members are carefully
selected on the basis of skill, experience and personality.

The client is considered to be an important member of
the team. Close communication between all members
of the team is encouraged and ideas are integrated to
achieve a complete response to the brief.

The firm responds to compliance with time and cost
programmes and is committed to providing a high
standard in all aspects of its services.

The firm is particularly aware of the need to respond
to change. Awareness of the trends in property
development, architectural design and construction
are considered essential to the success of the project.

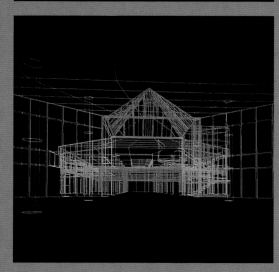

WALTER BROOKE AND ASSOCIATES PTY LTD

Directors – Architecture
John Walter Dip. Arch. S.A.I.T. F.R.A.I.A. (centre)
Stephen Brooke Dip. Arch. S.A.I.T. M.ARCH
  M.I.T. F.R.A.I.A. (left)

Director – Project Management
John Bray S.A.I.T. (right)

Associate
Ian Russell Dip. Arch. S.A.I.T. A.R.A.I.A.

Established
Partnership 1974
Incorporated 1976
Walter Brooke & Associates Pty Ltd 1981

Address
49 Greenhill Road
Wayville, S.A. 5034

PO Box 162
Goodwood, S.A. 5034

Telephone
(08) 272 4166

Facsimile
(08) 272 0143

Number of Employees
25

Sphere of Operations
South Australia
Northern Territory
Victoria
New South Wales
Queensland

Project Types
Commercial
Office, Retail

Community/Recreation
Sports Halls, Complexes, Pools

Education
Schools, Colleges, Universities

Local Government
Councils, Civic Centres, Libraries

Medical
Health, Hospitals, Clinics

Hospitality
Hotels, Motels, Restaurants

Finance
Banks, Building Societies

Industrial
Factories, Warehouses

Residential
Homes, Public Housing, Apartments

Ecclesiastical
Churches, Schools, Retirement Villages

Disciplines
Architecture
Project Management
Heritage Studies
Interior Design
Graphics

Person to Contact
John Walter
Stephen Brooke
John Bray

Some Current and Recent Projects
Commercial: Offices

Flinders Street, Adelaide 1983	$1.0M
St Kilda Road, Victoria 1984	$0.8M
North Terrace, Adelaide 1983/84	$1.6M
66 Greenhill Rd, Wayville 1985	$1.0M
48 Greenhill Rd, Wayville 1986	$1.2M
47 Greenhill Rd, Wayville 1986	$0.5M
26 Greenhill Rd, Wayville 1986	$1.2M

Retail Centres

Hallett Cove and Seaton, S.A. 1986/87	$1.6M
Shops and offices, Walkerville, S.A. 1987	$1.1M
Brashs Prospect and Edwardstown, S.A. 1987	$1.0M

Community/Recreation
City of Tea Tree Gully

Modbury, Highbury Centres, S.A. 1980	$1.1M
Commonwealth Dept of Housing & Construction Woodside Army Barracks, Recreation Complex 1987	$2.1M

Education

College of T.A.F.E., Marleston, S.A. 1982/83	$5.5M
St John's Grammar School Inc, Belair various ongoing 1984-87	$0.75M
S.A.I.T. School of Nursing, Adelaide Design Studies 1986	$13.0M
S.A.I.T. Labs and Lecture Stage I and II 1986/87	$2.2M
University of Adelaide – various projects 1987	

Government and Local Government

City of Enfield, Civic Centre study 1986/87	$1.0M
Hindmarsh Council, Works Depot Study 1986/87	$0.7M
Commonwealth Dept of Housing and Construction Woodside Army Barracks, redevelopment 1983/86 Architects in assoc. Walter Brooke Hodgkison Matthews	$18.0M
Stirling Council, office expansion 1986	$0.6M

Medical

St Andrew's Hospital, Adelaide – New theatre suite	$1.5M
Drug and Alcohol Services Council, clinics 1986/87	$1.0M
S.A. Health Commission, colocation project 1987	
Design study, Elizabeth, S.A.	$1.5M

Hospitality

Fitzroy Island, Qld Master planning 1983	$1.0M
Birdsville, Qld Hotel/Motel redevelopment 1984/87	$0.5M
South Australian Brewing Company: Retail liquor outlets 1984/87	$1.3M
Hotel refurbishments 1987	$1.0M
Restaurants, Blue Whale and Maxims 1985	$0.75M
Pepper Tree, North Adelaide 1985	$0.2M

Finance

Commonwealth Bank branches 1983/87	$0.1-1.5M
National Australia Bank, Westpac, State Bank	
Adelaide Permanent Building Society 1983	$1.0M
Various branches	$0.5M
Citicorp, Adelaide refurbishment 1986	$1.0M
Hindmarsh Adelaide Building Society 1986	$1.5M

Industrial

Office warehouse developments 1982/87	$0.1-$1.2M
Industrial Park, Marlon Rd, S.A. 1985/86	$1.25M
Taminga Factory, S.A. 1986	$2.5M
Bus depot, warehouses, Hindmarsh, S.A. 1985/86	$0.5M
Office workshops, Dry Creek, S.A. 1983/85	$0.6M

Residential

Townhouses, East Tce, Adelaide 1982/86	$0.25M-$1.25M
Houses: Adelaide, West Beach, 1986/87	$0.75M-$0.5M
Bridgewater, Mt Pleasant	$0.75M-$0.6M
Public Housing: Devon Design Construct S.A.H.T. Renown Pk, Pt Adelaide, Morphett Vale 1985/87	$12.0M

Ecclesiastical

Salvation Army, S.A. Catholic Church, various	$0.6M
Baptist Church, Care Village Stage I and Christian Care School 1983/87	$3.0M

The Company
Walter Brooke and Associates Pty Ltd is a state-of-the-art professional practice incorporating the broad spectrum of disciplines necessary to cover the total Architectural design solutions and needs of today's and tomorrow's clients.

The Directors and staff have significant experience in a wide cross section of Architecture since, and prior to, the company's incorporation. The experience of the practice is also augmented by a background in project development, cost management and consortia liaison which benefits to considerable effect, the project and Architectural package.

The office acts as a forum for project involvement with Directors ensuring personal participation from inception to completion.

Often the project is instigated with the client and our extensive portfolio of services commences with preparation of a brief and feasibility study and carries through research, analysis, synthesis, design, documentation, production, project team management and contract administration to completion.

These significant capabilities allow and encourage very close co-operation and involvement with clients at a human level, as well as production of innovative and progressive results.

Professional and Technical Services
The following services are offered as part of the professional scope of work carried out by the practice.

Problem Analysis	Documentation
Presentation of Ideas	Contract Administration
Solution Synthesis	Research
Feasibility Studies	Historical Assessment
Sketch Design	Heritage Evaluation
Design	Graphic Design
Drafting	Interior Design
Design Presentation	Landscape Design
Construction Detail	Model Making
Specifications	Materials Selection

The firm is versatile in current modern architectural and design idioms, also sensitive restoration and refurbishment. It has an established reputation for excellence in the design field and the directors have the respect and recognition for top architectural design amongst their contemporaries.

Creative sensitivity in design is best exhibited in the practice being consistently amongst local competition and award winners since 1978.

Architectural Philosophy
Put succinctly without the confusion of eclectic philosophical language our aim is to achieve high quality architecture that successfully resolves the parameters and constraints set by the clients' needs.

Our work transcends architectural notions to acknowledge also the requirements of performance, efficiency, cost effectiveness, relationship with society and the environment in general.

Design Expression
Our rationale is realized by analysis and synthesis testing the conceptual by both vertical and lateral methodology. Recent moves into the field of 3D computer aided design has provided the practice with design and production capabilities keeping us in the forefront of achievement.

Production Technology
This involves the progression of the design through subjective and objective review of construction technique, fabrication, materials and finishes to ensure the proper evaluation of the project as a whole. Office automation with word processing and computerisation supports the validity of solutions and strengthens our expertise in team project and construction management.

Contract administration is therefore well supported and performance maintained at a high level throughout all aspects of the architectural process, including the most important area of client confidence and rapport.

1

1 Woodhead Australia Offices, Darwin
2 University Offices, Darwin
3 Wallace Residence, Port Douglas
4 S.A.M.F.S. Headquarters and Fire Station, Adelaide
5 Alice Springs Travellers' Village

2

3

4

5

WOODHEAD AUSTRALIA – ARCHITECTS

Directors (left to right)
Brent Blanks B. Arch. FRAIA
Gary J. Hunt B. Arch. ARAIA
Robert D. Hall B. E. FSASMI LFRAIA
William R. Giles B. Arch. FRAIA AIArbA
Peter McLennan B. Arch. ARAIA
David King-Jones B. Arch. ARAIA
Hans Vos

Established
1927

Addresses

Adelaide
26-28 Chesser Street
Adelaide, S.A. 5000

Telephone
(08) 223 5013

Facsimile
(08) 232 0028

Darwin
19 Lindsay Street
Darwin, N.T. 5794

Telephone
(089) 81 9177

Facsimile
(089) 81 8279

Alice Springs
70 Elder Street
Alice Springs, N.T. 5750

Telephone
(089) 52 5173

Facsimile
(089) 52 8675

Cairns
163 Lake Street
Cairns, Nth Qld 4870

Port Douglas, Cairns
12 Macrossan Street
Port Douglas
Nth Qld 4871

Telephone
(070) 98 5525

Facsimile
(070) 98 5534

Perth
41 Hampden Road
Perth, W.A. 6009

Telephone
(09) 386 8955

Facsimile
(09) 386 3639

Number of Employees
130 (1987)

Value of Commissions
Commissions for works
in excess of $1,000M in 1987

Project Types
Tourism/Leisure
Commercial
Retail
Industrial
Health
Restoration/Recycling
Educational

Other Disciplines
Architecture
Resort & Urban Design
Interior Design
Project Development

Persons to Contact
Adelaide
Brent Blanks
David King-Jones

Darwin
Hans Vos
William R. Giles

Alice Springs
Gary Hunt
Stewart Brooks

Port Douglas
Gavin Lee

Perth
Ian Howard

Current and Recent Projects

Tourism/Leisure

Redevelopment, Adelaide Railway Station,
Hotel/Convention Centre
In association with John Andrews
International Sydney — $189M

Sheraton Mirage Resort, Port Douglas, Nth Qld
Condominium units, golf club, support facilities
and master planning.
In association with Media 5, Southport — $100M

Desert Springs Country Club Estate
Alice Springs, Northern Territory
18 hole golf course, golf club, residential, hotel
and village centre — $27M

Prodev Pty Ltd, Resort, Mauritius
300 room hotel, condominiums, golf course and
ancillary facilities — $180M

Darwin Marina Estate, Northern Territory
Marina, hotel, condominiums
and ancillary facilities — $80M

Aser Property Trust Group Casino,
Adelaide Railway Station — $25M

Commercial

Office Building, Adelaide
South Australia Super Fund Investment Trust — $38M

Office Building, Adelaide
South Australia Super Fund Investment Trust — $13M

Office Building/Convention Centre,
Adelaide, South Australia
Public Buildings Department — $16.5M

State Bank of South Australia
Grenfell Street, Adelaide — $8.5M

Office Building, Adelaide, South Australia
Wyatt Benevolent Institution Inc. — $9.5M

Retail

Office/Retail Development, Adelaide, South Australia
Pennant Property Trust — $26M

Retail/Carpark Development,
Adelaide, South Australia — $22M

Retail Redevelopment, Adelaide, South Australia
Aust. Mutual Provident Society — $8M

The Gallerie Shopping Centre,
Adelaide, South Australia
National Mutual Life Association of Australasia — $5M

Industrial

Assembly Plant, South Australia
Chrysler Australia (Mitsubishi Motors) — $35M

S.A. Metropolitan Fire Services Headquarters
and Fire Station, South Australia — $14.5M

Northern Power Station Buildings
Electricity Trust of South Australia — $4M

Bus Depots, Morphettville, Aldgate
and Elizabeth, South Australia
State Transport Authority (S.A.) — $7.6M

Workshop redevelopment, Randwick, New South Wales
Urban Transit Authority of N.S.W. — $1.6M

Extensions to existing facilities, Stage 1
Port Stanvac, South Australia
Petroleum Refineries (Aust.) — $1.7M

Redevelopment of Reynella Winery, South Australia
Thomas Hardy & Sons — $3.5M

Health

Wallaroo Hospital Redevelopment
as a regional medical centre, South Australia — $6M

Berri Regional Hospital Redevelopment
South Australia — $6M

Royal Adelaide Hospital
New Admissions centre and redevelopment
of operating theatre, South Australia — $12M

Modbury Hospital
Expansion and redevelopment, South Australia — $3M

New Medical Resource Centre
South Australian Medical Library — $4M

Defence Projects

HMAS Coonawarra Naval Base,
Darwin, Northern Territory
Dept. of Housing & Construction — $13.5M

Local Government

Retail/Carpark, South Australia
Corp. of the City of Adelaide — $2.85M

Civic Centre, South Australia
District Council of Angaston — $0.5M

Education Projects

Hartley College of Advanced Education,
South Australia, Public Buildings Department — $5.5M

Alterations and extensions, South Australia
Whyalla Technical College — $6M

Willunga High School, South Australia — $2M

Regency Park Centre
Crippled Children's Association
of South Australia — $5.5M

Chemical Technical Building
South Australia Institute of Technology — $2M

Telecom Training Centre, Pasadena, South Australia
Department of Housing & Construction — $2.5M

Profile

Woodhead Australia – Architects, is a nationally operated architectural Group which provides design solutions in direct response to a client's specific brief and site. Our strength rests in our ability to:

- Create buildings which aesthetically combine form and function while working within predetermined financial parameters.

- Integrate specialised user requirements into the built form.

By providing efficient professional attention and detailed consideration to clients across the full range of architectural services, we have come to reap the rewards of an extremely loyal clientele.

As part of our overall belief that "Good design is an investment for the future", Woodhead Australia offers corporate, individual, institutional and government clients a range of capabilities that include: development of brief, design, contract documentation, contract administration, post contract assistance, and interior design. Our level of contribution may be tailored to meet specific project requirements.

Due to our size and lengthy period of operation, we have the capability to provide both depth and diversity. While, over the years, a great number of different building types have been added to our portfolio, we have developed particular expertise in developing commercial, retail, industrial and tourist projects.

Although all our work must address the fundamental issues of purposes, place and people, our goal is to continue producing innovative, cost efficient, quality design, free from the temporary influence of fads or trends.

The Teams: Experienced teams are assembled to suit each particular project requirement, drawing upon the diverse skills contained within the Group. Each project comes under the control of a Company Director or Regional Director for its full duration. Each project team seeks to include a client's representative as a key member, enhanced on a need basis with multi-disciplinary expertise from various engineering, management, design and cost consultants who may be engaged and co-ordinated by Woodhead Australia on behalf of the client.

National Reach: Woodhead Australia provides architectural services throughout Australia via offices in Adelaide, Darwin, Alice Springs, Port Douglas, Cairns and Perth, with permanent offices planned in other major population centres throughout Australia. Senior personnel are highly mobile and are accustomed to the provision of detailed management and technical skills wherever they may be needed.

Negotiating Ability: Today, zoning analysis, feasibility studies, submissions for grants, efficient project management and associated tasks, call for the use of experienced negotiating abilities. Woodhead Australia offers a full range of these services.

Specialised Design: Our extensive nation-wide experience allows us to offer clients climatically sensitive design in such divergent locations as Mediterranean, tropical and arid regions.

Additional Services: Woodhead Australia, upon request, can provide total concept to include architecture, landscape and interior design; co-ordination of special plant and equipment into building structures; furnishing and artwork selection; special studies; litigation and arbitration attendances.

WOODHEAD
AUSTRALIA
ARCHITECTS

1

2

4

6

7

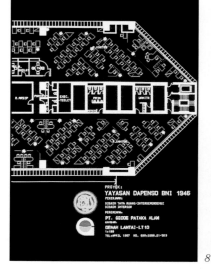

8

1 *Four Seasons Cooinda Hotel,*
  Kakadu National Park, N.T.

2 *Headquarters for*
  Health Insurance Commission,
  Tuggeranong, A.C.T.

3 *Standard Chartered Bank*
  (Australia) Limited, Head Office,
  Adelaide, S.A.

4 *Elizabeth City Centre,*
  Elizabeth, S.A.

5 *Commonwealth Banking Corporation*
  South Australian Capital Office,
  Adelaide, S.A.

6 *Diamond Beach Hotel Casino,*
  Darwin, N.T.

7 *Bridgewater Mill wine labels*
  for Petaluma Pty. Ltd.

8 *Layout plan for Bank Negara Indonesia*
  1946, Jakarta, Indonesia

WOODS BAGOT PTY LTD

3

5

From its foundation in 1869, Woods Bagot was destined to become one of Australia's leading architectural companies.

Today the practice operates from its Adelaide base throughout the Asia-Pacific region and is one of the largest design groups in Australia with a staff of over 160 persons.

Woods Bagot has firmly established traditions of analytical and managerial expertise and dedication to rational innovation in design. The company's full service team includes architects, interior and graphic designers, landscape architects and planners. These are talented people with a developed technical knowledge. People who appreciate quality . . . understand the constraints of time . . . the disciplines of budgets.

Woods Bagot is as much at home as architect of the landmark commercial development for Adelaide's CBD as it is rationalising office space and accommodation for a major client in Hong Kong.

The company's strength has always been its commitment to purposeful, directed management throughout the design and construction process. This ensures each project is aesthetically pleasing, technically sound and commercially viable.

Woods Bagot has been a part of the pioneering move to an acceptance of quality and new design standards throughout Australia. It is continuing to build this reputation beyond Australia's shores. Projects in every Australian mainland State and Territory, Indonesia and Hong Kong are a testament to this.

Specialised services, some of which are provided by independently managed organisations within the Group, include:

Architecture
Interior Design
Briefing Services
Facilities Programming
Pre-project Analysis
Health Planning and Design
Space Planning
Graphic Design
Urban Planning
Landscape Architecture
Computing
Architectural Models

Head Office
Woods Bagot Pty. Ltd.
99 Gawler Place, Adelaide
South Australia 5000
Telephone (08) 212 7600
Fax (08) 231 0026, Telex AA82864
(and in other States)

Woods Bagot International Ltd.
1202 East Point Centre
Hong Kong
Telephone 5-833 9987
Fax 5-72 0350
Telex 82811 WB1 HX

For further information on
Woods Bagot's services
and resources contact:
Group Chairman, Bill Steele, or
Managing Director, Alistair Angus
on (08) 212 7600

L A N D S C A P E · A R C H I T E C T S

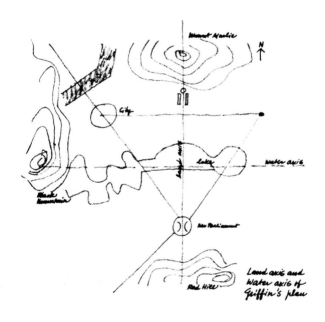

Land axis and
Water axis of
Griffin's plan

1

2

3

4

5

1 Thurgoona Park Estate, Albury

2 National Botanic Gardens Rockery
   Complex, Canberra

3 Goodwin Retirement Village, Canberra

4 Glebe Park, Canberra

5 Bruce TAFE College, Canberra

DEVERSON SCHOLTENS BOMBARDIER
Landscape Architects

Principals
Paul Bombardier, BLA FAILA ASLA
Paul Scholtens, MAIH ARAIPR

Established
1979

Address
Deakin Chambers
14 Hannah Place
Deakin, A.C.T. 2600

Telephone
(062) 851955

Facsimile
(062) 816668

Number of Employees
10

Project Types
Commercial
Offices, Resorts

Ecclesiastical/Institutional
Churches, Cemeteries, Prisons,
Court House

Educational
Schools, Colleges, Universities

Engineering
Lakes, Transportation Corridors,
Irrigation

Environmental
Restoration, Assessment

Health
Hospitals, Nursing Homes

Industrial
Land Restoration and Conservation,
Factories

Recreational
Sporting Fields, Parks, Pools,
Playgrounds

Residential
Homes, Public Housing,
Aged Persons Units

Urban/Municipal
Malls, Plazas, Streetscapes

Person to Contact
Paul Bombardier

Principals
Paul Scholtens, Paul Bombardier

Profile
The Practice of Deverson Scholtens Bombardier, Landscape Architects, provides private clients, Architects, Engineers, Planners and Government agencies with creative design skills supported by sound technical knowledge in all aspects of Landscape Architecture.

The basis of our work is the development of imaginative and innovative concepts which are in sympathy with the surrounding environment and are appropriate to our client's needs. At the same time we are concerned with efficient planning and implementation within defined budgets and time constraints.

The firm is structured to act as consultant for projects involving Architecture, Engineering, Urban Planning and Environmental Sciences. In this capacity, we are responsible for evaluation, design, documentation, tendering, co-ordination and supervision of each project to its completion.

Our highly experienced design and administration team has expertise in site masterplanning, landscape and environmental studies, horticulture, conceptual site design, detail landscape and irrigation design, construction documentation, site supervision, and contract administration.

Current and Recent Projects
Educational
Chisholm High School, Canberra
Bruce TAFE College, Canberra
Lawton Special School, Qld
St Marys School, Myrtleford, Vic.
Clyde Cameron College, Wodonga, Vic.

Engineering
Tuggeranong Dam and Lake Landscaping,
  Canberra
Bruce Highway Deviation, Qld
Elizabeth Mitchell Drive, Albury, N.S.W.
Eastern Parkway, Canberra

Industrial
Mitchell Industrial Estate, Canberra
Melrose Drive Industrial Estate, Wodonga
Thurgoona Industrial Park, Albury

Institutional
Everton Park Medical Centre, Qld
Embassies of Greece, Brazil, Indonesia, Korea, India,
  New Zealand, in Canberra
EEC Chancery, Canberra
Parklea Prison, Sydney
Clyde Mail Exchange, Sydney

Recreational
Fadden Pines District Park, Canberra
Thurgoona Town Park Masterplan, Albury
Pelerman Gardens Tourist Development, Qld
National Botanic Gardens, Garden for the Disabled,
  Canberra
Dog on the Tuckerbox Redevelopment, Gundagai, N.S.W.
National Botanic Gardens, Rockery Complex,
  Canberra

Residential
Corry's Wood Neighbourhood Landscaping, Albury
Yarralumla Town House Development, Canberra
Federation Park Neighbourhood Landscaping,
  Wodonga, Vic.
Australian Defence Forces Academy, Canberra
Government Housing, Richardson, Canberra

Urban/Municipal
Tuggeranong Town Centre and Lake
  Landscape Development, Canberra
Thurgoona Town Centre Masterplan, Albury
Glebe Park, Canberra
Veteran's Park Development, Canberra
Streetscape Redevelopment, Narrandera
Town Parks and Streetscape Redevelopment, Corowa
Woden Town Park and Cemetery, Canberra

Member
Australian Institute of Landscape Architects

Deverson
Scholtens
Bombardier

MOUNT PIPER POWER STATION

Great Western Highway

WALLERAWANG

MEADOW FLAT

RYDAL

LITHGOW

O'CONNELL

TARANA

SODWALLS

FISH RIVER

HAMPTON

LANDSCAN PTY LIMITED
Landscape Architects and Environmental Planners

Directors
John Ladd-Hudson B.Arch., F.R.A.I.A.,
Dip. L.D., A.A.I.L.A. Affiliate N.Z.I.L.A.
David Louden R.A.I.P.R.
Jacinta McCann B.L. Arch. A.A.I.L.A.

Associates
Karen Prichard B.L. Arch. A.A.I.L.A.
Carolyn Tallents B.L. Arch. A.A.I.L.A.
Sally Ash B.A.

Established
1981

Address
115 Sailors Bay Road
Northbridge, N.S.W. 2063
P.O. Box 151
Northbridge, N.S.W. 2063

Telephone
(02) 958 1533

Facsimile
(02) 958 2126

Telex
AA 72998

Number of Employees
18

Person to Contact
David Louden

Profile
Landscan offers a comprehensive range of landscape design and environmental planning consultancy services.

Since the formation of the company in 1981, Landscan has grown rapidly to meet the new demands set by market trends. Today, it comprises a multi-disciplinary team including experienced landscape architects with expertise in all areas of commercial design, master planning and environmental assessment studies.

The key directors and associates have been with the firm since its inception and, as individuals, have up to fifteen years experience in all forms of landscape architecture.

Current projects are located throughout Australia and involve feasibility and master planning, site assessment, visual assessment, environmental studies, landscape design, documentation and contract administration.

Recent growth in the practice has been in commercial office park development, rural master planning, resort development and landscape and visual assessment studies.

In 1986, Landscan received the Australian Institute of Landscape Architects inaugural National Design Award for landscape planning and design of the National Headquarters for IBM Australia Limited at West Pennant Hills.

Current major commercial projects have landscape budgets ranging from two hundred thousand dollars to four million dollars.

Landscan will continue to maintain high standards of design excellence and client service upon which its reputation as one of Australia's leading landscape architectural practices has been established.

Upper left
IBM National Headquarters
Epping Corporate Park
EIS Visual Assessment Plan,
Mt Piper to Marulan

Upper right
Four Mile Beach Resort, Port Douglas
American Express Atrium
Quay Apartments
Sanctuary Cove Resort Master Plan

Professional Services
Planning and Environmental Studies
Master Planning

Site Investigation

Site Analysis

Visual Analysis and Assessment

Environmental Studies and Reports

Forestry Management and Maintenance

Rural Master Planning

Design, Documentation and Contract Administration
Concept Design

Design Development

Graphic Presentation and Rendering

Planting and Grading plans

Schedules and Specifications for tender

Cost Analysis, Estimates and Cost Control

Construction and Contract Administration

Coordination of External Works

Other Services
Landscape Maintenance Manuals

Technical and Horticultural Advice

Computer Drafting and Cost Analysis

Feasibility Studies

Plantstock Pre-ordering

Location of Specimen Plant Material

Current and Recent Projects
Hotels and Resorts
Pelican Beach Resort, Coffs Harbour
Sheraton Darwin Hotel
Sheraton Hobart Hotel
The Beachcomber Resort Hotel, Noosa, Queensland
Sanctuary Cove Resort Community, Queensland
St Bees Island Resort, Whitsunday Passage
Broadbeach Hotel, Redevelopment, Ocean Place, Gold Coast

Commercial Office Developments and Office Parks
IBM National Headquarters, West Pennant Hills, Sydney
American Express Headquarters, Macquarie Corporate Park, Sydney
Cityview Office Park, Pennant Hills, Sydney
Southbank Corporate Park, Brisbane
St George Building Society Headquarters, Sydney
Waterfront Place, Brisbane
Pymble Corporate Centre, Sydney
Amory Gardens, Ashfield, Sydney

Urban Design
Aetna Office Towers, Sydney
Central Park Commercial Tower and Plaza, Perth
Chatswood Connection, Chatswood, Sydney
Centennial Plaza, Sydney CBD
Prince Alfred Park Project, Sydney
The Interchange, Chatswood, Sydney
National Australia Bank House Refurbishment, Sydney
The Maritime Centre, Sydney
Darling Harbour Western Boulevard Aquarium, Sydney

Retail and Industrial Development
Casuarina Shopping Square, Darwin
Charlestown Shopping Centre, Newcastle
W.D. and H.O. Wills Headquarters, Sydney
Bay Village, Noosa Heads

Residential Developments and Retirement Communities
'Tantallon', Sydney
'Essex House', Sydney
'Pilochory', Sydney
'The Shores', Sydney
'St Johns Wood', Sydney
'Warringah Place', Sydney
East Lindfield Garden Village, Sydney
'Glenaeon', Sydney

Education and Community Facilities
M.S. Western Region Centre, Sydney
Mater Hospital, North Sydney
The King's School, Parramatta
Abbotsleigh Girls School, Sydney
Port Macquarie T.A.F.E.
Narellan Primary School, N.S.W.
Masada College, Sydney
Knox Grammar School, Sydney
Calwell High School, Canberra
Pymble Ladies' College, Sydney

Recreation Facilitites
Sydney Football Stadium, Moore Park, Sydney
Rosehill Racecourse, Sydney
Raleigh Park, Sydney
Dunbar Park, Sydney
Epping Recreation Complex, Sydney
Southbank Corporate Park Recreation Centre, Brisbane
'Kincumber Waters' Caravan Park, N.S.W.

Rural Property Master Planning and Design
Arrowfield Stud, Hunter Valley
Woodlands Stud, Jerry's Plains , N.S.W.
Blandford Park, Murrurundi, N.S.W.
Cudlipp Property, Paddy's River, N.S.W.
Carbine Lodge, Melbourne
Crown Lodge Stables, Warwick Farm
Nebo Lodge Stables, Rosehill
Lord Ben Stables, Rosehill

Landscape Management Plans and Environmental Protection
IBM Australia Limited, Cumberland Forest, Sydney
Mulgoa Valley Regional & Environmental Study
Penrith Lakes Scheme, Sydney

Visual and Landscape Assessment
Lismore to Armidale Proposed Transmission Line EIS
Lismore to Mullumbimby Proposed Transmission Line EIS
Mt Piper to Marulan Proposed Transmission Line EIS
Bateman's Bay Marina EIS
Bermagui Marina EIS
Jervis Bay Naval Relocation EIS
Millers Point Landscape Conservation Study

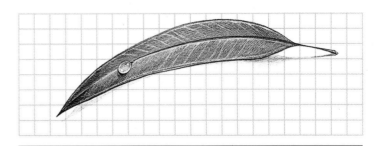

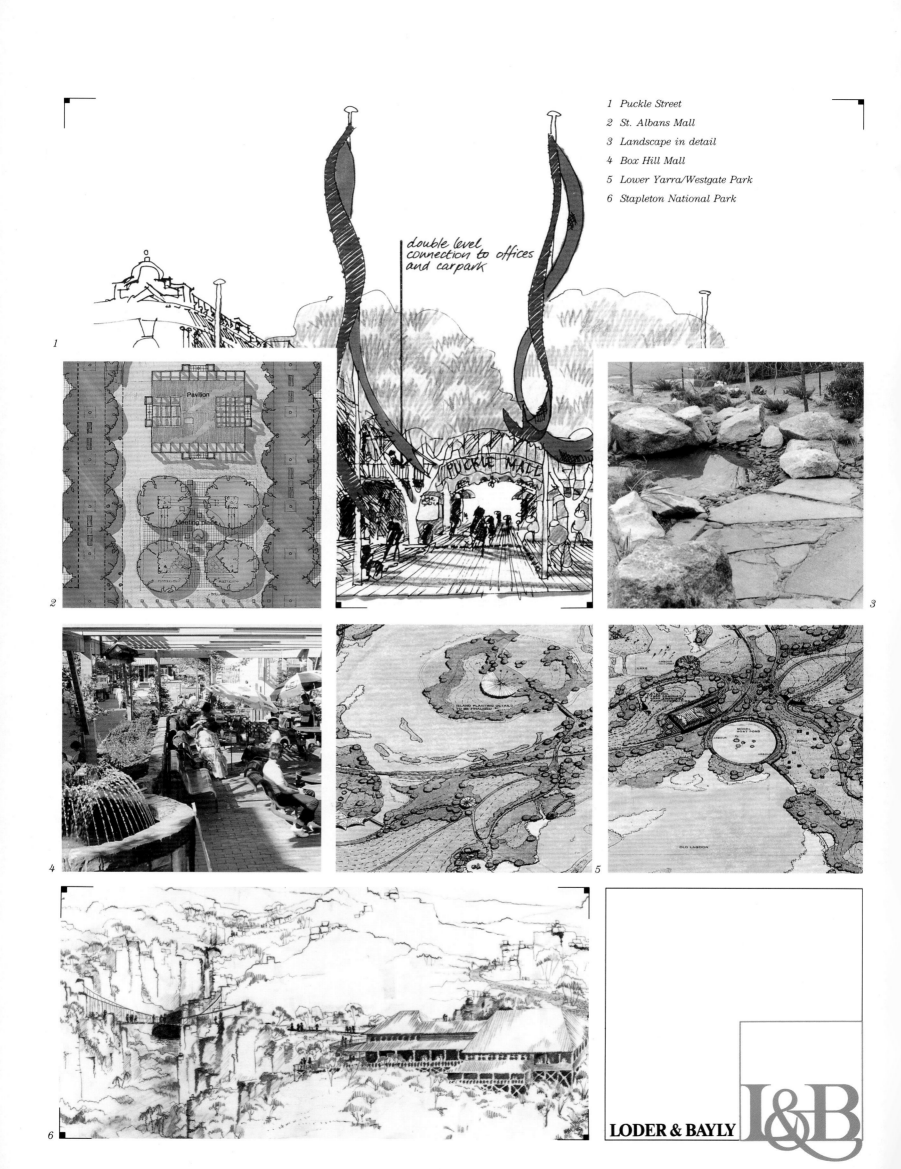

1 Puckle Street
2 St. Albans Mall
3 Landscape in detail
4 Box Hill Mall
5 Lower Yarra/Westgate Park
6 Stapleton National Park

double level
connection to offices
and carpark

LODER & BAYLY

LODER & BAYLY PTY LTD

Landscape/Design Personnel

(left to right)

Nick Safstrom
Landscape Architect
Dip. Arch. (R.M.I.T.)
Dip. Land. des. (R.M.I.T.)
A.A.I.L.A. M.R.A.I.P.R.

Jan Martin
Urban Design
B. Arch. (Melbourne)
Dip. T.R.P. (Melbourne)
M.R.A.P.I.

Brian Scantlebury
Site Engineering
B.E. (Hons) (Monash)

Ian Wight
Recreation Planner
M.A. Geog. (Edinburgh)
M.C.D. (Masters – Town Planning) (Liverpool)
M.R.A.P.I. M.R.T.P.I.

Mike Smith
Landscape Architect
Dip. Hort. Sci. (Burnley)
Grad. Dip. Land. Des. (R.M.I.T.)
A.A.I.L.A. M.R.A.I.P.R.

Craig Eldridge
Landscape Design
B.A. Sci. Land. Arch. (R.M.I.T.)

Peter Haack
Landscape Design
Dip. App. Sci. (Horticulture) (Burnley)

Christina Banco
Graphic Design
B.A. Vis. Com. (R.M.I.T.)

Other Senior Personnel and Disciplines

William Chandler
Urban Planning, Architecture

Bridget Cramphorn
Social Planning

Malcolm Daff
Traffic Planning

Don Glasson
Urban Planning

Natalie Gray
Urban Planning

John Loder
Transport, Planning and Economics

Michael Read
Urban Planning

Josephine Connellan
Civil Engineering

Anthony Martini
Civil Engineering

Address
79 Power Street
Hawthorn, Vic. 3122

Telephone
(03) 819 1144

Facsimile
(03) 819 1665

Landscape & Design Services Provided

Site Analysis, Planning, Design & Development
Visual Assessment
Recreation Research Planning & Design
Urban Design
Landscape Design
Resort Planning, Feasibility & Development
Estate Planning
Access Planning

Current and Recent Landscape and Design Projects

Housing

Walker Street Estate	$0.45M
Gronn Place Estate	$0.35M
Boyd Crescent Estate	$0.35M

Lilydale Retirement Village

Wolmersley Friendship Village

Williamstown Rifle Range Estate

Newmarket Saleyards Redevelopment

Mont Park Residential Feasibility

''Mock Street''
Low-energy, more affordable housing

Parks

Greenvale Recreation Reserve, 85 ha.

Lower Yarra/Westgate	$5M
Barham Lakes, 80 ha.	$2M

Royal Park
Competition finalists

Blue Rock Dam Recreation Areas

Yarra Park, Melbourne, Upgrade

Yarra Valley Bike Paths

Altona Foreshore & Wetlands

Traralgon Creek

Gardiners Valley Recreation

Malvern City Recreation Assessment

Moorabbin Recreation Study

Kilcuna Play Park, Lakes Entrance

Ballam Park Playground

Resorts

Cape Schanck Country Club and 36-hole Golf Course

Mt. Stirling Alpine Resort

Stapleton National Park (NT)

Storth Ryes
Residential, Marina and Golf Course

Promlee
Residential, Marina and Golf Course

Mt. Buller Resort Centre

Urban Design

Box Hill Mall

St. Albans Mall

Haymarket Precinct

Puckle St. Mall
Competition winners

Maryborough Centre

Shepparton Mall
Competition finalists

Cranbourne Centre

The Practice

Loder & Bayly's landscape and design consultancy is a vital part of our practice.

The firm was founded on an inter-disciplinary approach. The individual members of the firm are committed to inter-disciplinary problem-solving and, as a group, we offer project teams who provide this approach at a senior level.

The senior professionals in the group take individual and shared responsibility for the work of the firm and its reputation. All professionals of the group share involvement in deciding major policy matters and are responsible for sustaining the standards of the firm.

A practice can only perform to the limits of the ability of those whose services are available in it. The recruiting policy of the firm has always been to employ good people when they are available.

The structure of the firm very much reflects the basic aims of the group: experienced professionals from a range of disciplines working closely and co-operatively together in order to provide a useful and efficient service for private and public clients in planning and design, engineering and landscape.

We offer at all times independent, authoritative, solution-oriented advice within the skill areas that the group encompasses.

For all projects, large or small, Loder & Bayly nominate a project officer. He or she will be an experienced manager and a senior professional with expertise in the 'lead' discipline.

The majority of the professional group have multiple qualifications and substantial experience. This apparently top-heavy structure is a matter of policy: it ensures that senior professionals work on, and take real responsibility for, each project in the office. Lesser experienced professionals and support staff play an important role.

The use of part-time assistance ranges from clerical and drafting help, to sub-consulting advice from the most eminent specialists available, to extend or reinforce our own capability in response to the needs of the clients.

While the practice has developed a wide range of skills, it enjoys the opportunity to work with other leading designers and architects. Our services include either becoming part of other consultancy teams, providing isolated specific advice or design, or bringing others into our teams to tackle specific projects.

Our services are supported by data base and direct screen input C.A.D. systems specially developed for site development, earth moulding as well as landscape design. Our computer systems also include sophisticated traffic analysis capability – 3D highly-manipulable financial analysis packages, and project management systems.

The skills encompassed within the group include:

Urban Planning	Traffic Engineering
Transport Planning	Geography
Landscape Architecture	Architecture
Urban Design	Graphic Design
Civil Engineering	Economics
Sociology	Financial Analysis

1 Lake St. Clair Study

2 Darling Harbour Redevelopment project

3 D.H.P. CAD Documentation

4 Mackenzie Street Playground

5 Mitchell & Clouston Head Office Sydney

MITCHELL + CLOUSTON GROUP
Landscape Architects, Environmental Consultants, Planners

Directors (left to right)
James Mitchell Dip LD, Dip Hort, AAILA, ARAIPR
Brian Clouston Dip LD, NDH, DH, PPLI, FILAM
Alun Chapman BA, MA(LD), ALI, AAILA

Associate Planning
Vaughan McInnes BRTP, MRAPI, GDLA

Established
Mitchell + Clouston Planning   1987
Mitchell + Clouston   1984
James Mitchell & Associates Pty Ltd. 1972
Brian Clouston & Partners Limited   1961

Addresses
Sydney
53a Ross Street
Glebe, N.S.W. 2037
Telephone
(02) 660 7744
Facsimile
(02) 660 6243
Canberra
36 Grey Street
Deakin, A.C.T. 2600
Telephone
(062) 73 2264
Facsimile
(062) 73 3637

Number of Employees
10

Associated Offices
Brian Clouston & Partners Asia Ltd.
Hong Kong
Kuala Lumpur
Singapore

Brian Clouston & Partners UK Ltd.
Durham
London
Bristol
Birmingham
Chester
Huddersfield

Number of Employees
200

Project Types
Cemeteries
Educational
Engineering
Health
Industrial
Leisure
Parks
Recreation
Rehabilitation
Residential
Resorts
Retirement Villages

Person to Contact
Sydney
James Mitchell
Canberra
Alun Chapman
Planning
Vaughan McInnes

Profile
Mitchell Clouston Group is a multi-disciplinary consultancy practising in the fields of landscape architecture; recreation, regional, town and environmental planning; with offices in Sydney, and Canberra and associated offices in the United Kingdom, Singapore, Hong Kong and Kuala Lumpur.

The consultancy has undertaken commissions for a wide range of clients including Local, State and Commonwealth government departments and private organisations.

The practice can provide the following services:

Mitchell + Clouston
Environmental Impact Assessment and Appraisal
Visual Analysis
Landscape Design
Park and Recreation Design
Documentation and Specifications
Contract Administration and Supervision
Urban Design
Mine Rehabilitation
Site Management and Maintenance Advice

Mitchell + Clouston Planning
Local Environmental Studies
Local Environmental Plans
Policy and Development Plans
Planning Schemes
Development Control Plans
Town Centre Studies
Commercial and Industrial Planning
Feasibility Analysis and Project Appraisals
Tourism, Leisure and Resort Planning

We have forged links with a wide range of experts in the environmental sciences enabling us to solve technical problems while adopting an individual design approach to each situation.

The preparation of detailed reports, plans and cost estimates to make applications for and to gain funding through Employment Programmes, Tourism, Steel Industry and Boat Launching Grants, etc. has proved to be a useful service to local government departments.

Mitchell + Clouston have the design expertise and resources to work closely with engineering, architectural and economic consultants, both in Australia, the Middle East and Pacific Region.

Professional Approach
We are committed to the creation of viable projects that demonstrate design excellence with technical competence and longevity.

To achieve this, we believe in the creative resolution of design problems with flair and originality.

Group Philosophy
As the environmental, employment and economic implications of development comes increasingly under focus, there is a need for rational and practical planning solutions which offer the opportunity for development stimulus, within the requirements of good planning practice.

Our approach to solutions offers professional and creative advice on a range of planning matters. It is comprehensive and has a flexible management structure, enabling the group to undertake a wide range of projects without difficulty.

Landscapes are for people to enjoy. Without their enjoyment of a landscape any design will fail.

We believe our first principle is to provide environments that people appreciate and that they wish to come back to.

Landscapes should be memorable. The design of a landscape should demonstrate an originality that is lasting and which will mature with time.

Design should be technically feasible and original, co-existing alongside technical adequacy, if it is to succeed.

Whether we are undertaking the feasibility studies of tourist resorts in Queensland, the planning of New Towns in the Middle East or Hong Kong, the design of condominium and hotel environments in Singapore and Kuala Lumpur, or the development of Darling Harbour Park in Sydney, we are able to utilise the considerable knowledge and experience of our talented staff to generate the right design solution to suit our clients' preferences.

Current and Recent Projects
Urban Design
Darling Harbour Park and Promenade, The Authority
Work included early planning involvement, design documentation of harbourside park, promenade and pavements, fountains and lakes, exhibition building forecourt, acquisition of palms and fig tree and site supervision.

Port Macquarie Town Green
Hastings Shire Council
Design of entrance plaza playground and riverside walk.

Community
Botany Cemetery and Eastern Suburbs Crematorium, The Trust
Preparing masterplan, design documentation of vaults and crypts, new entrance and open spaces.

Institutional
Tallawarra Power Station,
Electricity Commission of N.S.W.
Undertaking a landscape study of existing and proposed facilities completing impact assessment and preliminary development plans.

Resorts
Tam O'Shanter Mission Beach, Sefano Pty Ltd.
Appraisal of existing facilities and proposals for extensions.

Jindabyne Resort Development – owner
Environmental Impact Assessment and preliminary planning.

Parks
Mackenzie Street, Leichhardt Municipal Council
Design documentation of small community park and play facilities.

Australian Garden Festival,
Victorian Tourism Commission
Preliminary planning and initial assessment study.

Gungaderra Creek,
National Capital Development Commission
Concept design of creek side park in Gungahlin, Canberra.

Natural Areas
Jerrabomberra Wetlands,
National Capital Development Commission
Ecological Assessment, masterplan and landscape development of a major wildlife resource on the edge of Lake Burley Griffin.

Roads
Gungahlin Internal Roads,
National Capital Development Commission
Design and layout proposals for Canberra's New Town Development

Industrial and Business Parks
Unanderra Industrial Park, Wollongong City Council
Masterplan and detail design.

Health
The New Fairfield Hospital, Department of Health
Landscape Assessment, design documentation and supervision of a major western suburbs health facility.

Commercial
Kambah District Centre –
National Capital Development Commission
Design of Neighbourhood Centre Environs.

Recreational
Davidson Park Walking Track Study
National Parks and Wildlife Study
Planning of 72km walking tracks and associated facilities around Middle Harbour.

Lake St Clair Recreation Study
Singleton Shire Council
Detailed recreation and management study of the Glennies Creek catchment area in the Upper Hunter Valley.

1   Boomerang Beach Resort, N.S.W. (Tourist development)

2   110 Walker Street, North Sydney (New Head Office of Rice Daubney)

3   Charter Grove Commercial Complex, St Leonards, N.S.W. (Office Development)

4   Merritts Base Station Facility, Thredbo, N.S.W. (Tourist development)

5   Boomerang Beach Resort, N.S.W. (Tourist development)

RICE DAUBNEY
Landscape Architects

Directors
Stephen Sanlorenzo
Principal Landscape Architect
Bachelor of Landscape Architecture
University of New South Wales
President NSW Group
Australian Institute of Landscape Architects

Established
1987

Address
97 Pacific Highway
North Sydney, N.S.W. 2060

Telephone
(02) 922 2955

Facsimile
(02) 959 3015

Number of Employees
6

Associated Offices
Rice Daubney
Level 1
Cnr Beach Road & Parnell Rise
Auckland 1, New Zealand

Telephone
(09) 37 8848

Facsimile
(09) 37 6600

Project Types
Urban Design
Commercial/Office
Educational
Health
Hotel & Leisure
Retail
Medium Density Housing
Parks & Recreation

Other Disciplines
Architects
Urban Planning
Interior Architecture
Building Diagnostics
Health Systems

Person to Contact
Sydney
Stephen Sanlorenzo

New Zealand
Warren Dixon

Natural Resource Assessment
Blue Mountains Eastern Escarpment Visual
Assessment Study
Visual assessment and policy planning study of
22 sq km area between Penrith and Kurrajong Heights
for the Department of Environment and Planning.

Master Planning
Thredbo Alpine Village
Site analysis, concept design and presentation of
proposal to expand village facilities and infrastructure
for Kosciusko Thredbo Pty Ltd.

Mitchell Park Estate
Site planning and landscape concept design of a
multi-storey medium density housing estate in
Blacktown, N.S.W. for Trikon Corporation Ltd.

International Corporate Centre, Terrey Hills
Environmental design guidelines, allotment layout and
development controls of a 60 ha site for Dainford Pty Ltd.

Boomerang Beach Tourist Resort
Site evaluation, concept layout and presentation of
proposals for 100 residential units, conference and
recreation facilities in northern NSW for Turner
Corporation Ltd.

Landscape Design and Documentation
Lutanda Retirement Village
Site planning, earthworks, hard and soft works for
4.5 ha retirement village in Pennant Hills, N.S.W. for
Jennings Industries Limited.

Charter Grove Commercial Complex
Urban design and planting layout of a city office park
focusing on a central plaza for Chase Corporation.

Office and Showroom Complex, St Leonards
Streetscape design and facade treatments including
documentation of drainage and irrigation systems for
Lucas and Tait Development.

Centrecourt, North Ryde
Design for new carpark and landscape work to
Epping Road frontage for MEPC Australia Pty Ltd.

Timber Processing Plant, Homebush Bay
Foreshore buffer zone proposals and design of outdoor
timber display complex for Weyerhaeuser (Australia)
Pty Ltd.

Chullora Administration Centre
Design, documentation and construction supervision of
an outdoor eating area, carpark and river enhancement
programme for the State Rail Authority of N.S.W.

Commercial Development, Bankstown
Pedestrian circulation areas, carparking and planting
proposals for Caralis Holdings Pty Ltd.

Balgownie, Retail Development
Tropical setting to retail centre including entry,
courtyard, beer garden and frontage landscaping of a
Wollongong retail facility for A J Whitty Pty Ltd.

Clydoak Commercial Centre, Bankstown
Plaza, pedestrian circulation and carparking design
for commercial building for Zenith Development
Corporation.

Merritts Base Station, Thredbo
Building forecourt plaza, 600 vehicle car and coach
parking areas, creek rehabilitation and ski slope design
for Kosciusko Thredbo Pty Ltd.

History
Rice Daubney Landscape Architects was formed in 1987
as an independent consultancy within the Rice Daubney
Company. Stephen Sanlorenzo is the Principal
Landscape Architect.

The Landscape Group has established a reputation for
the effective development of planned environments on
a regional and local scale. Rice Daubney Landscape
Architects work with established Rice Daubney clients
and also provide consulting services to a broad spectrum
of independent clients.

Capabilities
The capabilities of Rice Daubney Landscape Architects
include site master planning, landscape and environmental studies, conceptual and detail landscape design,
construction documentation and supervision
of construction where required.

Rice Daubney Landscape Architects prefer an early
involvement with the overall design process to ensure
that their contribution is an integral part of the total
project.

With a commitment to achieving harmony between
man-made structures and the natural environment,
Rice Daubney Landscape Architects design unique
spaces which will bring unexpected pleasures to many
people, for many years to come.

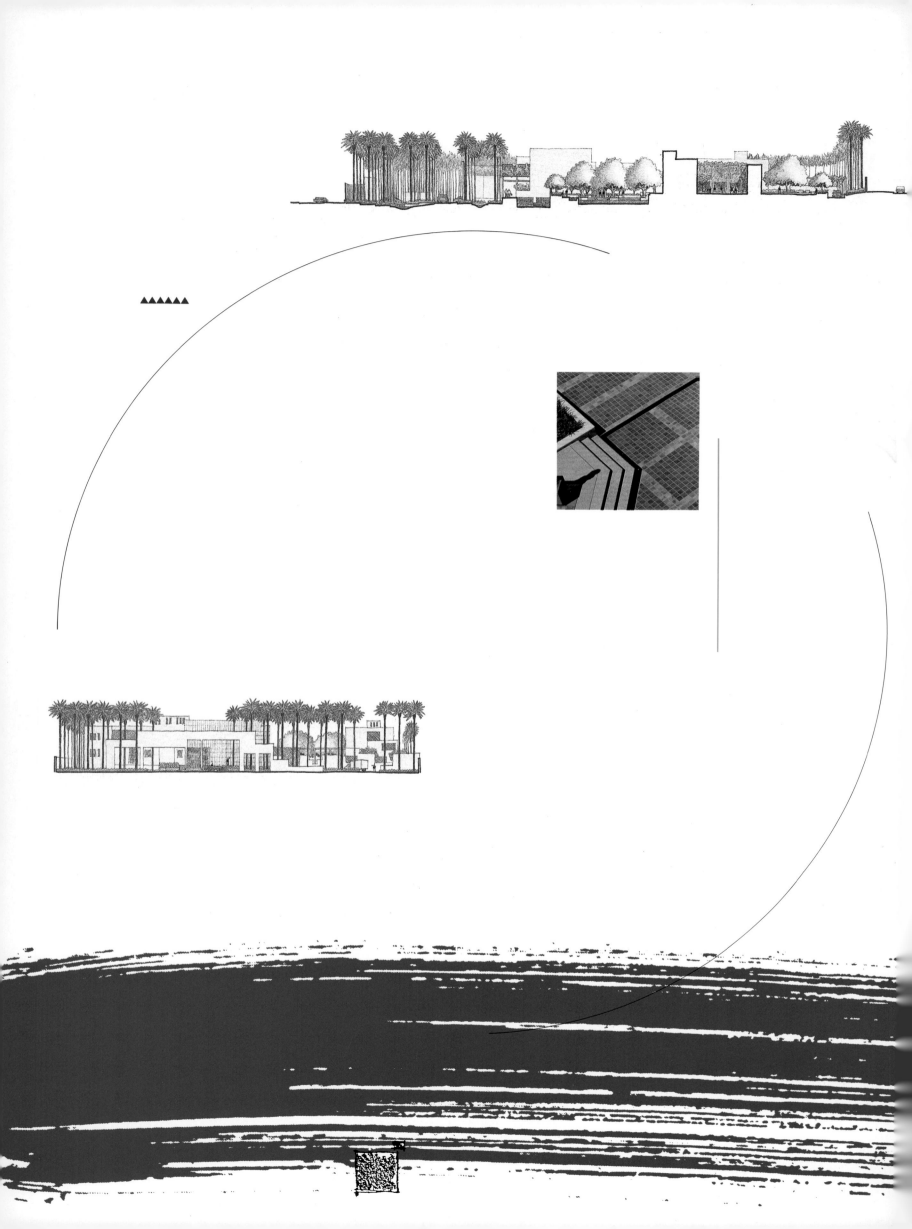

TRACT CONSULTANTS
Landscape Architects, Urban Designers and Planners

Directors
Howard McCorkell B.Arch., Dip. T.R.P.,
 F.R.A.I.A., F.R.A.P.I.
Rodney Wulff B.L.A., M.L.A., Ph.D., A.A.I.L.A.
Stephen Calhoun B.S., M.L.A., A.A.I.L.A.
Chris Dance B.Econ., Grad. Dip. L.D., A.A.I.L.A.
George Gallagher B.E. (Civil), Grad. Dip. L.D.,
 M.I.E. (Aust), A.A.I.L.A.
Tim Biles B.A., Dip T.R.P., M.R.A.P.I.
Stuart Pullyblank Dip. Hort. Sci.,
 Grad. Dip. L.D., A.A.I.L.A.
Barry Murphy Dip. Hort. Sci., Grad. Dip. L.D.,
 M.L.A., A.A.I.L.A.

Associates
Michael Stokes B.Arch.
Suzy Boyd B.Arch.
Stewart Somers B.App.Sci.(Plg),
 Dip.App.Sci.(Urb and Reg. Plg), M.R.A.P.I.

Cathy Heggen B.T.R.P., M.R.A.P.I.

Established
1970

Addresses
Melbourne
195 Lennox Street
Richmond, Vic. 3121

Telephone
(03) 429 6133

Facsimile
(03) 429 5925

Perth
1327 Hay Street
West Perth, W.A. 6005

Telephone
(09) 481 1878

Facsimile
(09) 481 1885

Number of Employees
30

Person to Contact
Melbourne
Howard McCorkell, Rodney Wulff
Perth
Barry Murphy

Tract Consultants provide services as landscape architects, urban designers and planners to a diverse range of clients in the private sector and to Government authorities at all levels.

Philosophy
The practice aims to produce site sensitive, high quality and appropriate solutions that stand the test of time. Emphasis is focused on a critical and rigorous analysis of the client brief and of all design and siting issues as a basis for the evolution of practical and creative solutions.

Background
In the 70's, Tract were an integral part of the Merchant Builders Group in Melbourne. In this relationship Tract contributed measurably to the promotion of landscape design as a primary design skill in the land and building development process.

Scope of Work
The practice is especially involved with landscape projects including concept and schematic designs, construction documentation, site supervision and contract administration.

The urban design work of the practice focuses on civic, municipal and commercial projects closely integrated with architectural and engineering solutions for structured urban spaces.

As town planners, the practice is involved with physical planning, strategic and statutory planning including the formulation of amendments to Planning Schemes, negotiated planning and advocacy in Planning Appeals and Hearings.

Tract have been involved in a considerable number of foreshore and urban design projects across the country. Amongst these are included the Foreshore Master Plan for St. Kilda commenced in the late 70's, Newcastle Harbourside Park, the State Government Precinct in Brisbane, the Parliamentary Triangle studies for the NCDC in Canberra and the Forrest Place Perth projects.

The practice is a participant in the Sandridge City Development Company which has been selected by the Victorian Government as preferred tenderer for the $600M redevelopment of the Station Pier, Port Melbourne precinct.

Tract have provided landscape design services on numerous building projects that have received Institutional Awards and commendations. Examples include the Prahran Market redevelopment, Vermont Park Cluster Housing, Portland Aerodrome, The Bakery Office redevelopment, and the Knox Schlapp Public Housing Scheme.

Current and Recent Projects
A selection of current and recent projects undertaken by the practice are as follows:
Urban Planning and Design
Forrest Place, Perth
This project comprises a major urban square in the centre of Perth incorporating underground car parking, plazas and water features, and interfacing with major commercial, retail and civic functions. Tract as the urban designer are part of a multi-disciplinary consultant team. For completion 1988.

Riverside Quay, Melbourne
A $300M|project incorporating 7 office buildings on the south bank of the Yarra River. Godfrey Spowers, Architects. Our work includes all urban design and landscape components. Completion due 1988, stage one.

Brisbane Government Precinct
Selected from a list of 18 firms across Australia, Tract were appointed to Master Plan an area of 10 city blocks adjoining Parliament House. Documentation and construction for Stage 1 (2 city blocks) with a landscape/ urban design component of $2M was completed in 1986.

Newcastle Foreshore Competition
Upon winning the National Competition from a field of 75 entries, Tract were appointed by the Newcastle Council as principal consultants for the detailed design and documentation for the major landscape components for half of the project. Completion due, 1988. Overall budget approximately $13M.

Landscape Planning and Design
Our involvement in landscape planning and design ranges from small site specific projects across broad scale sites where skills in analysis and interpretation must be first used to define the opportunities and problems for the development. A selection of projects include:

Australian Embassy Riyadh
Landscape and external design works of the new Australian Embassy as sub-consultants to Daryl Jackson Architects. Completed 1987. Site works budget approximately A$3M.

National Tennis Centre Melbourne
Landscape architects for the project designed by Philip Cox Architects of Sydney with Peddle Thorpe and Learmonth. Our brief includes all external site works, and landscaping.

Melbourne Cricket Ground Precinct
Landscape design, documentation and construction supervision for the restoration of the precinct to the Cricket Ground upon the completion of major building works including construction of the National Gallery of Sport. Budget $1M. Completion 1987.

Brickmakers Park Oakleigh
Landscape design and documentation for the creation of a municipal park on the former quarry and tip site in Oakleigh.

Fairfield Park Northcote
Proposals for the rehabilitation and upgrading of the historic Fairfield Park adjoining the Yarra River in the City of Northcote.

Camerons Cove Sydney
Landscape design, documentation and implementation for a medium density scheme for 60 town houses adjoining a water front park on the harbour edge in Balmain, Sydney.

Flowerdale Estate
Preparation of site planning and landscape proposals for the conversion of a historic farm estate outside of Melbourne into a major corporate training and hospitality centre.

Site Planning and Design
St Kilda Harbour Redevelopment
Following preparation of a master plan for the St. Kilda foreshore in the early 80's, more recently Tract have been involved in the site planning and design for the major St. Kilda Harbour redevelopment incorporating a Marina facility for 1,000 boats.

Mount Martha Valley Country Club
Preparation of planning proposals for an integrated golf course and housing development at the entry to the Mornington Peninsula in Dromana.

Fawthrop Lagoon Portland
Conversion of the Fawthrop Lagoon and Swamp in the centre of Portland into a major conservation and recreation amenity for the town as a major Victorian Sesquicentennial project.

Healesville Sanctuary
Preparation of a master plan for staged improvements to the Healesville Sanctuary outside Melbourne. Several significant stages have been implemented.

SEC Morwell
Study for the Electricity Commission to produce rehabilitation plans for the major overburden dump (300 hectares) and open cut mine at Morwell.

Physical and Statutory Planning
Tract Consultants are experienced in the leadership and management of complex planning projects where specialist sub-consultant assistance may be engaged such as soils engineers, geologists, botanists, foresters, meteorologists, engineers or others.

Examples of Physical Planning Projects include:
Shire of Tambo
Review of the Lakes Entrance Planning Scheme including proposals for future of commercial, industrial, tourist and residential strategies. Preparation of a strategy plan and statutory controls for the village of Metung.

Shire of Alexandra
Preparation of a strategy plan incorporating design and siting guidelines for the township of Marysville.

Shire of Bairnsdale
Review of the Gippsland Lakes land use strategy plan incorporating Paynesville and the rural area.

The work of Tract Consultants spans a rich diversity of projects, large and small, throughout Australia. The practice seeks to integrate creative skills with practical and achievable solutions, appropriate to the context of the task. The results are evidence of this success.

ARCHITECTURAL · COMPONENTS

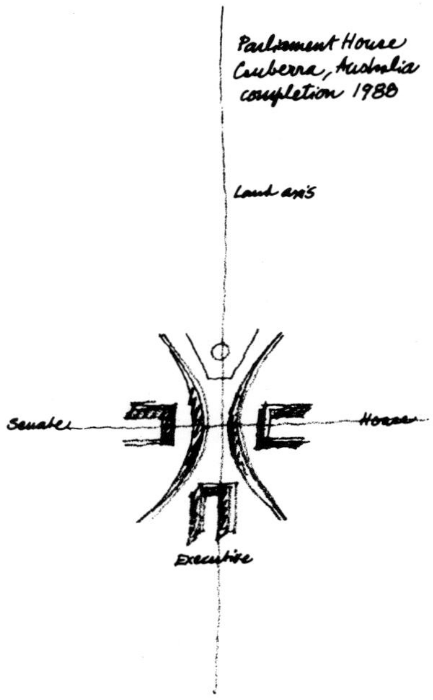

Parliament House
Canberra, Australia
completion 1988

Land axis

Senate   House

Executive

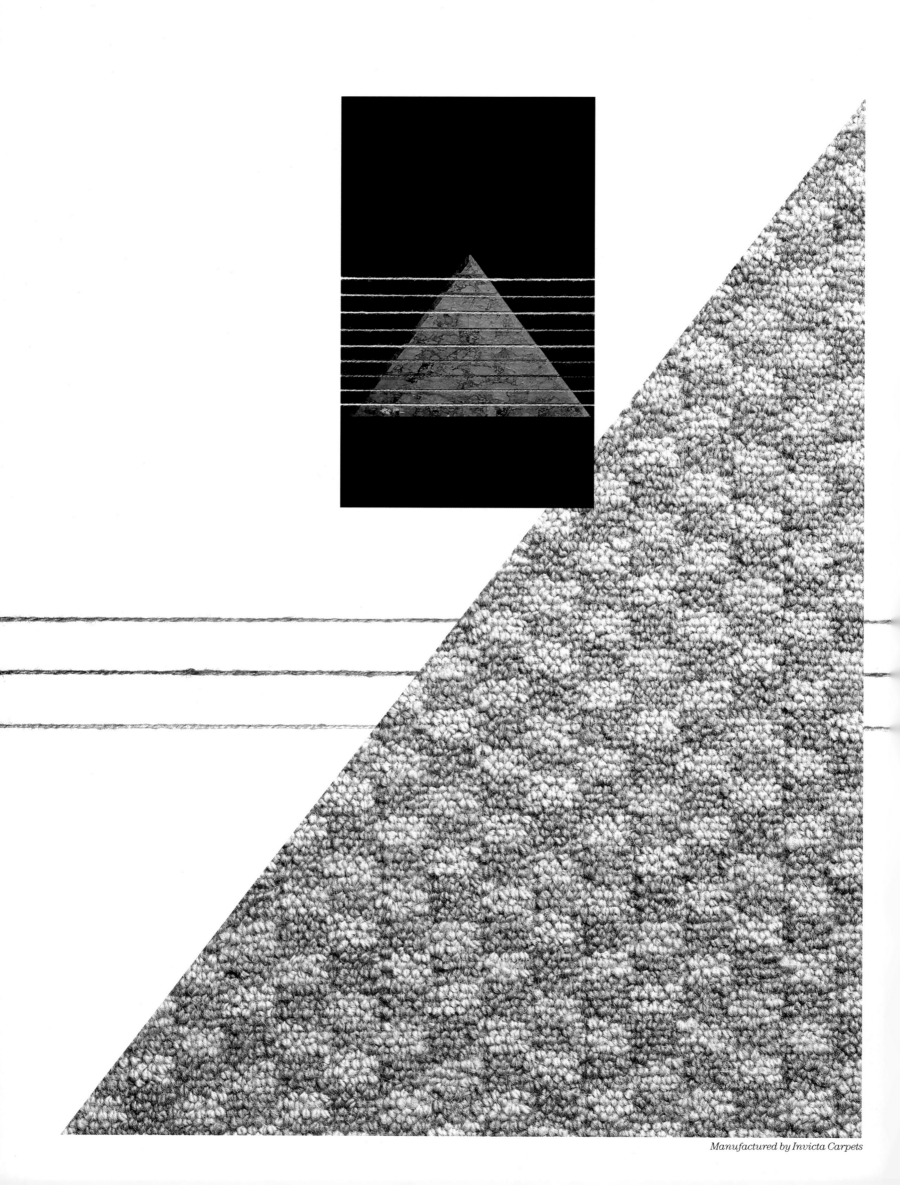

Manufactured by Invicta Carpets

AUSTRALIAN WOOL CORPORATION

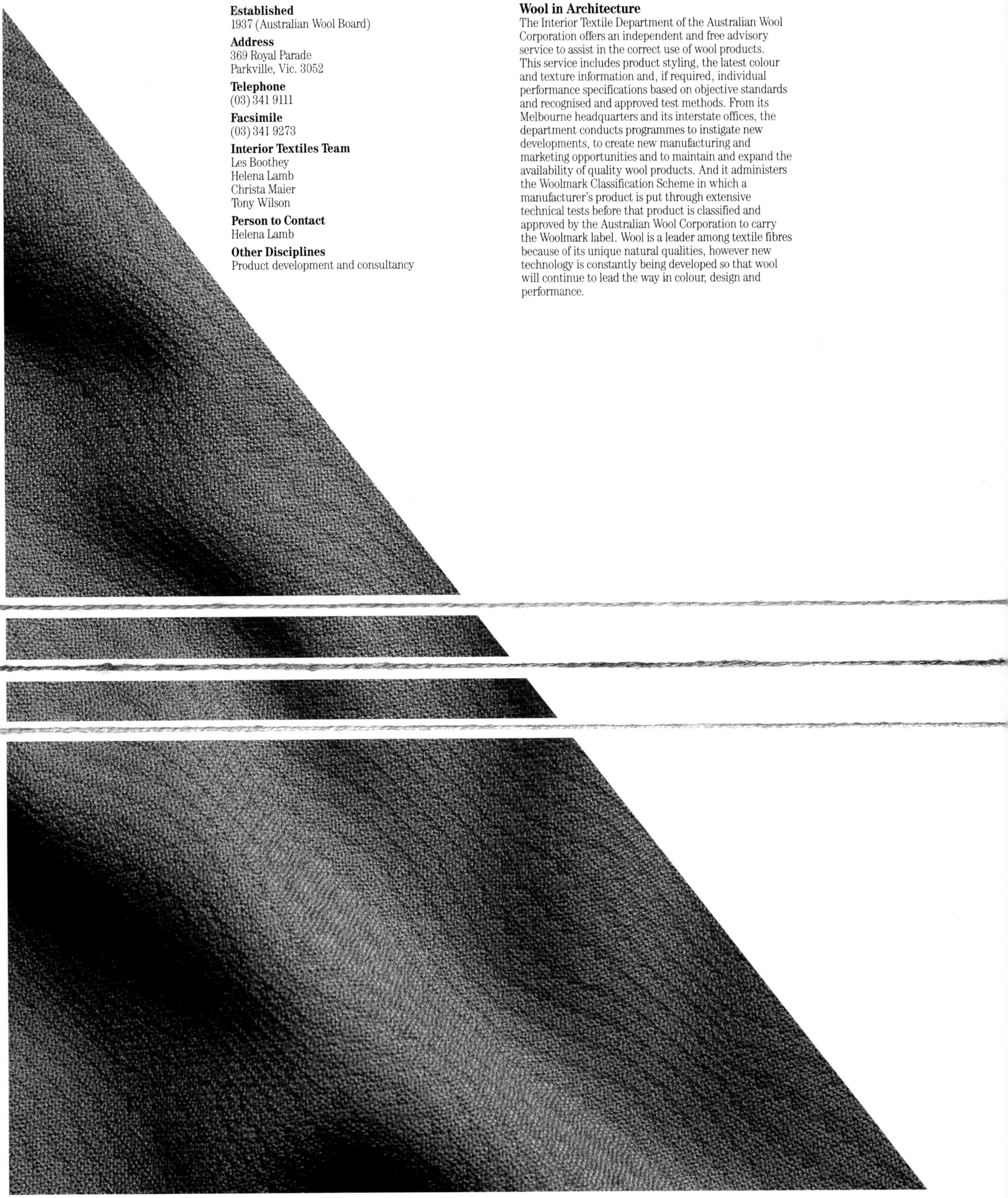

Established
1937 (Australian Wool Board)

Address
369 Royal Parade
Parkville, Vic. 3052

Telephone
(03) 341 9111

Facsimile
(03) 341 9273

Interior Textiles Team
Les Boothey
Helena Lamb
Christa Maier
Tony Wilson

Person to Contact
Helena Lamb

Other Disciplines
Product development and consultancy

Wool in Architecture

The Interior Textile Department of the Australian Wool Corporation offers an independent and free advisory service to assist in the correct use of wool products. This service includes product styling, the latest colour and texture information and, if required, individual performance specifications based on objective standards and recognised and approved test methods. From its Melbourne headquarters and its interstate offices, the department conducts programmes to instigate new developments, to create new manufacturing and marketing opportunities and to maintain and expand the availability of quality wool products. And it administers the Woolmark Classification Scheme in which a manufacturer's product is put through extensive technical tests before that product is classified and approved by the Australian Wool Corporation to carry the Woolmark label. Wool is a leader among textile fibres because of its unique natural qualities, however new technology is constantly being developed so that wool will continue to lead the way in colour, design and performance.

Available from Potpourri

Designs on Wool

Wool is a very special textile fibre. It is the most complex textile fibre in the world and its very complexity has endowed wool with special qualities. It is a natural fibre – soft, warm, comfortable, strong and resilient. It has been woven by man for fabrics and carpets for 25,000 years. It took Stone Age man no great intellectual feat to realise that wool is warm in winter and cool in summer, that it resists liquids and is naturally flame-resistant. Such unique qualities continue to give wool the edge on all other fibres. The aesthetic advantages of the fibre make wool products the definitive choice for interior textiles. An appreciation of its psychological, acoustical and economic advantages has resulted in an enormous demand for wool in commercial buildings. Wool carpets, curtains and upholstery add a pervasive sense of style and quality to a building. The ability of the wool fibre to absorb and retain dyes, to act as a buffer to reduce peak humidity levels, to absorb sound energy, to resist flame, static electricity and soiling and to retain its shape are just some of the special characteristics that allow wool products to keep on looking good. These are the attributes which provide developers, architects and designers with the opportunity of combining economic viability with creative impact, comfort and practicality with inspiration and innovation. In terms of any design discipline, wool remains the fibre for the future.

Manufactured by Brintons Carpets

PURE NEW WOOL

Available from Marco Fabrics

BANG & OLUFSEN

Andrew Donaldson, Stuart Tolliday, Garry Bellairs (left to right)

Head Office
Bang & Olufsen Hi-Fi Pty Ltd
136 Camberwell Road
Hawthorn East, Vic. 3123

Telephone
(03) 882 1256

Facsimile
(03) 813 3705

Telex
31712

Person to Contact
Andrew Donaldson, Managing Director
Stuart Tolliday, Product Manager

Commercial Division
136 Camberwell Road
Hawthorn East, Vic. 3123

Telephone
(03) 882 1256

Facsimile
(03) 813 3705

Telex
31712

Person to Contact
Garry Bellairs, Manager

Showrooms
Melbourne
698 Burke Road
Camberwell, Vic. 3124

Telephone
(03) 882 7348

237 Swanston Street
Melbourne, Vic. 3000

Telephone
(03) 663 4881

Sydney
586 Oxford Street
Bondi Junction, N.S.W. 2022

Telephone
(02) 387 5878

Facsimile
(02) 389 0241

772 Pacific Highway
Gordon, N.S.W. 2072

Telephone
(02) 498 5005

Facsimile
(02) 498 5006

Adelaide
27 Gouger Street
Adelaide, S.A. 5000

Telephone
(08) 51 2124

Facsimile
(08) 212 5407

Project Types
Domestic Audio Systems
Domestic CTV & Video Systems
Round-the-House Hi-Fi
Commercial Audio/Video Systems

1 Domestic Interior: Totally integrated sound and picture

2 MX Television: Winner of International Design Awards

3 Beolink Terminal: This single remote control commands both sound and picture anywhere in the home

4 Audio/Video Integration: The ultimate in design, quality and performance

Furnishing with Integrated Picture and Sound

Bang & Olufsen is a comparatively small Danish Company with over sixty years experience in the increasingly competitive audio and video market. The secret to their survival is the unique and somewhat paradoxical blend of extreme simplicity of operation with some of the world's most advanced technology. The pure design of their products, executed with meticulous attention to detail and the finest materials, allows them to blend with any environment.

The Museum of Modern Art in New York has fourteen Bang & Olufsen products on display in their Permanent Design Collection. They have also held a separate exhibition of thirty-four Bang & Olufsen products – the first time in the history of the Museum that the products of one manufacturer have been so honoured. That similar exhibitions have since been held at museums around the world bears witness to the integrity of Bang & Olufsen's product design but sometimes overshadows the technical innovations and landmarks which are contained therein.

Bang & Olufsen currently produce various sized television receivers, each capable of outstanding definition and colour accuracy with unmatched hi-fi stereo sound, plus state-of-the-art video recorders, tuner-amplifiers, compact disc players, turntables and tape decks complemented by an extensive loudspeaker collection to provide for any application or environment.

All of Bang & Olufsen's hi-fi, televisions and video products are fully remote controlled. A single hand-held remote control is all that is required to operate every unit in the system. Bang & Olufsen can extend this simplicity to enable the distribution and control of high quality sound and picture to as many rooms or areas as required. This facility is called the Beolink System and Bang & Olufsen are the only people in the world who can provide the high degree of control and flexibility offered therein. This total audio/video integration provides sound and picture distribution in an area in which Bang & Olufsen are many years ahead of the rest of the market. Their products are also "future safe" and designed to be able to take advantage of technological advances as and when they occur.

With a view to an ever-increasing involvement in the electronics of the future, Bang & Olufsen has initiated a consortium with two other Danish companies to research and develop the integration of all electronic information in the home. The Home Information Network will incorporate the Bang & Olufsen products of today to provide numerous extra facilities and benefits. The outstanding sound and picture quality, combined with the convenience of full remote control from anywhere in the home or office complex, makes Bang & Olufsen a logical choice for any sophisticated environment.

Bang & Olufsen have been represented in Australia for over twenty years and they have established an enviable reputation for both the quality of their products and their after sales service.

Bang & Olufsen Hi-Fi Pty Ltd offer a comprehensive service from the personalised design of an audio/video system through the highest standard of installation, to an unequalled service and back-up facility.

Ideally, as with air-conditioning, lighting and other such services, an integrated Bang & Olufsen audio/video system requires consideration at the design stage of a project. By involving a Bang & Olufsen consultant at the beginning the design can take into account the appropriate placement of the hardware, the loudspeakers, the control points and associated wiring. However, should the need arise, an integrated Bang & Olufsen system can be fitted retrospectively.

The newly established Commercial Division of Bang & Olufsen Hi-Fi offers a service specifically for Architects and Designers to assist in the design and specification of integrated audio and video systems. There are many applications for such systems which are particularly suited to boardroom, managerial offices and other professional environments.

Bang & Olufsen Hi-Fi also operates Showrooms in Adelaide, Melbourne, Sydney and Brisbane. Each Showroom is designed to demonstrate the full potential of the products and incorporates a professionally staffed Service Department and the services of a fully trained installation team.

The outstanding quality of Bang & Olufsen's products and the flexibility they offer, coupled with the professional back-up support provided by Bang & Olufsen Hi-Fi make them the only alternative.

1 Ansett Domestic Terminal, Sydney
Eight moving pathways.

2 Hyatt on Collins Hotel, Melbourne
Four escalators and thirteen lifts.

3 Queensland Cultural Centre Complex
Six escalators and twelve lifts.

4 Queen Victoria Building, Sydney
Fourteen escalators and seven lifts.

5 Malvern Shopping Centre, Melbourne
Ten moving pathways and three lifts.

6 Overseas Passenger Terminal,
Circular Quay, Sydney
Two outdoor escalators.

JOHNS PERRY LIFTS

A.J. (Tony) Hough,
National Marketing Manager

Established

Established in 1856, a division of Boral Johns Perry Industries Pty Ltd (Inc. in Victoria); designers/manufacturers and suppliers of lifts (all types), escalators, moving pathways, rising stages and platforms, vehicle turntables, cranes, hoists, winches and wool presses; other activities include long term maintenance, repair, modernizations and 24 hour emergency servicing of vertical transport and other equipment.

Principal Address
Australian Head Office, Manufacturing & Research Centre located at:
45 Wangara Road, Cheltenham,
Victoria 3192

Telephone
(03) 584 3311

Facsimile
(03) 584 8978

General Manager
P.G. Langton

Branch Managers
Victoria – B. McKenzie – (03) 329 5700
New South Wales – A.C. Hill – (02) 29 1374
A.C.T. – D.C. Taylor – (062) 80 5943
Queensland – J.F. Meuris – (07) 252 7688
South Australia – W.J. Ridgwell –
(08) 223 1939
West Australia – D.J. Bright –
(09) 322 1522
Tasmania – D. Van Rijn – (002) 28 0365
Northern Territory – F. Van Der Loos –
(089) 85 2069
Auckland (NZ) – C.J. Burbridge – 394 236

Moving high density pedestrian traffic

Introduction

For grace of form and functional efficiency, there is little that can match a building's architecture so well as escalators and moving pathways. They are now the most common and fastest means of carrying people for retail and other high density applications. Indeed, think of each step of an escalator or pallet of a pathway as a miniature lift, smoothly and continuously carrying a stream of passengers.

Such is their acceptance by the architectural profession that our company alone has installed in recent years nearly 250 escalators and 100 pathways in shopping centres, railway stations, airline terminals, office buildings and racecourses throughout Australia. When installed in 1974, the Ansett Domestic Terminal at Sydney Airport (8 units) and Melbourne's Whitehorse Plaza Shopping Centre (6 units) were the first major pathway installations in the country and introduced new concepts in passenger transport. Pathways, of course, have the added advantage of being able to carry laden shopping trolleys, strollers, luggage and wheelchairs, otherwise unsuitable for movement on escalators.

This article offers guidance on equipment available and highlights important considerations in the building design stage. References apply to escalators and pathways unless otherwise noted.

Basic Data

In Australia, the maximum inclination for escalators is 30^0, with $27^0 30'$ being permitted for reduced rises. Pathways may vary between 0^0 and 12^0. Obviously, escalators need less space than pathways and are easier to accommodate. Depending on the room available and the rise, we supply escalators with step widths of 600, 800 and 1000mm, with respective capacities of 4,500, 6,750 and 9,000 persons per hour. Pathways are available in pallet widths of 800 and 1000mm for capacities of 6,750 and 9,000 persons per hour. However, widths of 1200 and 1400mm are being suggested for busy overseas airports and the like where passengers need to pass others standing with luggage. Future developments will no doubt see them in Australia. Top and bottom transition curves are recommended for pathways in shopping centres for the safer carriage of shopping trolleys.

Arrangements

A criss-cross or parallel formation of units in a shopping centre can be crucial to the flow of traffic and its effect on business.

Parallel formations give more immediate access between two points, whereas a criss-cross arrangement distributes traffic more evenly over different levels, which is often advantageous for shopping malls and other retail areas. Parallel units may leave some shops inconveniently out of reach, leading to unsatisfied traders and subsequent loss of acceptable rental returns. This is not as accentuated with escalators where walking distances are not as great.

Pathways can be provided for any combination of rises and horizontal spans. Over very long distances speed loses its advantage and it may be wiser to consider other options. In any case pathways are ideal for linking shopping levels to car park floors and transport terminals.

Structural and Access Considerations

Longer span pathways may need one or more intermediate structural supports (which can become aesthetic features), provided the area below is not intended for exhibitions or entertainment use. Intermediate supports may be avoided through increased truss depth, although this may be a more expensive solution. Should a pathway span a building construction joint then structural engineers should make due allowance for expansion and construction in the bearing plates. Column foundation loads also need to be checked for dynamic loads imposed.

As escalators and pathways are brought to site fully assembled, suitable access and adequate temporary floor slab supports should be provided. Building designers may find that installation costs rise substantially and the construction programme suffer delays where these requirements are not observed.

Aesthetic and Functional Aspects

Of the finishes we offer, clear or a range of tinted glass balustrades are the most often installed, followed by the so-called solid balustrade finishes such as vitreous enamel or laminate (not for outdoor use) and the more expensive stainless steel. Standard units have natural anodised aluminium decks, however, many other attractive finishes are available.

Under handrail lighting and combplate lights are also options. The units are normally provided with smooth finish prime painted truss cladding, except for outdoor equipment which features galvanized cladding and an environmentally protected water dispersal system. Where a decorative finish is to be applied to the truss, consideration should be given to its fire-resistance properties and the added weight. In many cases a satisfactory finish is achieved by merely painting the truss cladding.

Floor inspection plates can be ribbed aluminium or rubber inlay. Marble and the like should be avoided because of weight. Yellow demarcation lines are standard on escalator steps and optional for pathway pallets.

For escalator rises in excess of 6 metres, we recommend the option of a minimum of three horizontal steps to aid passenger confidence.

Incidentally, we are providing units with four level steps for the Darling Harbour Development (12 escalators and 20 lifts), a large NSW Bicentenary Project.

Our units are often required to operate in noise sensitive environments such as the Queensland Cultural Centre. We appreciate being made aware of any special low noise requirements so that maximum attention can be applied to producing the quietest possible equipment.

The ability to service the equipment with minimum downtime is vital and can be performed easily without removing escalator steps as with other types of systems. All units, by the way, come complete with many safety features, including handrail inlet switches and combplate and skirt-switch shutdown protection. A digital diagnostic display aids in establishing the reason for a shutdown, facilitates the unit's return to service and is available as an optional feature.

Our company, through its extensive branch network, is always pleased to provide more information on any aspect of vertical transport.

BORAL

1

2

3

4

5

1 Pratt & Co., Rialto Twin Towers

2 & 5 Merrill Lynch (Australia) Pty Ltd,
    No. 1 Collins Street

3 IBM Australia Ltd, 484 St. Kilda Road

4 Cargill Australia, 432 St. Kilda Road

PAR-TEK

Director
Chris Morris

General Manager
Hamish Richardson

Established
1984

Address
311-315 High Street
Prahran, Vic. 3181

Telephone
(03) 525 1600

Facsimile
(03) 529 2448

Representative List of Clients and Architects

Client

Australia & New Zealand Banking Group Limited
Aitken Walker & Strachan Solicitors
American International Group
Australian Merchant Holdings Ltd
Bache Cortis & Carr Ltd
The Ball Partnership
Union Bulkships Ltd
Cargill Australia Ltd
Carrington Confirmers Pty Ltd
Clayton Utz
Commonwealth Golf Club
Corrs Pavey Whiting & Byrne Pty Ltd
Deloitte Haskins & Sells
GRE Insurance Ltd
George Tauber Imports Pty Ltd
IBM Australia Ltd
Kleinwort Benson Australia Ltd
Macquarie Bank Ltd
Merrill Lynch Australia Pty Ltd
Morgan & Banks Pty Ltd
McCaughan Dyson & Co. Ltd
McDonnell Douglas Information Systems Pty Ltd
McIlwraith, McEacharn Ltd
McIntosh Hamson Hoare & Govett Ltd
Multiplex Pty Ltd
National Mutual Corporation Pty Ltd
National Mutual Royal Bank Ltd
Petrofina Exploration Services
Pratt & Co. Financial Services Pty Ltd
SEC Superannuation Fund
Shell Company of Australia Ltd
Solution No. 6 Directionale Design Pty Ltd
Transport Industries Insurance Co. Pty Ltd
J. W. Thompson Australia Pty Ltd

Architects and Interior Designers

Barrack Douglas & Co. Architects and Planners
Bates Smart & McCutcheon Pty Ltd
Best Overend Architects
Biancino & Associates Pty Ltd
Bruce Henderson Architects Pty Ltd
Clerehan Cran Architects Pty Ltd
Geyer Design Pty Ltd
Godfrey and Spowers Australia Pty Ltd
Graeme H. Jasper Architects Pty Ltd
Kiessling & Mullerow Architects Pty Ltd
Meldrum Burrows & Partners
Nexus Design Pty Ltd
Terry Danks Design
Whitford & Peck Architects Pty Ltd
Woods Bagot Pty Ltd
Wragg & Bristow Consultant Designers Pty Ltd

Designed Divisions

Par-Tek has made the creation of office environments into an art form.

We love what we're doing. We enjoy working with Architects and Interior Designers to create the exceptional office interior, and we are committed to finishing the project on time to the complete satisfaction of the client.

Par-Tek was established in 1984, but our involvement in the industry and our understanding of the impact of the work environment on employee morale and productivity dates back more than two decades.

We've experienced and contributed to the major breakthroughs in partitioning that have occurred over that time, including the introduction of plasterboard partitioning in the 1970's.

Our people were also directly involved in initiating the trend towards on-site construction of partitions, made feasible by the introduction of innovative components for the fixing of partitions to floors and ceilings.

This increasing versatility in partitioning, which is continuing, inspired a new and refreshing attitude to the aesthetics of office interiors. The expanding range of stylish furniture, fittings, floor and partition finishes and colours has added momentum to this change, so that now Architects and Interior Designers are creating many highly innovative and beautiful interiors.

We're involved in refurbishing existing buildings and fitting out new ones. We accept each assignment on its own merits, and, if required, we will manage all aspects of a fitout.

Our contribution begins with the interpretation of the plan in collaboration with the Designer. We're interested in the subtleties of the design as well as the overall environment we're helping to create. We like to see ourselves as part of a team. In this way we also develop an emotional involvement with the success of a project.

Our care in this interpretation, and our ability to imagine two-dimensional drawings as three-dimensional interiors, helps to ensure accurate quoting. We are also often asked to advise on developments in finishes and fittings, on a consultancy basis, prior to design documentation.

Following the approval to proceed, there's the critical pre-production phase when all the elements must be organised and, most importantly, possible problems identified.

Coordination is a complex task and the opportunity for error is ever-present. At this stage our experience really helps us plan the job thoroughly.

Our approach is to take nothing for granted. We have developed practical production systems and work hard to maintain strong relationships with suppliers and sub-contractors. It would be unrealistic of us to pretend that every job runs like clockwork, but we are proud of our record of reliability in containing costs and meeting deadlines.

For the duration of a major project, we have a supervisor on-site and maintain clear lines of communication so that all involved remain informed of progress. Our own partition system, which has received wide acceptance, was developed as a response to changing needs in the industry.

We keep ourselves informed of advances in architecture and interior design, and travel regularly in order to study developments and maintain contact with partitioning contractors overseas.

By now you've probably realised that we enjoy a challenge, and the chance to apply innovative techniques and introduce new materials and components.

PAR-TEK

1 Zenith Centre – Sydney
   Austwin sealed insulating glass
   units, 6mm Suncool TS21 on
   green glass, 12 mm airspace,
   6 mm clear, float glass

2 New South Wales State Bank,
   Sydney
   Planar Armourfloat Assembly

3 Perth Airport
   12mm Grey Armourfloat Planar
   and Suspended Assembly

4 Burswood Island Casino – Perth
   A wide range of Pilkington ACI
   glass used to create an exciting
   building

PILKINGTON ACI

PILKINGTON ACI

Mr. David Cleland, General Manager of the Architectural Glass Division, Pilkington ACI Pty Ltd.

Address
Pilkington ACI Operations Pty Ltd
Greens Road
Dandenong, Vic. 3175

Telephone
(03) 797 6222

Facsimile
(03) 791 8600

Telephone Numbers of the Pilkington ACI Interstate Offices
Adelaide
(08) 373 0022
Perth
(09) 367 7222
Sydney
(02) 438 3722
Brisbane
(07) 839 0827

Facsimile Numbers of the Pilkington ACI Interstate Offices
Adelaide
(08) 373 0043
Perth
(09) 367 8308
Sydney
(02) 438 4904
Brisbane
(07) 832 1592

Glass Reflecting Australia

Glass has played a vital role in the development of Australia, ever since the first sheets of glass arrived here as carefully stored cargo with the First Fleet.

In fact, the development and use of glass in this country in many ways reflects the growth of Australia as a nation.

As the early Australia grew and the settlers began to extend over this harsh land, Australia was a major importer of glass from England and Europe.

From 1856 one of the major suppliers of window glass was the English company, Pilkington Brothers.

The first large scale commercial manufacture of glass occurred in 1872, when the Melbourne Glass Bottle Works was established by Alfred Felton and Alexander Grimwade – two names that have become famous in Australian history.

In 1880 Melbourne's Exhibition Building, with its extensive use of glass was completed, in 1881 William Farmer's Drapery Store in Sydney installed the first plate glass windows in Australia and in 1898, Sydney's Queen Victoria Market building, with its barrel vaulted glass ceiling, providing light and protection for the traders and shoppers below, began serving its first patrons.

The Melbourne Glass Bottle Works of Felton and Grimwade had become so successful, it had acquired other bottle making companies in Adelaide and Sydney, and in mid 1915 these were amalgamated to form Australian Glass Manufacturers' Limited.

Australian Glass Manufacturers' Limited expanded and grew into what is now ACI. In 1931 it formed Australian Window Glass and began manufacturing flat glass near Sydney in competition with imports. This soon led to a close association between Pilkington Brothers and Australian Glass Manufacturers' for almost 40 years, which saw them eventually come together in the joint venture glass manufacturer Pilkington ACI in 1972.

So the birth, growth and development of Pilkington ACI has mirrored, in many ways, the coming of age of Australia.

Today, Pilkington ACI is Australia's largest float glass manufacturer, offering a range of architectural glass equal to the highest international standards.

The company's aim is to assist architects and developers make the most of the enormous potential glass has to offer, safe in the knowledge that they are dealing with an Australian company that has developed a product range to suit the Australian market.

Among their quality products is the **Suncool High Performance** Series, which comprises a range of glasses, each with metallic oxide coating applied to one surface, giving a distinctive appearance, as well as a high solar control performance.

In the **Suncool** series there are four standard coatings available which may be applied in a range of densities to clear or tinted base glass. The resulting combinations of coatings and base glass present a broad range of colour and solar control performances to suit a variety of needs.

The **Suncool** range is suitable for single glazing applications and is available annealed where appropriate, toughened, heat-strengthened, laminated or incorporated in sealed insulating glass units.

Suncool Reflective Laminated Glass combines the outstanding performance and visual appeal of Suncool High Performance Glasses with the properties and benefits of laminated glass.

Suncool Reflective Laminated Glass is characterised by:

low visible distortion
safety and integrity
ultraviolet screening
coating protection in exposed situations
heat and glare control
enhanced noise control
ease of handling, distribution and storage
workability

Suncool Reflective Laminated glass can be used in monolithic glazing and in insulating glass units.

Another Pilkington architectural development is **Austwin** Insulating Glass Units. The primary function of Austwin Insulating Glass Units is to reduce air-to-air heat transfer.

The units consist of two or more pieces of glass separated by metal spacers, which have both primary and secondary seals and a desiccant to prevent the formation of condensation within the air space.

Austwin units, which are a feature of the eye-catching High Court building in Canberra, are extremely versatile and can be manufactured to meet different design requirements.

The main benefits of **Austwin** factory sealed insulating units are increased thermal insulation, improved sound insulation, greater comfort, and except in extreme circumstances, condensation is virtually eliminated.

This allows for greater use of glass in wide frontages and west facing walls which still allow buildings to remain cool – and quiet.

Colourclad is another Pilkington ACI product to prove popular with architects.

A ceramic coated, heat-strengthened glass, it is a virtually maintenance free cladding material.

This is because the ceramic coating is permanently fused to the inside surface of the glass, making the coating resistant to weathering and atmospheric pollution.

The main use for **Colourclad** is for infill or spandrel panels in curtain wall construction where an opaque area is required, but still retaining the surface integrity of the glazing.

Colourclad is available on Clear or Tinted Float glass.

Pilkington Architectural **Armourfloat All Glass Assemblies** are suspended glass facade systems designed to provide a method of glazing large openings in buildings without the use of mullions or frames of any kind. In conventional framed systems, the visual amenity is obstructed by the frame supporting the glass. Armourfloat All Glass Assemblies overcome this restriction. They give the appearance of a complete glass facade, which maximises through vision.

A further development by Pilkington is the **Planar Assembly,** in which instead of each panel being suspended from the one above, panels are separately fixed to the building. The Planar System uses Armourfloat Toughened glass, employing an ingenious technique of having countersunk holes in the glass, combined with an interior angle fitting which, because of its flexibility, prevents high stress build-up when the glass comes under load.

The Planar System is a patented system and the resources of the Pilkington ACI Structural Glass Design Service are on hand to design a suitable system for your particular requirements.

Armourview Balustrading is a free-standing system developed by Pilkington ACI, which exploits the structural strength capabilities of toughened glass to produce stunning, clean, dramatic and cost effective balustrading. Unlike other glass balustrade systems, Armourview is completely free-standing, with just the bottom edge of the glass set into the floor. This completely eliminates the need for framing and fixing systems and exceeds the strength requirements of Australian Standards.

Architectural glass technology is certainly one of the fastest expanding fields in the building and construction industries.

To meet the challenges being asked of architectural glass, Pilkington ACI has developed its Technical Service Group, which is staffed by qualified engineers who are experts in their own field. One of the primary ways in which they assist architects is by employing highly specialised computer programs to theoretically compare, with great accuracy, potential and proposed glazing alternatives. These alternatives increasingly involve environmental as well as structural design applications, including thermal and structural loading, tinted and reflective glasses for solar control, free standing glass balustrading and glasses capable of withstanding human and missile impact.

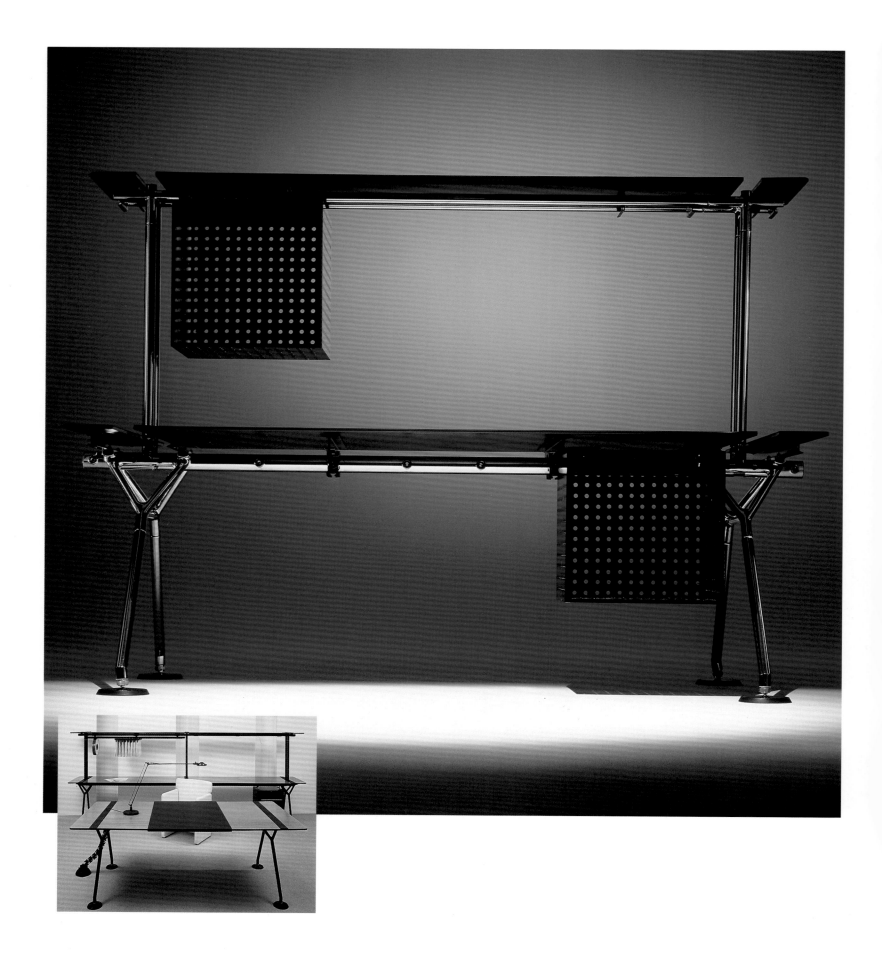

TECNO FAR-EAST PTY LTD

Established
1954, Tecno Milano

Addresses
Victoria
Tecno Far-East Pty Ltd
Collins Place
45 Collins Street
Melbourne, Vic. 3000

Telephone
(03) 654 3922

Facsimile
(03) 654 3176

Telex
AA31252

New South Wales
Tecno Far-East Pty Ltd
207-229 Young Street
Waterloo, N.S.W. 2017

Telephone
(02) 698 1477

Facsimile
(02) 319 3169

Queensland
Tecno Far-East Pty Ltd
348 Edwards Street
Brisbane, Qld 4000

Telephone
(07) 832 2377

Facsimile
(07) 832 0447

Manufacturing Facilities
Tecno Far-East (Mfg) Pty Ltd
26-30 Connell Road
Oakleigh, Vic. 3166

Telephone
(03) 568 0366

Facsimile
(03) 569 8266

Telex
AA154436

Project Application
Office
Institutional
Hotels
Residential
Design
Supply

Installation
Total Turnkey Operations
Furniture Systems
Partitions
Storage Systems
Textiles
Lighting

New Era Furniture for Australia
History & Design Philosophy

The beginnings of the present day company, can be traced to Italy in 1927 with the name Tecno first being used in 1953. Since this time, the name Tecno has summed up the style worked out by Osvaldo Borsani – advanced technology in a rigorous, high quality, long lasting design.

The first Tecno products to make their presence felt on the international design scene were the P40 armchair and D70 sofa – both designed by Osvaldo Borsani in 1954. In 1968, at the XIVth Triennale in Milan the 'Graphis' office system in white laminate was introduced, thus innovating office furnishing traditions. It was completed in 1972 by the 'Modus' seating system and in 1985 by the version in 'Supergrain' wood.

With the advent of the Seventies, the 'Centro Progetti Tecno' was formed around Osvaldo Borsani.

Through this facility, the original concept of the company was extended from the manufacture and supply of furniture, to the control and creation of the environment in which Tecno products are used.

The scope of this department now extends from simple commercial and domestic areas, to large open space projects such as City Centres, Airports and Conference facilities. Using some of our latest products, 'WS' indoor/outdoor public seating, theatre seating P767/757 with multi-lingual translation facilities etc., we are able to meet any requirements where man-made environments are concerned.

The 1984 'Compasso D'Oro' (Golden Compass) was awarded to Tecno for their design and execution of the coordinated image of Alitalia Passenger Agencies.

In 1986, the 'Nomos System' designed by Foster Associates in conjunction with the Tecno Group signalized a new approach which reopened the debate on the age-old distinction between furniture for the office and for the home, as well as, perhaps, the very concept of Furniture.

Now, with a new venture, namely Tecno Far-East Pty Ltd, the company has opened a large modern manufacturing facility in Melbourne to supply the Australian and Asian markets directly and to guarantee the ability of the Tecno group to fill large orders in any country whatsoever.

Production management has been imported from Milan to ensure the same high level of technology and quality of finish that has made Tecno world renowned for over 30 years.

Summary
If your requirement calls for uncompromising high quality and advanced technology we would be pleased to include you in our already impressive list of clients.

International

Lloyd's of London, Head Office

Fiumicino International Airport, Offices and Facilities

Alitalia, Passenger Agencies in Italy and abroad

Porsche, Head Office, Europe

ICI, Head Office, Europe

Yale University, USA

Australia

Wardley Australia Pty Ltd

ANZ

University of Tasmania

Electrolux Australia Pty Ltd

RACV

Joint Coal Board

AAMI

BMW (Australia)

Lanes Motors

Malaysian Airlines

Ansett Golden Wings

Qantas

Local Authority Superannuation Board

IBM Australia Ltd (Qld)

National Mutual Centre

INDEX

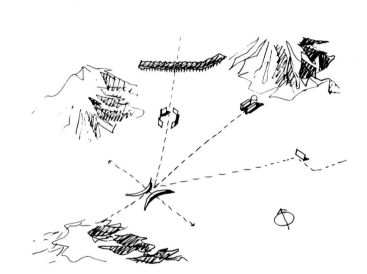

NAME OF PRACTICE	Pages	Overseas Countries Serviced						Project Types														Other
		S.E. Asia †	Europe	Pacific ††	U.S.A.	China	Middle East	Commercial	Ecclesiastical	Educational	Environmental	Health	Industrial	Interior Design	Landscape	Municipal	Recreational	Residential	Restoration	Retail	Town Planning	

Architects

NAME OF PRACTICE	Pages	SE	EU	PA	US	CN	ME	CO	EC	ED	EN	HE	IN	ID	LA	MU	RE	RS	RT	RL	TP	Other
Ancher Mortlock and Woolley Pty Ltd	14-15	●		●				●	●	●	●	●	●	●	●	●	●	●	●	●	●	
Bates Smart & McCutcheon Pty Ltd	16-17	●	●	●	●	●		●	●	●		●	●	●	●	●	●	●	●	●	●	Engineering-Mechanical/Electrical/ Structural/Hydraulics Project Management
Edward F Billson & Associates Pty Ltd	18-19	●		●				●	●	●		●	●	●			●	●	●	●		
Bligh Jessup Robinson	20-21							●	●	●	●	●	●	●			●	●	●	●	●	
Blythe Yeung & Menzies	22-23							●	●	●	●	●	●	●	●	●	●	●	●	●	●	
Boddam Whetham + Dorta	24-25	●		●				●						●	●	●				●		Space Planning, Product Design, Corporate Graphics, Entertainment
The BPA Group BPA Australia Pty Ltd BPA Interiors + Space Planners Pty Ltd	26-27		●	●	●			●			●	●	●	●			●	●	●	●		Retail Consultant Development Consultant Project Management
Brown Falconer Group Pty Ltd	28-29							●	●	●		●	●	●	●	●	●	●	●	●	●	Aged Care, Tourism
Dino Burattini & Associates	30-31			●	●			●	●	●	●	●	●	●			●	●	●	●		
Cameron Chisholm & Nicol Pty Ltd	34-35	●	●	●	●	●		●	●	●		●	●	●		●	●	●		●	●	
Cann Architects Pty Ltd – Perth, Sydney, Surfers Paradise	36-37	●		●				●		●	●	●	●	●		●	●	●		●		Hotels, Resorts
Christou & Vuko Pty Ltd	38-39	●		●				●		●		●	●	●		●	●	●		●		Laboratories, Toursim
Collard Clarke & Jackson Pty Ltd	40-41							●		●		●	●		●		●	●				
Conrad & Gargett Pty Limited	42-43	●		●		●		●	●	●	●	●	●	●	●	●	●	●	●	●		Hotels, Resorts
Tony Corkill Pty Ltd	44-45							●		●	●		●	●	●	●	●			●	●	Resorts
Philip Cox, Richardson, Taylor & Partners Pty Ltd – Sydney, Canberra Philip Cox, Etherington, Coulter & Jones Pty Ltd – Perth Philip Cox, Sanderson & Partners Pty Ltd – Melbourne	46-47	●		●				●	●	●	●	●	●	●	●	●	●		●	●	●	
Davenport Campbell	48-49	●		●	●	●		●	●	●	●	●	●	●		●	●	●	●	●		Strategic Facility Planning, Development Management
Michael Davies Associates Pty Limited	50-51							●		●		●	●	●	●	●	●	●		●		Hotels, Resorts, Tourism, Sport and Recreation
De Angelis Taylor & Associates Pty Ltd	52-53							●	●	●		●	●	●	●	●	●	●		●		
Demaine Partnership Pty Ltd	54-55							●	●	●		●	●	●	●		●	●	●			
Devine Erby Mazlin Australia Pty Limited	56-57			●				●	●	●	●	●	●	●	●	●	●	●	●	●	●	Tourism, Resort Planning
Douglas Daly Bottger Architects Pty Ltd	58-59							●	●	●		●	●			●	●	●		●	●	
Edwards Madigan Torzillo Briggs International Pty Ltd	60-61	●		●				●		●	●	●	●	●	●	●	●	●	●	●	●	Entertainment Centres

† Hong Kong, Indonesia, Macau, Malaysia, Philippines, Singapore, Taiwan, Thailand

†† Fiji, New Zealand, Papua New Guinea, Vanuatu

Architects

NAME OF PRACTICE	Pages	Overseas Countries Serviced						Project Types														
		S.E. Asia †	Europe	Pacific ††	U.S.A.	China	Middle East	Commercial	Ecclesiastical	Educational	Environmental	Health	Industrial	Interior Design	Landscape	Municipal	Recreational	Residential	Restoration	Retail	Town Planning	Other
Figgis & Jefferson Pty Limited	62-63	●		●				●	●	●		●	●	●			●	●	●		●	
Firth, Lee + Partners Pty Ltd	64-35			●	●			●		●		●	●	●			●	●	●	●	●	●	Resorts, Materials/ Handling and Space Planning
Forbes and Fitzhardinge	66-67	●						●				●	●	●			●		●		●	●	Security Refurbishment
Frank Kolos + Partners Pty Ltd	68-69	●		●			●	●	●	●	●	●	●	●			●	●	●	●	●		
Gibbon Hamor & Associates	70-71	●		●		●		●		●	●	●	●	●			●	●	●	●	●	●	Project Management, Tourism and Leisure, Development and Urban Planning
Godfrey and Spowers Australia Pty Ltd	72-73	●						●		●	●	●	●	●			●	●	●		●	●	Urban Design
Goodwin and Southwell Architects	74-75							●	●	●		●		●			●	●	●	●	●		Tourism and Resorts
Greenhatch & Partners Pty Ltd	76-77							●						●	●		●	●	●	●	●		Project Management, Development Analysis
Harkness Group	78-79							●	●	●	●	●	●		●		●	●		●			Legal
Haysom Group Architects	82-83							●					●	●			●	●	●	●	●		Graphics
Hodgkison Matthews & Partners Pty Ltd	84-85	●	●	●	●			●	●	●		●	●	●			●	●	●	●	●	●	Defence, Hospitality, Computer Modelling, Project Management, Urban Design
Hoffer Reid and Coombs	86-87			●	●			●		●	●	●	●	●			●	●	●	●	●	●	Hotels, Resorts
Howlett & Bailey Architects Pty Ltd	88-89	●				●	●	●	●	●		●	●	●	●	●	●	●	●	●	●		Project Management, Urban Design
Lawrence H Howroyd & Associates	90-91			●				●	●	●	●		●	●			●	●	●	●	●	●	Commissioned Reports
Daryl Jackson Pty Ltd	92-93	●	●	●			●	●	●	●	●	●	●	●	●	●	●	●	●	●	●	●	Research, Reports, Building Briefs, Urban Design, Hotels, Resorts
Jackson Teece Chesterman Willis & Partners Pty Ltd	94-95	●		●				●		●	●	●	●	●	●	●	●	●	●	●	●	●	Urban Design, Development Economics, Construction Management
John Bruce + Partners Pty Limited	96-97			●	●			●	●			●		●	●		●	●		●	●		Hotels, Leisure Resorts, Project Management
Kann Finch + Partners Pty Limited	98-99	●		●				●	●	●		●	●	●	●	●	●	●	●	●	●	●	Computer Facilities Hotels, Leisure Resorts
Keers, Banks and Maitland Pty Limited	100-101	●	●	●			●	●		●		●	●	●			●	●	●	●		Institutional
Lawrence Nield and Partners Australia	102-103	●	●	●				●		●	●	●	●	●			●	●	●	●	●		
Leighton Irwin-Garnet Alsop (Aust.) Pty Ltd Leighton Irwin Pty Ltd	104-105			●				●	●	●	●	●	●	●	●	●	●	●		●	●		
McConnel Smith & Johnson Pty Ltd	106-107	●		●				●	●	●	●	●	●	●	●	●	●	●	●	●	●	●	Graphics, Urban Redevelopment
City of Melbourne Urban Design and Architecture	108-109							●		●	●	●	●	●	●	●	●	●		●	●	●	Maintenance, Urban Design, Project Management
Meldrum Burrows & Partners Pty Ltd (Inc. in Vic.)	110-111	●	●			●	●	●	●	●	●	●	●	●	●	●	●	●	●	●	●	●	Computer Facilities, Institutional, Urban Design

† *Hong Kong, Indonesia, Macau, Malaysia, Philippines, Singapore, Taiwan, Thailand*

†† *Fiji, New Zealand, Papua New Guinea, Vanuatu*

NAME OF PRACTICE	Pages	Overseas Countries Serviced						Project Types														Other
		S.E. Asia †	Europe	Pacific ††	U.S.A.	China	Middle East	Commercial	Ecclesiastical	Educational	Environmental	Health	Industrial	Interior Design	Landscape	Municipal	Recreational	Residential	Restoration	Retail	Town Planning	

Architects

NAME OF PRACTICE	Pages	S.E. Asia †	Europe	Pacific ††	U.S.A.	China	Middle East	Commercial	Ecclesiastical	Educational	Environmental	Health	Industrial	Interior Design	Landscape	Municipal	Recreational	Residential	Restoration	Retail	Town Planning	Other
Millar Smith Partnership	112-113							●	●	●		●	●	●		●	●	●	●	●	●	
Mitchell/Giurgola & Thorp Architects	114-115		●	●	●			●	●	●	●	●	●	●	●	●	●	●	●	●	●	Urban Design, Campus, City Planning
MLE Architects	116-117	●		●				●	●	●		●	●	●	●	●	●	●	●	●		
Mockridge Stahle & Mitchell Pty Ltd	118-119							●	●	●		●	●			●	●	●	●			Master Planning, Fire Protection
John M Morton Architects Pty Ltd	120-121							●	●	●	●	●	●	●	●	●	●	●	●	●	●	
Napier Thomas Mantesso Healey Pty Ltd	122-123							●	●	●		●	●	●		●	●	●	●	●		Tourism
John Nicholas & Partners Pty Limited	124-125							●						●	●	●	●	●	●	●		Project & Construction Management, Building Programming, Cost Control Management
Oldham Boas Ednie-Brown	126-127	●	●		●			●	●	●	●	●	●	●	●	●	●	●	●	●		Tourism
Peddle Thorp Partnerships in Australia	128-129	●	●	●	●		●	●	●	●	●	●	●	●	●	●	●	●	●	●	●	
Ross Perrett Pty Ltd	130-131									●	●		●		●		●	●				Land Development, Golf Course Design, Site Planning
Perry Bland & Partners Pty Ltd	132-133			●				●	●	●		●	●	●		●	●	●	●	●	●	
Peter Hunt Pty Ltd	134-135	●	●					●	●	●	●	●	●	●	●	●	●	●	●	●		Project Management
Philip Follent Architect	136-137							●		●				●	●		●	●				Government, Playground and Play Equipment Design
Powell, Dods and Thorpe	138-139							●	●	●	●	●	●	●	●	●	●	●	●	●	●	Media and Communications, Tourism
Rice Daubney	140-141			●				●		●	●	●	●	●	●	●	●	●	●	●	●	
Robertson & Marks Pty Ltd and Guy Fuller Cook Pty Ltd	142-143			●				●		●	●	●	●	●	●	●		●	●	●	●	High Rise Residential
Robinson Loo Wyss & Schneider Pty Ltd	146-147	●		●				●		●		●	●			●	●		●	●		
Rod Roach Architecture Pty Ltd	148-149							●	●	●			●	●		●	●	●		●		
Rogers & Co. Pty Ltd	150-151							●		●		●	●	●		●	●	●	●	●	●	Tourism, Planning and Development
SHK Architects (NSW) Pty Ltd	152-153							●		●	●	●	●	●	●	●	●	●	●	●		
E. Smrekar Pty Ltd	154-155							●	●	●		●		●			●	●		●		
Stenders + Partners	156-157	●	●	●	●		●	●		●	●		●	●	●	●	●	●	●	●	●	Tourism
Stephenson & Turner Sydney Pty Ltd	158-159	●		●				●					●	●		●	●	●		●	●	Hotels, Resorts
Tasman Storey & Associates Pty Ltd	160-161							●		●				●	●	●		●	●	●		

† *Hong Kong, Indonesia, Macau, Malaysia, Philippines, Singapore, Taiwan, Thailand*

†† *Fiji, New Zealand, Papua New Guinea, Vanuatu*

INDEX

Name of Practice	Pages	Overseas Countries Serviced						Project Types														Other
		S.E. Asia †	Europe	Pacific ††	U.S.A.	China	Middle East	Commercial	Ecclesiastical	Educational	Environmental	Health	Industrial	Interior Design	Landscape	Municipal	Recreational	Residential	Restoration	Retail	Town Planning	
Architects																						
Straesser Poli Little & Associates Pty Ltd	162-163		●					●		●	●	●	●	●		●	●	●	●	●		Tourism, Office Planning, Feasibility Studies, Refurbishments
Tasarc Pty Ltd	164-165							●	●	●	●	●	●	●	●	●	●	●	●	●	●	
Tompkins, Shaw & Evans Pty Ltd	166-167							●		●			●	●		●	●		●	●		
Travis Partners Pty Ltd	168-169			●				●		●	●	●	●	●	●	●	●	●	●	●	●	Waterfront Redevelopment, Cost Planning, Quantity Surveying, Adaptive Re-use, Government (Federal, State, Local), Tourism
Tsigulis & Zuvela Pty Ltd	170-171							●	●	●		●	●	●		●	●	●		●	●	
Walter Brooke and Associates Pty Ltd	172-173							●	●	●	●	●	●	●	●	●	●	●	●	●		Military
Woodhead Australia – Architects	174-175	●		●	Mauritius			●	●	●		●	●	●	●	●	●	●	●	●	●	Tourism, Industrial Design, Graphic Design
Woods Bagot Pty Ltd	176-177	●		●				●	●	●	●	●	●	●	●	●	●	●	●	●	●	Graphic Design, Computing, Model Making, Computer Programming, Predevelopment Analysis, Hotels & Resorts
Landscape Architects																						
Deverson Scholtens Bombardier	180-181							●	●	●	●	●	●	●	●	●	●	●	●	●	●	
Landscan Pty Limited	182-183			●				●	●	●	●	●	●		●	●	●			●	●	Resort Planning, Rural & Stud Farm Master Planning, Interior Landscape Design
Loder & Bayly Pty Ltd	184-185	●		●				●		●	●		●		●	●	●	●	●	●	●	Urban Design, Roads, Graphics
Mitchell + Clouston Group	186-187	●		●			●	●	●	●	●	●	●	●	●	●	●	●	●	●	●	Roads, Hotels, Resorts, Urban Design, Cemetry Master Planning
Rice Daubney Landscape Architects	188-189			●				●		●	●	●	●	●	●	●	●			●	●	Tourist Resort Master Planning, Business Park and Medium Density Housing Site Planning
Tract Consultants	190-191			●				●	●	●	●	●	●		●	●	●	●	●	●	●	Site Analysis and Design, Urban and Civic Design, Design Guidelines

For a complete list of Architects, contact the relevant State or Territory Chapter of the Royal Australian Institute of Architects.

† *Hong Kong, Indonesia, Macau, Malaysia, Philippines, Singapore, Taiwan, Thailand*

†† *Fiji, New Zealand, Papua New Guinea, Vanuatu*